CRICKET'S

GREATEST
Characters

CRICKET'S GREATEST Characters

Fantastic Stories of Cult Heroes, Colourful Figures and Oddballs

GEOFF TIBBALLS

JR BOOKS

First published in Great Britain in 2008 by
JR Books, 10 Greenland Street,
London NW1 0ND
www.jrbooks.com

A catalogue record for this book is available from the British Library.

ISBN 978-1-906217-28-0

3 5 7 9 10 8 6 4 2

Typeset by SX Composing DTP, Rayleigh, Essex
Printed by MPG Books Ltd, Bodmin, Cornwall

CONTENTS

INTRODUCTION   1

A LAW UNTO THEMSELVES
Sid Barnes: A Man Misunderstood   3
Ian Botham: Boys' Own Hero   7
Geoffrey Boycott: The Quest For Perfection   11
Brian Close: Captain Courageous   17
Phil Edmonds: A Difficult Opponent   22
Andrew Flintoff: Larger Than Life   24
E.M. Grace: The Coroner   26
W.G. Grace: The Doctor   29
George Gunn: The Individual Approach   33
Tony Lock: Best Supporting Artist   37
Ted Pooley: Gambler Anonymous   40
Dermot Reeve: The Improviser   42
Phil Tufnell: Rebel, Rebel   44
Shane Warne: Spin Genius   48

UNLIKELY ATHLETES
Warwick Armstrong: The Big Ship   52
David Boon: The Keg On Legs   54
Mike Gatting: The Fat Controller   56
Inzamam-ul-Haq: Heavyweight Hero   59
Ken 'Slasher' Mackay: An Immovable Object   62
Colin Milburn: The Jolly Buccaneer   64
Charles Palmer: Master Of The Lob   68
Jack Simmons: Flat Jack   72
David Steele: The Bank Clerk   74
William Buttress: The Ventriloquist   78

THE JOKERS
Ray East: The Essex Jester   80
'Chuck' Fleetwood-Smith: The Bird Impersonator   84
Patsy Hendren: Alias Elias   88
Allan Lamb: Dickie's Nemesis   91
Arthur Mailey: The Art Of Self-Deprecation   94
Cecil Parkin: The Mad Magician   96
Derek Randall: Rags To Riches   100
Bryan 'Bomber' Wells: A Leisurely Approach   104

MEN OF SUBSTANCE
Denis Compton: Father Of Invention   108
Learie Constantine: The First West Indian Superstar   112

C.B. Fry: A Man For All Seasons   115
Colin Ingleby-Mackenzie: Cavalier Captain   120
Imran Khan: Role Model   123
Keith Miller: Matinee Idol   126
K.S. Ranjitsinhji: A Prince Among Men   130
Vivian Richards: Master Blaster   133
C. Aubrey Smith: From Hove To Hollywood   137
Lionel Tennyson: The Aristocratic Touch   139

BIG HITTERS
George Bonnor: The Colonial Hercules   145
Harold Gimblett: A Tortured Soul   147
Gilbert Jessop: The Croucher   151
Kevin Pietersen: Striking A Pose   154
Charles Thornton: Bun Lover   158
Albert Trott: A Sad Decline   160
Arthur Wellard: The Terror Of Taunton   164

FAST AND FURIOUS
Billy Bestwick: An Unquenchable Thirst   166
Roy Gilchrist: Jamaican Firebrand   168
Merv Hughes: The Walrus   171
John Jackson: The Foghorn   174
Dennis Lillee: The Ultimate Competitor   177
Fred Spofforth: The Demon   180
Fred Trueman: Fiery Fred   182
Sammy Woods: Champagne And Lobsters   187

LIVES LESS ORDINARY
George Brown: High And Mighty   190
Bob Crisp: The Adventurer   192
Monty Panesar: Cause For Celebration   193
Bobby Peel: Drunk In Charge   196
Jack Russell: A Creature Of Habit   199
Frank Ryan: Undercover Agent   204

THE MEN IN WHITE COATS
Dickie Bird: Star Turn   206
Brent 'Billy' Bowden: The Crooked Finger   211
Frank Chester: Fearless Frank   213
Cec Pepper: A Sharp Tongue   216
Bill Reeves: A Way With Words   219
David Shepherd: At The Hop   220
Alec Skelding: The Prince Of Kidders   224

BIBLIOGRAPHY   229

INTRODUCTION

The history of cricket, probably more than any other sport, has produced a wonderful array of colourful characters, men whose escapades have been retold and whose quirks embellished to subsequent generations in front of pavilions across the globe, from leafy Cotswold villages on a tranquil Sunday afternoon to the hustle and bustle of the Gabba at the height of an Ashes series. The very nature of the game has somehow always lent itself to eccentricity, particularly in the days before prying television cameras. Figures such as Albert Trott, George Gunn, C.B. Fry, Patsy Hendren and, of course, the incomparable Grace brothers delighted spectators wherever they played, not only for their brilliance but also for their individualism, which in some cases extended to bending the rules to breaking point. The pressures of the modern game have made this breed an endangered species, although the likes of Jack Russell, Phil Tufnell and Derek Randall deserve honourable mentions.

Whilst many of the 70 characters in this book are giants of the game – Compton, Botham and Miller, to name but three – they have not been selected for inclusion here in terms of ability; these are the greatest characters, not necessarily the greatest players, although it is comforting that excellence and personality can sometimes cohabit harmoniously. Otherwise, one of the joys of cricket is that so many delightful characters have operated solely at county level without ever troubling the Test scorers – forgotten heroes like 'Bomber' Wells, Ray East and Colin Ingleby-Mackenzie. Nor are personalities confined to players – hence the presence of a gaggle of charismatic umpires such as Dickie Bird, Cec Pepper, Alec Skelding and David Shepherd. Along with assorted mavericks and showmen – the artful, the aristocratic, the rebellious and the rotund – they are all part of a glorious fraternity known collectively as cricket's greatest characters.

Naturally this list is purely subjective (among those who nearly made it were Albert Knight, the Leicestershire batsman who used to pray at the crease before the start of an innings, and Yorkshire's Ted

Wainwright, who habitually took his bat to bed), so if your favourite cricketing personality does not feature I can only apologise. However, I hope you will agree that those I have chosen live up to the billing.

This book would not have been possible without the game's past chroniclers, who have so perfectly captured the essence and flavour of players from bygone eras, nor without the guidance and encouragement of my publisher, Jeremy Robson.

Geoff Tibballs

A LAW UNTO THEMSELVES

Sid Barnes
A Man Misunderstood

The Australian Sid Barnes is invariably depicted as a sour individual, a loner, whose eventual suicide was the almost inevitable outcome of years of bitterness and hostility. Although he was certainly not one for toeing the party line – to the extent that the Australian Board of Control once dropped him from the Test team on grounds 'other than cricket ability' – he had a talent for demonstrating his disaffection in a humorous manner. Instead of boorish physical or verbal outbursts, he often registered his protest in a quirky fashion designed to mock authority but which was no less effective for its apparent lack of spite. The most famous example was his reaction to being overlooked by the selectors for a Test against South Africa in 1953. Frustrated, Barnes asked whether he could be 12th man for New South Wales against South Australia at the Adelaide Oval and at the drinks interval strode out to the square dressed as a butler in grey suit with a red carnation. He carried a tray with a scent spray, a portable radio and cigars, which he proceeded to offer to the players and umpires. He combed the luxuriant hair of Keith Miller and held up a mirror so that his friend could admire the results. The charade lasted more than eight minutes and there was a distinct feeling among the 9,000 spectators that Barnes had outstayed his welcome. For after initially laughing at his antics, they became increasingly impatient for play to resume, as a result of which his overdue departure was greeted with catcalls. The South Australian Cricket Association were even less impressed and sent a letter of protest to New South Wales regarding Barnes's behaviour.

By that stage in his career, Barnes probably expected nothing less, having been repeatedly labelled in some quarters as the 'bad boy' of Australian cricket. His critics cited the incident at Melbourne Cricket Ground where, refused entry by a gateman because he did not have a pass, Barnes vaulted the turnstile. An Australian Board official described the episode as 'childish' and 'undignified' but team-mate Ernie Toshack subsequently claimed that Barnes had generously given his own ticket to an old lady. Barnes had also upset protocol on the 1948 tour to England when, as part of a home movie chronicling the trip, he filmed King George VI at Lord's. It later emerged that Barnes had obtained permission from the MCC President to film in the hallowed area but this cut no ice with the Australian Board of Control.

Then there were the occasional run-ins with umpires. After English umpire Alec Skelding had rejected an appeal on the 1948 tour, Barnes rounded up a stray dog and presented it to him with the comment: 'Now all you want is a white stick.' Barnes was pilloried for the remark yet it amounted to nothing more than the culmination of a series of lively but amicable exchanges with the equally witty Skelding. Similarly in New Zealand, after an umpire had finally granted an lbw appeal, Barnes removed the umpire's hat and, to the delight of the crowd, playfully patted the official's bald head. Captaining New South Wales against South Australia at Sydney in 1952, Barnes was so dismayed when an appeal for a catch was turned down that he began to lead his side from the field. The umpires ordered their return, whereupon Barnes, in his inimitable style, promptly called for drinks, even though only 20 minutes remained until the tea interval. He was very much a law unto himself.

Sidney George Barnes was born on 5 June 1916 at Annandale, Sydney. He had a tough upbringing and trained as a fitter until cricket proved his salvation. An aggressive right-hand opening batsman and useful leg-break bowler, he hit 40 runs off a nine-ball over in a grade match, and after just one full season for New South Wales he was the youngest player chosen for Donald Bradman's party to tour England in 1938. The adventure started inauspiciously when he fractured his wrist playing deck games on the voyage, an injury that kept him out of action until the end of June. Nevertheless, he scored 720 runs at an average of just over 42 and played in the Fifth Test at the Oval, the occasion on which Len Hutton hit his record-breaking 364 for England.

Resuming his career after the war, Barnes shared in a record fifth-wicket partnership of 405 with Bradman against Wally Hammond's English tourists at the 1946 Sydney Test. Both men scored 234, although Barnes, adopting a more dogged approach than before, batted ten-and-a-half hours for his. He later claimed that he had deliberately ended his innings at precisely the same total as Bradman's so that he would forever be linked numerically with the great man – and with his own name taking alphabetical precedence. Barnes had also been the bane of the English at the First Test in Brisbane when, during a break in play for a thunderstorm, he pushed a heavy block of ice down the pavilion awning so that it crashed a few feet in front of the startled tourists. Not for the last time, his joke was not immediately appreciated.

By now Barnes had become something of a wheeler-dealer around Sydney and delighted in exhibiting his newfound wealth in the form of sharp suits and flash cars. In the summer of 1947 he played Lancashire League cricket with Burnley, combining his duties with work as a wine and spirits sales rep, but found that his apparent prosperity did not go down well with the locals. Indeed, the traditional collections for his 50s yielded such a meagre return that the following Saturday, in order to avoid alienating the working-class spectators, he decided to park his car some distance from the ground and to wear a grubby raincoat and a cloth cap to the match. The impoverished look paid off and his collection swelled to £28.

For his second tour of England in 1948, Barnes put £8 on himself at odds of 15 to 1 to score a century in the Lord's Test – something that he was particularly keen to do as the MCC had refused to allow him to have a net at Lord's when he was in England the previous year. After bagging a duck in the first innings, he landed his bet with a majestic 141 in the second. A fluent back-foot player specialising in square strokes on either side of the wicket, Barnes enjoyed an outstanding series, averaging over 82 in the Tests and compiling 1,354 runs in all first-class matches. Competitive and audacious, he was also a brave short-leg fielder, earning the nickname 'Suicide Sid'. True to form, he was roundly criticised for standing just five yards from the bat, and he suffered the consequences in the next Test, at Old Trafford, when a full-blooded blow from Dick Pollard smacked him in the ribs. He tried to bat in Australia's innings but collapsed at the crease after running a single and was hospitalised for 10 days.

Barnes was at the peak of his powers and deferred to no man. He even had a rubber stamp made of his signature, carrying it along with an inked pad in his pocket so that he could get through more autographs than his team-mates. Little could he have anticipated, therefore, that the Oval Test – his 13th appearance for his country – would prove to be his last.

First, he declined to tour South Africa in 1949–50 because he didn't think the Australian Board were paying him enough. He further incurred their wrath by penning a series of outspoken articles in the press under the provocative heading *Like It or Lump It*. He was selected to make a comeback in the Third Test against the West Indies at Adelaide in 1951–52 but, in an unprecedented move, the ABC demanded that he be left out of the side. When Barnes sued a correspondent who had written a letter on the subject to the editor of a national newspaper, the Board's secretary was obliged to produce the minutes of all meetings that had led to the contentious decision. The author of the letter withdrew his criticism in court and the Board's intervention appeared to have been based on little more than the Melbourne turnstile incident.

Barnes retired from first-class cricket in 1953, having amassed 8,333 runs at an average of 54.11. His Test average was 63.06. He became a full-time cricket writer, seemingly taking delight in criticising players and officials whenever possible. On 16 December 1973, the offbeat character who had once delighted spectators by taking strike with a child's bat during Bradman's testimonial match committed suicide at his Sydney home by swallowing a fatal dose of tranquillisers. It was said that he never forgot a good turn and never forgave a slight. Sadly, all too often he had greater experience of the latter.

Ian Botham
Boys' Own Hero

With a bat or ball in his hand, Ian Botham was a hero straight out of a *Boys' Own* comic, a swashbuckling adventurer capable of deeds beyond the reach of mere mortals. But away from the cricket field he demonstrated on a depressingly regular basis that, far from being a superhero, he was every bit as flawed as the next man – especially if the next man happened to be Vlad the Impaler. At one point the tales of brawling and aggression – coupled with allegations of drug-taking and womanising – threatened to undo all his brilliance on the pitch but then Botham reinvented himself as a charity crusader. Channelling his seemingly boundless energy into more worthwhile areas, he has raised more than £10 million on his epic long-distance walks in aid of leukaemia research, work that contributed greatly towards him receiving a knighthood in 2007. It was an honour that once seemed highly unlikely ever to come his way. Indeed, back in the 1980s the odds on a knighthood for Ian Botham would have been about as long as those on England winning the famous Headingley Test of 1981 in which Botham himself played such an unforgettable role.

That Test against Australia epitomised everything that was remarkable about Botham the cricketer. He had bagged a pair in the Second Test at Lord's, thereby bringing down the curtain on his unhappy spell as England captain. Mike Brearley, whom Botham had replaced as captain, was the safe pair of hands needed for the Third Test at Headingley, but there was little indication of an improvement in fortune as England, forced to follow on 227 behind the Australians, lurched to 6 for 1 in their second innings at close of play on the third day. With bookmakers offering 500 to 1 on an England victory, Australian wicketkeeper Rod Marsh and fast bowler Dennis Lillee controversially placed bets on England to win, claiming that such odds were ridiculously generous in a two-horse race. However, as England slumped to 135 for 7 and an innings defeat appeared inevitable, the odds began to look miserly. Botham had already taken six wickets in Australia's innings followed by a top score of 50 in

England's sorry reply but now, with apparently nothing to lose, he really came into his own. As Graham Dilley joined him at the crease, Botham said: 'Right then, let's have a bit of fun.' With first Dilley (56) and then Chris Old (29) offering admirable support, Botham blasted the Australian attack to all parts of the ground in a devastating display of hitting, finishing on 149 not-out as England established a lead of 124. Bob Willis completed the fairytale with 8 for 43 as the shell-shocked Australians were skittled for 111, giving England the most incredible victory in Ashes' history.

Botham followed this up with further heroics – a match-winning 5 for 1 in 28 balls at Edgbaston and a typically pugnacious 118 at Old Trafford – as England clinched the series 3-1. In December he was voted BBC 'Sports Personality of the Year'. It was a no-contest.

Botham had always been a fiercely independent spirit. Born in Heswall, Cheshire, in 1955, he was raised in Somerset, where his sole ambition at school was to play sport, ideally for the county cricket team although he did also have an offer to play football for Crystal Palace. His careers master told him: 'Fine, everyone wants to play sport, but what are you really going to do?' But Botham remained single-minded in his approach and, after leaving school at 15, duly joined Somerset. He has said that he only ever had about six hours of coaching in his career. 'I've never tried to play perfectly. Some cricketers try to master a technique, so that every muscle in their body is absolutely under control. That isn't my way. They are like classical pianists who spend hours every day practising, whereas I'm like a jazz saxophonist who has a pretty good technique and wants to go into orbit.' However, he has acknowledged the help he received with his bowling from the experienced duo of Brian Close and Tom Cartwright at Somerset. Cartwright – the master of medium-paced accuracy – encouraged the youngster to develop an economical run-up and taught him how to move the ball off the pitch and through the air while Close (the Somerset captain) added pace and aggression to the mix. An early demonstration of Botham's raw talent came in a 1974 Benson & Hedges Cup quarter-final against Hampshire at Taunton. In reply to the visitors' 182, Somerset were toiling on 113 for 8 with 15 overs left. Botham came in at number nine and West Indian Andy Roberts, one of the fastest bowlers in the world, was brought back to finish off the Somerset innings. Almost immediately Botham took a nasty blow to the mouth from a Roberts' bouncer but, unfazed, he spat out a couple of broken teeth, downed a glass of water and then set about hammering Roberts around the ground. He finished on 45 not-out as Somerset got home by one wicket with an over to spare.

Botham's county form earned him an England call-up against Australia in July 1977 – the first of 102 Tests. Yet he had already made his mark on the Australians four months earlier, when he was involved in a Sydney barroom brawl with former Australian captain Ian Chappell during the Centenary Test. Taking exception to Chappell's derogatory remarks about England, Botham had sent him flying across the bar before chasing him into the street, where he was only dissuaded from inflicting further punishment by the appearance of a police car.

The image of being as handy with his fists as with a bat would stay with Botham, who sometimes struggled to realise that there was a fine line between macho and yob. He missed the start of the 1978 tour to Australia after putting his hand through a glass door in a pub and two years later was charged with assault following a nightclub incident in Scunthorpe. He was subsequently acquitted, saying, 'I'd rather face Dennis Lillee with a stick of rhubarb than go through that again,' but such escapades merely provided fuel for his critics. The *Daily Mail*'s Ian Wooldridge wrote: 'Botham's electrifying deeds on the cricket field have made him an incandescent figure whose influence on impressionable youth is probably greater than that of any other British sportsman. This carries a responsibility which all too often he has not acknowledged.' And of Botham's short reign as England captain, Ray Illingworth remarked acidly: 'Botham's idea of team spirit and motivation was to squirt a water pistol at someone and then go and get pissed.'

Botham had a running battle with certain sections of the press, demonstrating a surprisingly thin skin to criticism. In 1981 he was said to have jostled the respected Henry Blofeld following an uncomplimentary article. He then sued the *Mail on Sunday* over sex and drugs allegations on the 1983–84 tour of New Zealand but later withdrew the action and confessed to having smoked cannabis in the past, as a result of which he received a 63-day ban from cricket. Even his jokes landed him in trouble. When he said, 'Pakistan is the sort of place everyone should send his mother-in-law for a month…all expenses paid', he was fined £1,000 by the Test and County Cricket Board.

If he hoped that spending the winter of 1986–87 playing for Queensland would keep him out of the tabloid spotlight, he was sorely mistaken. When Allan Border and Greg Ritchie started arguing on a flight to Perth, Botham – predictably – got involved. He later wrote: 'Some of the passengers started to get agitated and as Ritchie went to the toilet, I tried to reason with Border. The next thing I knew, someone turned around and started complaining about the language. I put my hands on his shoulders, redirected his gaze to the front and told him to mind his own business.' On arrival at Perth, a police officer presented Botham with a bat to sign and then charged him with assault. Border agreed to stand bail, as did Dennis Lillee, who arrived at the jail with a six-pack of beer and his 12-year-old son who had told his father he wanted to be able to tell his mates he'd seen Botham behind bars. Botham was fined £400 and Queensland terminated his contract.

He had quit Somerset in 1985 in protest at the sacking of his friends Viv Richards and Joel Garner and went on to play for Worcestershire until 1991. The following year he joined County Championship newcomers Durham before retiring midway through the 1993 season. Appropriately, his last match was against the touring Australians. David Boon, who faced Botham's final over in first-class cricket, recalled: 'It included the exposure of parts of the human anatomy not usually seen on the cricket field, the pulling of faces and the mimicking of various bowlers' actions.' Botham finished the day's play by keeping wicket for an over without pads or gloves. He bowed out with 5,200 Test runs and 383 Test wickets to his name, to cement his reputation as one of the greatest-ever all-rounders. Viv Richards said admiringly: '"He who dares wins" is his attitude. He didn't care if he was hit for four successive boundaries in an over if he thought he could get the batsman out with the fifth or sixth delivery.'

Botham was never likely to go quietly. In 1996 he lost an expensive libel action against former Pakistan captain Imran Khan, and in 2001 he was forced to confess to a two-year affair with Australian waitress Kylie Verrells. He had previously managed to brush off claims by former Miss Barbados Lindy Field that during England's 1986 tour of the West Indies she and Botham had enjoyed such wild sex that they broke a bed, but this time there were no denials and he apologised unreservedly to long-suffering wife Kath.

Throughout his career, Botham has inspired loyalty and hostility almost in equal measures. While many in the game have defended him stoically, Frances Edmonds, wife of former England spinner Phil, wrote that Botham was in no way inhibited by a capacity to over-intellectualise, adding: 'I'd always been brought up to mistrust anyone whose bodyweight in kilos was numerically superior to his IQ.' Certainly his nicknames of 'Guy the Gorilla' and 'Beefy' (although he considered changing this to 'Sir Loin of Beef' after his knighthood) scarcely hinted at a New Man and Botham himself once stated: 'I don't ask my wife to face Michael Holding, so there's no reason why I should be changing nappies.'

Yet Kath Botham insists that her husband has mellowed of late, while Botham contends that many of the stories about him have been exaggerated anyway. 'If I'd done a quarter of the things of which I'm accused,' he says, 'I'd be pickled in alcohol, I'd be a registered drug addict and would have sired half the children in the world's cricket-playing countries.'

That may be too much to ask even of a superhero, but Botham has always specialised in pushing back the boundaries and defying the laws of probability. Recalled after his 1980s drug ban to face New Zealand, with his second and 12th balls he captured the two wickets needed to pass Lillee's world record of 355 Test wickets, whereupon Graham Gooch just looked at him incredulously and asked: 'Who writes your scripts?'

Geoffrey Boycott
The Quest For Perfection

It would be fair to say that Geoffrey Boycott did not take well to criticism of his playing ability. When a young Bob Woolmer was relaxing in the bath with Boycott after an MCC game, he casually mentioned that his Kent team-mates believed that Boycott had a weakness down the leg-side. Boycott reacted to the suggestion with such fury that Woolmer later recalled: 'It was either a very brave or very naïve statement. For the next few minutes I was gasping for breath under water.'

Boycott's sensitivity arose from his overwhelming desire and determination to be the best batsman in the world. He may not have been blessed with the natural gifts of a Sobers or a Compton, but he resolved to compensate for any deficiencies through sheer hard work. He practised longer and harder than anybody else, kept his body in the best possible condition by going to bed earlier than anybody else and when he was at the crease set out to bat for a greater length of time than anybody else. His single-minded approach to his craft came at a cost. He was not one for socialising with his team-mates and became branded a loner, a curmudgeon. 'People have a herding instinct,' he once lamented. 'If a guy does not drink and goes off to practice or have dinner, they think you are weird. You are not: you are different.' He didn't suffer fools gladly – at times he didn't suffer anyone gladly – and often used Yorkshire bluntness as an excuse for downright rudeness. He developed a reputation for meanness yet could be kind – even generous – to those he trusted. Sadly, they were few and far between, the walls of privacy that he erected around him being worthy of Fort Knox. David Gower perfectly summed up Boycott's contradictory nature when he said of him: 'He has the ability to be extremely charming, and an equal ability to be a complete sod.'

Boycott often seemed utterly ruthless in his aim for world domination. His selfishness at the crease was legendary, with batting partners being readily sacrificed in order to preserve his own infinitely more precious wicket. The phrase 'looking after number one' never rang truer than when Boycott was opening the batting. This egocentricity was apparent from his early days in club cricket with Barnsley. When Dickie Bird pushed a ball to the leg-side for a comfortable single that would have given him his 50, he called for a single and set off, only to find his partner, Boycott, firmly anchored in his crease. 'Keep running, Dickie,' said Boycott as Bird reached his end. 'Keep running all the way back to the pavilion.'

A similar fate befell England vice-captain Ted Dexter at the Port Elizabeth Test on the 1964–65 tour of South Africa. Boycott had been keeping strike by taking a single at the end of each over but the fielders had grown wise to the ploy and moved in for the last ball. Dexter recounted: 'Then Boycott called me for a run and I was flat out, head down, straight through. Yet Boycs hardly moved down the pitch at all. All he did was put his bat down to make sure he wasn't out.' Dexter had the distinction of being Boycott's first Test run-out victim…but not the last.

The only time Boycott expressed a hint of remorse was on running out local hero Derek Randall during the 1977 Trent Bridge Test against Australia – but even then his regret was born more out of fear for what the Nottinghamshire supporters might do to him. Randall had made just 12 at the time and Boycott's fatal call for a tight single prompted a chorus of boos from the home support. Boycott concluded that the only way to make amends was to compile a century, which he duly did, but he remains convinced that the Nottingham public never forgave him.

Occasionally the boot was on the other foot. After accidentally running out Boycott in a Test match, Dennis Amiss went on to make 50. As the England players applauded the half-century from the balcony, a distraught Boycott shouted: 'They're my runs you're clapping. My runs!'

Then in 1978 Boycott achieved his dream of captaining England when he led the side in New Zealand in place of the injured Mike Brearley. His relentless pursuit of his own personal goals did little to foster team spirit, and on the fourth day of the Second Test at Christchurch he was deemed to be scoring so slowly that he was in danger of costing England the match. Eventually frustration in the dressing room boiled over to the extent that Ian Botham, then a precocious newcomer, was promoted to number four with the order from vice-captain Bob Willis: 'Go and run the bugger out.' When Botham succeeded by calling for a wildly improbable single, a despairing Boycott was heard to mutter: 'What have you done, what have you done?' Boycott was still sitting sulking with a towel over his head – his standard response to being out cheaply or in a disappointing manner – half an hour later, asking himself rhetorically: 'What am I doing? Playing with children?' He had not forgiven Botham by the following morning and refused to talk to him even when he was bowling, instead sending messages via other fielders. Botham remembered: 'Whoever was fielding at cover or mid-off would be sent over to me to say "Boycs wants to know if you want another slip" and I would respond, "That would be nice." The fielder would trot over to Boycs and pass on the message.'

As one who guarded his wicket so fiercely – 'given the choice between Raquel Welch and a hundred at Lord's,' he said famously, 'I'd take the hundred every time' – the very thought of throwing it away appalled him. On the opening day of the 1970–71 tour of Australia, he showed himself to be in prime form by making an undefeated 173 against South Australia. In order to give others a chance of much-needed batting practice, the next morning captain Ray Illingworth suggested that once Boycott had reached his double century he should surrender his wicket. Boycott reacted angrily and was so upset that he was out to the third ball of the day. He refused to speak to Illingworth for several days afterwards but a compromise was eventually reached and in the next match, against Queensland, Boycott retired hurt on 124.

Batting was never anything other than a serious matter. Controversially given out lbw during a game against the Leeward Islands on England's 1980–81 tour of the West Indies, Boycott was returning glumly to the dressing room when he spotted an attendant laughing and pointing at him. Displaying his customary disregard for diplomacy, an incensed Boycott threw a glass of water over the man, who picked up a brick in retaliation but fortunately was restrained before he could do any damage with it. In fact, Boycott crossed swords with more people than Errol Flynn, prompting Derek Hodgson to write in *Wisden*: 'He has a facility for making enemies much faster than he made runs.'

Boycott was born in the Yorkshire mining village of Fitzwilliam in 1940. Fed up with being teased in the playground, the small boy with poor eyesight announced that he was going to be the greatest batsman ever and, night upon night after school, made two changes on the bus to travel to an indoor cricket venue 20 miles away. At 13 he played in a senior League game for Hemsworth and, batting at number nine in spectacles, short trousers and outsize pads, coolly struck the winning boundary against Knaresborough. A few years later he was again batting for his local club when his progress was halted by a message asking him to report to Headingley the next day for nets with Yorkshire. He left the field immediately, pursued by the opposition captain who demanded: 'Is it not courtesy to ask permission to leave the field in the middle of an innings?' 'I've finished with your class of cricket,' sneered Boycott. And off he went.

He made his Yorkshire debut in 1962 and, concentrating on the virtues of an impenetrable defence, soon earned a reputation for being able to occupy the crease for hours and grind out high scores. Many of his runs were accumulated by the on-drive or by forcing through the covers off the back foot; a swashbuckling, match-winning 146 in the 1965 Gillette Cup final was so out of character that it probably caused him sleepless nights. He made his first England appearance in 1964 and went on to become the first English cricketer to pass 8,000 Test runs. He scored 8,114 runs in 108 Tests at an average of nearly 48, his value to the team being such that only 20 of those Tests ended in an England defeat. Indeed England never lost a Test when Boycott scored a century – and he managed no fewer than 22. He was also a useful bowler of medium-paced inswingers – sometimes delivered while wearing his cap back-to-front – which had the knack of being able to break long partnerships. In the early part of his career, according to one team-mate, Boycott 'used to throw a bit like a woman', but in this area, too, he worked hard and developed into a highly competent fielder.

His highest Test score was a 10-hour 246 not-out against India at Headingley in 1967 but even though England went on to win the game, Boycott was sensationally dropped for the next Test for slow scoring. Boycott was understandably aggrieved, taking some comfort from the words of West Indies' spinner Lance Gibbs who told him: 'If you had been a West Indian, you would have been a hero. No West Indian would ever get dropped for making a double century.'

The scandalous decision made the chip on Boycott's shoulder bigger than ever. He had always seen himself as a working-class hero and made little secret of his contempt for players who had been to university, the Oxbridge 'gin and tonic brigade' as he called them. 'England seems to have a fixation with so-called leadership qualities,' he moaned, 'and it usually means background.' When he was overlooked in favour of Mike Denness for the England captaincy in 1974, he suddenly made himself unavailable to England for three years. The two events may or may not have been connected. Some have claimed that his self-imposed exile enabled him to avoid the likes of Dennis Lillee, Jeff Thomson, Andy Roberts and Michael Holding at their fastest, but there is little factual evidence to support such claims. They are more likely the result of mischief-making from anti-Boycott factions, although Lillee, for one, could hardly be counted a fan, once describing Boycott as 'the only fellow I've met who fell in love with himself at a young age and has remained faithful ever since.'

Opposition to Boycott became more plentiful after he was appointed captain of Yorkshire in 1971. As would prove the case with England, his style of leadership created dressing-room unrest. Yorkshire fast bowler Tony Nicholson said: 'It didn't matter what the rest of us did, Geoff was only concerned with his own performance. It was no way to captain a side.' In 1978 – the year in which Boycott was relieved of the captaincy after failing to win a single trophy – another team-mate, Richard Hutton, wrote of him in the *Cricketer*: 'On the slow and wet pitches which abounded in Yorkshire, he displayed a technique which none of us possessed, in that at times he made batting look horribly difficult. He could get bogged down to such an extent that his only way out was to call for and run desperate singles without reasonable regard for his partner's safety. Furthermore, the temptation to concentrate the strike on himself in favourable conditions was not always resisted. All this created pressure on the other batsmen.' Boycott's dismissal as captain was divisive even by Yorkshire standards, for whilst he fell out with senior figures at the club such as Illingworth, Fred Trueman and Brian Close, the crowds backed him to the hilt and it was a revolt by members that forced his reinstatement as a player.

He finally retired in 1986, having scored more than 40,000 runs for the county in all forms of cricket. Since then he has battled throat cancer and resurrected his commentating career after being sacked following a conviction in France for allegedly assaulting a former lover. The panama hat and lopsided grin have become familiar – and welcome – sights on the nation's television screens as Boycott dispenses no-nonsense advice and scathing criticism in a manner befitting the world's greatest batsman. Not even his detractors could ever accuse him of false modesty.

One's mind flashes back to the time when he opened the England batting with Dennis Amiss. 'Good luck,' called Amiss, as they went to their respective ends. 'It's not luck,' rasped Boycott dismissively. 'It's skill.'

Brian Close
Captain Courageous

Comedian Eric Morecambe used to say: 'You know the cricket season has arrived when you hear the sound of leather on Brian Close.' Both as a batsman facing the wrath of the West Indies' pacemen and as a short-leg fielder, Close demonstrated bravery above and beyond the call of duty in the days before helmets and protective padding. Unflinching and fearless, he took many a blow to the body but never rubbed an injured area on the field of play because he did not want to give his assailants the satisfaction of knowing they had ruffled him. As a captain he always believed in leading by example. Playing for Yorkshire, he was fielding in his familiar position when Gloucestershire batsman Martin Young hammered a ball from Ray Illingworth. The ball hit Close on the head and rebounded to Phil Sharpe, who caught it at first slip. Later Gloucestershire's Arthur Milton said: 'Brian, if that ball had struck you full on the temple, it would have killed you.' 'Yes, that's true,' agreed Close, 'but then he would have been caught at cover.'

Age failed miserably to make him more cautious. As a forty-something fielding at silly point for Somerset, he was cracked on the head by a square cut from Gloucestershire's South African star Mike Procter, the ball looping towards fielder Dennis Breakwell. However, the latter watched the man rather the ball and joined the rush to see if the captain was OK. When he came to, Close's first words were: 'Did we get him?' He was none too pleased to discover that his pain had been in vain and that Breakwell had failed to take the catch.

Close made no apologies for the fact that his positioning was designed to intimidate the batsmen. He said: 'You soon get to know the players who like a fight and those who don't, and you can make cricket a very difficult game for them. I only had to perch myself at short leg and just stare at some of 'em to get them out. They'd fiddle about and turn away and then look back to see if I was still staring at 'em. They didn't stay long.'

Ian Botham, one of his pupils at Somerset, described Close as 'one of the hardest, if not the hardest competitor I encountered during my playing career.' He was so tough he made old boots look like flip-flops. This mental and physical fortitude coupled with a fiercely stubborn streak made him a controversial figure, one who never shirked a challenge or shied away from confrontation. He was sacked as captain by both England and Yorkshire over separate issues and frequently fell foul of those in authority, as a result of which the mere mention of the name 'Brian Close' was enough to bring certain people out in a cold sweat.

Dennis Brian Close was born into a working-class family in Rawdon, Yorkshire, in 1931. His father Harry was a notable cricketer in the Bradford League and at primary school young Brian was taught by Grace Verity, sister of Yorkshire and England star Hedley Verity, who also hailed from Rawdon. Close went on to attend Aireborough Grammar School – Hedley Verity's old school – where he excelled at all sports. Indeed, he was such a promising footballer that he was signed as an amateur by Leeds United and represented England at youth level, but an injury forced him to focus his attention – temporarily at least – on cricket.

He made his first-class debut for Yorkshire in 1949, excelling more as a right-arm off-spin bowler than as a left-handed batsman, and was selected for the Players against the Gentlemen. On reaching his 50, he was congratulated by the Gentlemen's wicketkeeper, Billy Griffith, who said: 'Well played, Brian,' to which Close replied: 'Thank you, Billy.' However Close had unknowingly committed the cardinal sin of not referring to Griffith as 'Mister' – as the Gentlemen were expected to be addressed – and 10 days later he was summoned by Brian Sellers, a leading member of the Yorkshire committee, who reprimanded him for his effrontery.

That summer Close became, at 18 years and 149 days, England's youngest-ever Test player when he was called up to face New Zealand at Old Trafford. Although he made a duck, he achieved the double of 1,000 runs and 100 wickets in his first season of county cricket, earning him selection for England's 1950–51 tour of Australia. The tour was to prove a personal disaster for Close, who, by his own admission, was picked too early. As the only youngster in the party, he struggled to integrate with the senior players, none of whom took him under their wing. While the established players propped up the bar in the evening, Close drank nothing stronger than orange juice and, feeling increasingly isolated, became so unhappy that he sometimes cried himself to sleep at night. His occasional terseness and youthful arrogance further alienated his team-mates and when he was out cheaply to a rash stroke shortly before lunch in the Second Test, he returned to a silent dressing room. Informed that Close was disappointed in himself and needed consoling, England captain Freddie Brown replied: 'Let the blighter stew. He deserves it.' By the end of the tour Close, ordered to play despite nursing an injury, had acquired a reputation for malingering and insubordination and was not even on speaking terms with most of the England team. Few would ever again accuse Brian Close of malingering.

Reviving his football career, he signed for Arsenal in 1951 with the intention of combining it with his cricket duties. He obtained permission from Yorkshire captain Norman Yardley to leave the first match of the 1952 cricket season early in order to play for Arsenal but the decision was subsequently overturned in Yardley's absence. The result was that Close arrived late at Highbury and was sacked. He did go on to play for Bradford City but a serious knee injury ended his football career and restricted him to just two first-class cricket matches in 1953. Relishing a challenge as ever, he once swam across the River Severn in the dark after dinner at Worcester, prompting Yorkshire team-mate Dickie Bird, who spotted Close's clothes on the river bank, to rush into the hotel bar and exclaim: 'I think Closey is trying to drown himself!' According to those who survived to tell the tale, few things were more daring than getting into a car driven by Brian Close. Once, leaving Bristol, he was waving cheerfully to his team-mates as he overtook their cars and in doing so, missed a diversion sign indicating roadworks and plunged his vehicle down a deep hole. Viv Richards recalls of their time together at Somerset: 'I travelled miles with him. I'm not sure the rest of the side were that keen to go in his car – he had the habit of reading the *Sporting Life* as he was driving along and he was known to nod off just towards the end of the trip.'

Close was also known for never being out through any fault of his own. There was always someone – or something – else to blame. Watching from the pavilion at Chesterfield, he studied at length the action of Derbyshire seamer Les Jackson and proudly announced that he had identified when and where Jackson bowled his leg-cutter. When Close went out to bat, he shouldered arms and was clean bowled by Jackson with what was an off-cutter to him as a left-hander. Back in the dressing room, the Yorkshire team roared with laughter at Close's elementary miscalculation.

Close was appointed captain of Yorkshire in 1962 and, engendering a fighting spirit within the ranks, led the side to four County Championship titles in six seasons. He also earned one of his intermittent Test recalls in the 1963 series against the West Indies and achieved heroic status by standing up to a ferocious bombardment from Wes Hall and Charlie Griffith, notably in the Second Test at Lord's. In need of quick runs, he took the battle to the West Indies pacemen, even having the nerve to advance down the wicket to them. When he returned to the dressing room, having made a gallant 70, his body was black and blue. Photographs of his badly bruised torso made the front pages of national newspapers the following day. Nevertheless, he was not selected for the next series.

Despite his success with Yorkshire, he was a surprising choice to captain England in 1966. But he did so with distinction (winning six Tests and drawing one) until an unsavoury incident at county level in August 1967 led to him being stripped of the England captaincy. He was accused of unacceptable time-wasting and gamesmanship to prevent Warwickshire reaching a victory target at Edgbaston, Yorkshire contriving to bowl just two overs in the last 11 minutes. Roundly booed as he left the field, Close became involved in a verbal altercation with a spectator, while a man wielding an umbrella reportedly attacked Fred Trueman. Close maintained that he had done nothing wrong but the MCC vetoed his selection to captain the team on the winter tour to the West Indies. Colin Cowdrey would lead the side instead.

Three years later Close lost the Yorkshire job, too. Some believe it was because, in the heat of defeat, he had insulted the Lancashire president, Lionel Lister, after a match at Old Trafford but Yorkshire said they sacked Close because he disliked the new one-day game and had also allegedly failed to bring on the county's younger players. Yorkshire's loss proved to be Somerset's gain as the wily campaigner immediately set about turning around the fortunes of the West Country side.

Under Close's inspirational leadership, Somerset became born-again winners and anyone who failed to match his exacting standards was given short shrift. When Leicestershire needed 12 to win off the last two balls in a one-day game, Close told bowler Alan Jones exactly where he wanted them bowled. However, the instructions were not followed and both deliveries were despatched over the ropes to give Leicestershire an improbable victory. On reaching the dressing room, a raging Close grabbed Jones by the collar and screamed: 'You fucking pillock! My mother could have done better than that!'

He remained utterly fearless, and fielding at forward short leg to Middlesex's Clive Radley managed to take a catch with his hands behind his back between the cheeks of his bottom! The Somerset boys were suitably impressed. In 1976 the 45-year-old Close was rewarded with another surprise call-up to the England side, against the West Indies. In the Third Test at Old Trafford he stood up to the fire of Michael Holding, Andy Roberts and Wayne Daniel with the same courage that he had displayed against their countrymen 13 years earlier. 'The bouncers were flying,' recalled Close, 'and it was like being in a coconut shy. You were dodging balls whistling past your head.' When Close was hit in the chest by a ball from Daniel and slumped to the floor, Viv Richards, a team-mate at Somerset, was immediately concerned. 'OK, I was playing for my country,' said Richards, 'but this was my skipper on the ground and in pain. So I went up to him and asked him if he was OK. Closey eventually gathered himself together and bellowed, "Fuck off!" What a man!' Close may only have made 20 but he withstood the barrage for 162 minutes. Typically, he was dropped for the next Test. It would be the last of his 22 Test appearances.

He retired from county cricket at the end of the 1977 season and, somewhat ironically, became an England selector. In 1984 he was elected to the Yorkshire committee and two years later, aged 55, played his final first-class innings, for his own eleven against the touring New Zealanders at the Scarborough Festival. Needing just 10 runs to reach a career milestone of 35,000 first-class runs, he was caught behind for four. Afterwards the New Zealanders said that if they had known how near he was to the landmark, they would have let him stay – but Close would have none of it.

Thereafter, he helped coach Yorkshire's youngsters, occasionally captaining them in matches and still taking the short-leg position without a helmet. Yorkshire is renowned for being a county of hard bastards, but few were harder than Brian Close.

Phil Edmonds
A Difficult Opponent

'He's got a reputation for being awkward and arrogant,' said Frances Edmonds of her husband Phil. 'Probably because he is awkward and arrogant.' In the course of a distinguished career as a left-arm spinner with Middlesex and England, Philippe-Henri Edmonds was renowned for being almost as difficult a team-mate as he was an opponent. Outspoken and obstinate, he repeatedly fell out with his Middlesex captain, Mike Brearley, one argument ending with Edmonds pinning Brearley to the wall and warning him to 'lay off'.

Brearley's successor, Mike Gatting, also experienced problems controlling Middlesex's *enfant terrible*. Gatting recalled how Edmonds would sometimes get in a strop and refuse to bowl, so Gatting would send him down to the boundary where 'he would mess about with the crowd to make himself feel better. I would say to him afterwards: "You acted like a schoolboy, Philippe", whereupon he would turn around and laugh at me. He knew he was in the wrong but he wouldn't accept that he'd been childish. He likes to try and lead people on to see how angry they can get, and how far they can be pushed.'

Middlesex disciplined him in 1984 because, during the heat of battle, he preferred to lie flat on the ground in the outfield. Two days after he had helped England win the Ashes in 1985, he was named 12th man by Middlesex but, viewing the exercise as pointless, decided to go home instead. There was never any doubting his talent, but sometimes his attitude left a lot to be desired. He was a highly effective late-order batsman, with three first-class centuries and 22 fifties to his name, yet his career average was a modest 18.93. All too often he treated the loss of his wicket with casual disdain. His county team-mate Simon Hughes wrote that Edmonds would sometimes walk back to the pavilion 'chuckling with a mixture of mild disbelief and perverse pleasure.'

The son of a colonial property developer, Edmonds was born in Lusaka, Northern Rhodesia, in 1951. Moving to England, he played for Cambridge University before joining Middlesex. He made his Test debut in 1975 against Australia at Headingley and announced his arrival by taking 5 for 17 in his first 12 overs, using his height and strength to extract turn and bounce from the pitch. He complemented the graceful approach of a slow left-armer with the aggression of a fast bowler and was not averse to slipping the odd bouncer into an over, to the surprise of both batsman and wicket-keeper. When his irritation got the better of him and he aimed a bouncer at New Zealand's Richard Hadlee, he was immediately warned by the umpire about intimidating the batsman. Edmonds' response was to bowl another bouncer. It was partly because he was considered something of an unsettling influence within the side that he was restricted to 51 Tests over a 12-year period.

One person in the England set-up with whom he did identify was the equally awkward but intelligent Geoffrey Boycott. The Yorkshireman christened them the 'Fitzwilliam twins', on account of Boycott's place of birth and Edmonds' Cambridge college. Even so, Edmonds remained very much his own man, as illustrated during a boring Test in Calcutta when, fielding on the boundary, he showed his disapproval by picking up a newspaper and reading it.

More typically, he would field at short leg, demonstrating such fearlessness that batsmen said if they danced down the wicket to spinners, Edmonds would follow them. The position also enabled him to engage in none-too-friendly banter with batsmen, although some gave as good as they got. After Frances Edmonds had published *Another Bloody Tour*, her contentious account of the 1985–86 trip to the Caribbean, Australian wicketkeeper Tim Zoehrer responded to Edmonds' customary sledging by snapping: 'At least I have an identity. You're only Frances Edmonds' husband.'

Edmonds was rarely lost for words. When a reporter asked him what he was looking forward to most on returning home from a tour of India, Edmonds replied: 'A dry fart!' However, he surely regretted interacting with the Oval crowd as Pakistan piled up 708 in the Fifth Test in 1987. 'It's so depressing out here,' he called to spectators. 'Shout something encouraging you chaps!' To which one replied: 'This could be your last Test!'

The spectator proved an admirable clairvoyant: Edmonds never played for his country again. He retired from first-class cricket that year to concentrate on his business interests but, in response to a chronic injury crisis in the Middlesex team, he made a brief comeback in 1992, taking 4 for 48 at Trent Bridge. Afterwards he said he could hardly walk for a week. He later became chairman of the county side for whom he had taken over 1,500 wickets and was no less controversial in that role than he had been on the pitch. But being Phil Edmonds, he probably didn't give a damn.

Andrew Flintoff
Larger Than Life

On being awarded the freedom of his home town of Preston after England's memorable 2005 Ashes triumph, Andrew Flintoff mused: 'That means I can drive a flock of sheep through the town centre, drink for free in no less than 64 pubs and get a lift home with the police when I become inebriated. What more could you want?'

The sheep apart, such considerations appear, worryingly, to be uppermost in Flintoff's mind. While the 17-hour drinking session that resulted in him emerging bleary-eyed on the open-topped bus for the Ashes victory parade was dismissed as nothing more than youthful exuberance and simply served as further proof that he was a worthy successor to Ian Botham in every respect, the notorious 2007 incident with a pedalo called his judgement seriously into question. Hours after scoring a duck in England's World Cup defeat to New Zealand, Flintoff went on an eight-hour drinking marathon with team-mates and at four o'clock in the morning grabbed a pedalo from a beach near the team's Caribbean hotel. He dragged it a little way out to sea and was seen rocking it from side to side before it capsized, toppling him into the water, from where he had to be rescued by hotel staff. With coach Duncan Fletcher revealing that England's talismanic all-rounder had received a number of previous warnings regarding his behaviour, Flintoff was stripped of the vice-captaincy and suspended for the match against Canada two days later. This time few were willing to excuse his actions, former England fast bowler Bob Willis stating: 'I think Freddie has been making a fool of himself since the celebrations of the 2005 Ashes.' Whereas Flintoff's tremendous popularity ensured that the public forgave his earlier lapses (he turned up drunk for the official Ashes reception at Downing Street, although he denied claims that he had urinated in a flowerbed in the garden of Number 10), by 2007 his star was on the wane as he struggled against injury and general loss of form. He was no longer infallible or capable of winning matches almost single-handedly. He was in danger of becoming just another Test cricketer.

The career of Andrew 'Freddie' Flintoff (his nickname originates from the cartoon character Fred Flintstone) has had more than its fair share of highs and lows. Born in Preston in 1977, he was a fine all-round sportsman, playing centre-half for Preston schools at football and representing Lancashire schools at chess. But it was at cricket that the strapping youngster made his name, producing a breathtaking display of hitting to register 232 not-out in just 20 overs for St Anne's Under-15s. Snapped up by Lancashire at 16, he jeopardised his future when, angry at being out to a loose shot in a second XI fixture with Yorkshire, he smashed his fist against a pavilion wall, thereby fracturing his hand and putting him out of action for several weeks. And when he made his first-team debut against Hampshire, he scored 7 and 0 and dropped five catches.

Although he won a Test place in 1998, he still struggled for form at county level, but when his batting did come off, it was in explosive fashion. After Flintoff's match-winning 135 not-out against Surrey in the quarter-final of the 2000 NatWest Trophy, David Gower eulogised: 'We've just watched one of the most awesome innings we're ever going to see on a cricket field.' When concerns were still expressed about his fitness and weight, Flintoff responded with a 'Man of the Match' award in a one-day game against Zimbabwe, a performance that he rated as 'not bad for a fat lad.'

Dropped by England in 2001 and given a severe dressing-down by his own management team, he returned two stone lighter and with a remodelled bowling action. He began using his 6ft 4in frame to devastating effect, not only as a ferocious striker of the ball but also to generate bowling speeds in excess of 90mph, which, allied to his accuracy and mastery of reverse-swing, made him a formidable adversary. It seemed that he was finally about to realise his potential and he showed his joy at taking the wicket that enabled England to tie the one-day series in India in 2002 by ripping off his shirt in celebration. The spontaneous gesture predictably earned him a rebuke.

The Flintoff legend gathered pace with an innings of 167 against the West Indies at Edgbaston in 2004. One six was struck high into the stand, where the ball was almost caught, but ultimately dropped, by his father Colin! Everyone warmed to the amiable giant, particularly for his inspirational performances (402 runs and 24 wickets) in the 2005 Ashes series, during which he demonstrated his sportsmanship by consoling Australia's Brett Lee after the nail-biting Second Test at Edgbaston. He was named 'Man of the Series' and also BBC 'Sports Personality of the Year', the first cricketer to win the award since Botham in 1981. Freddie Flintoff was a superstar, and an admirably laid-back one at that. 'Until I'm the next but one in,' he revealed, 'I'm sitting around in my shorts, very relaxed. When I'm next man in, I put all my kit on and start to take an interest in what's going on. It helps me to remain chilled, and that helps my game.'

Grounded, relaxed and with a happy and stable family life, Flintoff had the world at his feet – until he started to relax a little too often. For the next two years the flashes of brilliance became increasingly rare. His batting was frequently embarrassing, his bowling was hampered by an ankle injury and he had the misfortune to lead England on the disastrous 2006–07 Ashes series in Australia, which resulted in a 5–0 whitewash. Then came the nocturnal boating jaunt, the 'Fredalo' incident…But this larger-than-life character has bounced back before from adversity. For the future of English cricket, it is to be hoped that he can do so again.

E.M. Grace
The Coroner

Edward Mills Grace, elder brother of W.G., was an argumentative soul. He argued with players, he argued with umpires, he even argued with spectators and was known to chase barrackers out of the ground before resuming his innings. Heckled by a drunk as he ran in to bowl at Bristol, E.M. (as he was always known) saw red, turned on his tormentor and charged after him, in the words of one witness, 'like a rhinoceros'. The chase continued out of the ground and away across Ashley Down. When E.M. finally returned and was asked nervously what he had done to the heckler, he replied: 'He's still running.'

As did his more illustrious brother, E.M. showed scant regard for the rules of the game, frequently twisting them to suit his own needs. Bowling for his club side, Thornbury, against Weston-super-Mare, he was struck for four successive sixes by F.A. Leeson-Smith. When the umpire called 'over', E.M. snapped: 'Shut up, I am going to have another.' And so he bowled a seventh delivery, off which the unfortunate Leeson-Smith was stumped. On another occasion, when a visiting captain announced in astonishment 'Well, I declare!' while batting, E.M. insisted on interpreting him literally, forcing the opposition to forego the remainder of their innings. Such was E.M.'s hold over umpires that at the start of one morning's play he successfully appealed for an lbw relating to the last ball of the previous evening!

Wisden wrote: 'But for the accident that his own brother proved greater than himself, E.M. Grace would have lived in cricket history as perhaps the most remarkable player the game has produced.' He was born in Bristol on 28 November 1841, and even as a schoolboy cricketer reacted angrily if a decision did not go his way. He was once so incensed by a borderline lbw at Long Ashton that he promptly snatched up the stumps and carried them from the field. Petulance was clearly in the genes. His grandfather, George Pocock, had been organist of the Portland Wesleyan Church at Kingsdown until a heated argument with the deacon resulted in Pocock resigning on the spot and taking the organ with him.

By the age of 21, E.M. was considered the most dangerous batsman in England. He was one of the first in the land to favour the pull shot and was renowned as a ferocious hitter. The Thornbury umpire (the village postmaster) would take to the field with the pockets of his coat bulging with as many as nine cricket balls in the expectation that E.M. would hit every one of them out of the ground. Grace had such a keen eye that in one season as captain he won the toss 38 times out of 40, explaining that his vision was so sharp that he could watch the coin at the top of the spin and call correctly. At representative level, notably with Gloucestershire, he specialised in fielding close to the bat – so close that when he caught Middlesex's Andrew Stoddart he was able to hand the ball back to the wicketkeeper without taking a step. Some opponents did not take kindly to his presence, Lancashire captain Albert 'Monkey' Hornby warning: 'If you stay there, E.M., I'll kill you.' To which Grace replied cheerfully: 'Kill away, Monkey.' His reflexes were remarkable, although whether it is true that he caught a swallow at point must be debatable.

In his early years E.M. was a fast round-arm bowler and took all 10 wickets in one innings for MCC against the Gentlemen of Kent at Canterbury in 1862, a match in which he also scored 192 not-out. But as a member of George Parr's team on the 1863–64 tour of Australia, he sustained an arm injury that forced him to perfect the art of bowling lobs instead. Playing against the United South team at the Oval in 1865, he tried to remove the obstinate Harry Jupp by cunningly pitching lobs high into the air so that they would land on top of his stumps. The tactic finally paid off, to the annoyance of Jupp and the spectators. With a riot a very distinct possibility, the match was stopped and Grace's men pulled up the stumps should they be needed as weapons. E.M. himself left no one in doubt as to his intentions. 'The first man who touches me,' he warned, 'will get the middle stump on his head.' The matter was resolved when poor Jupp reluctantly agreed to sacrifice his wicket. E.M. was not one for compromise.

With his mutton-chop whiskers and his handkerchief tucked in the strap at the back of his trousers, the autocratic E.M. was a familiar sight on cricket pitches at club, county and regional level. Even his duties as a coroner failed to interfere with his love of the game. Should there be a clash, he would simply announce that a post-mortem was needed and then go off to play cricket. In one more pressing instance, he had the corpse put on ice so that he could attend to it at close of play.

He played in only one Test, opening England's innings against Australia at the Oval in 1880 with W.G. and scoring 36 and 0. He continued to play for Gloucestershire until 1894, thereafter concentrating mainly on club cricket with Thornbury, for whom he took 352 wickets in 1906 at the age of 64. The following year his total was reduced to 212 but it was reported that 208 catches had been missed off his bowling. It has been suggested that E.M. himself kept a record of his fielders' failings, ready to use them in evidence. *Wisden* of 1908 calculated that in the course of his career E.M. had scored 76,705 runs and taken 11,959 wickets, although many of these were in club cricket.

In 1909 E.M. resigned as secretary of Gloucestershire – a post he had held for 38 years since the club's formation – and in the summer of 1910 he had to be carried from the field after collapsing through exhaustion. The following May he died. In a fulsome obituary, *Wisden* concluded: 'Barring W.G., it would be hard indeed to name a man who was a stronger force on a side or a more remarkable match winner.' And just occasionally E.M. did it within the rules.

W.G. Grace
The Doctor

In 1859 Martha Grace wrote a letter to George Parr: 'I am writing to ask you to consider the inclusion of my son, E.M. Grace – a splendid hitter and most excellent catch – in your England XI. I am sure he would play very well and do the team much credit. It may interest you to learn that I have a younger son, now 12 years of age, who will in time be a much better player than his brother because his back stroke is sounder, and he always plays with a straight bat. His name is W.G. Grace.'

Mrs Grace was a shrewd judge. Fine player though E.M. was, W.G. outstripped him in every respect. He scored over 54,000 runs and took nearly 3,000 wickets in first-class cricket, completed the seasonal double of 1,000 runs and 100 wickets on seven occasions, and hit 124 centuries, including seven double centuries and three triple centuries. Playing for his county, Gloucestershire, against Middlesex, he once carried his bat for 221, despite having spent the previous night at a patient's bedside. He played in 22 Tests, and just in the month of May 1895 scored 1,000 runs. Furthermore he was an outstanding athlete who, before his muscular 6ft 2in frame ballooned in weight, scored 224 for All England against Surrey at the Oval and then popped down to Crystal Palace to win the 440 yards hurdles at the National Olympian Association Championships. He also represented his country at lawn bowls and was a prime mover in the founding of the English Bowling Association.

In addition, he was more than E.M.'s equal in terms of games-manship, starting with the toss itself, where W.G. would call 'Woman' and then claim either Britannia or Victoria as his choice. He talked incessantly on the field and if E.M. also happened to be in the Gloucestershire ranks, the noise was unbearable. On one occasion the banter between the two provoked Lord Hawke to rebuke them for distracting the Yorkshire batsmen. Nor was W.G. above shouting 'miss it' just as a fielder was about to catch him. He even resorted to blackmail during a Gentlemen versus Players match at Lord's. Schofield Haigh had been granted permission by W.G. to leave the field early on the final day so that he could catch a train back to Yorkshire but as Grace's century drew near, the doctor hit what looked to be a certain catch in Haigh's direction. As Haigh waited for the ball to drop into his hands, W.G. yelled: 'Take the catch and you miss the train!' Keen to fulfil his travel arrangements, the compro-mised Haigh allowed the ball to hit the ground.

Grace saw nothing wrong in preserving his wicket at all costs. When one umpire gave him out early in an innings, he famously replied: 'They've come to see me bat, not you umpiring.' With that, he calmly replaced the bails and continued at the crease. Playing against Essex, W.G. was involved in a dispute with fast bowler Charles Kortright over a bump ball. Grace successfully won that argument, only to be clean bowled shortly afterwards, Kortright knocking two stumps out of the ground. As W.G. departed, Kortright mocked: 'What, are you going, Doctor? There's still one standing!' Such was his hatred of being out that he once declared an innings with the ball in mid-air before the fielder could catch him.

His desire to accumulate runs was insatiable – and often illegal. Having run three, he was surprised to see the ball lodge in the top of his pads as it was returned from the outfield, so, thinking on his feet, he ran another three. He then refused to give the ball back to the fielding side for fear of being given out for handling the ball. Grace tried the pad trick again in a match at Bristol after a bottom edge had seen the ball lodge in the top of his pad. Seizing the opportunity to add to his score, he waddled to the boundary with the ball intact and claimed four runs. To his disgust, the umpire refused.

One biographer wrote of Grace: 'He was a case of arrested development and remained, intellectually, always at the age of 16.' This showed not only in his gamesmanship but in his schoolboy-like determination to monopolise both the batting and the bowling. When his captain for the Gentlemen of the South had the temerity to suggest a change from W.G.'s bowling, Grace quickly offered: 'I tell you what, I'll go on at the other end.' Grace's bowling was deceptively effective. Like his brother, he started out by bowling fast until an expanding girth persuaded him to adopt a slower approach. Sir Arthur Conan Doyle said of him: 'He would lumber up to the wicket and toss up the ball in a take-it-or-leave-it style, as if he cared little whether it pitched between the wickets or in the next parish.' Although W.G. persisted in a round-arm action throughout his career, when most bowlers had long since switched to overarm, his first-class average of 18.14 was irrefutable evidence of his ability. Naturally he did everything he could to tip the scales in his favour, a favourite ploy being to draw the batsman's attention to an imaginary flock of birds flying across a bright sun and then bowl while the batsman's eyes were still dazzled. When it came to bending the rules, William Gilbert Grace simply could not help himself.

The master of manipulation was born in Bristol on 18 July 1848 into a cricket-loving family. His first-class career spanned 46 years. He opened for England at the age of 50 and was only omitted from the side in 1899, when his age and bulk made him a liability in the field. As late as 1902 he scored nearly 1,200 first-class runs in the season. His approach to batting was simple: 'Go for the bowling before it goes for you.' He is also said to have expressed a dislike for defensive shots, because 'you can only get threes'. He made run-making look ridiculously easy. In 1893 he surprised his team-mates by suddenly declaring the innings closed with his own score seven short of a century. He later explained that 93 was the one score between 0 and 100 that he had yet to make. He even batted with a broomstick in an exhibition at Cheltenham and made 35 – the second-highest score despite the fact that the other players were all using conventional bats. Few people unnerved him, although the delivery from Australian pace bowler Ernie Jones that reputedly whistled through the great man's bushy beard must have come close.

In spite of twisting the rules, Grace, a remarkably shy man in private, was generally a popular figure. As a doctor, he was described as brisk but jovial with a somewhat morbid sense of humour. After a troublesome birth, he told friends: 'Well, the baby's dead and I don't think there's much hope for the mother, but I do believe I shall pull the father through.' His medical skills were urgently required at Old Trafford in 1887 when, in trying to save a boundary, his Gloucestershire colleague Arthur Croome fell on the spiked railings in front of the pavilion and cut open his throat. Grace saved his team-mate's life and Croome later wrote appreciatively: 'They had to send out for a needle and thread to sew it up, and for nearly half an hour W.G. held the edges of the wound together. It was of vital importance that the injured part should be kept absolutely still and his hand never shook all that time.' As Croome noted, what made Grace's steadiness of hand all the more remarkable was that he had been toiling in the field for over 400 runs and had done his fair share of bowling.

Although W.G. was known to waive his patients' fees from time to time, he was decidedly grasping when it came to claiming his expenses from cricket. He may have officially been an amateur but one way or another he made a good living from the game. His financial demands brought him into frequent conflict with Gloucestershire but these squabbles were nothing compared to the embarrassment caused by his kidnapping of Australian Test star Billy Midwinter, the county's first professional. The Australian tourists had selected Midwinter to play for them against Middlesex at Lord's on 20 June 1878, but with Gloucestershire a man short, Grace decided in typically high-handed manner to press him into service against Surrey at the Oval. Midwinter was quietly practising at Lord's that morning when Grace and two team-mates – burly wicketkeeper Arthur Bush and brother E.M. – seized him and bundled him into a carriage bound for the Oval. The Australians gave chase, resulting in an angry altercation at the gates of the ground. As usual, W.G.'s voice won the day but a bewildered Midwinter could manage only 4 and 0 as Gloucestershire slumped to their first defeat for two years. A war of words followed between the county and the Australians.

Grace also brought the club into disrepute during a match against Middlesex. With Sir Timothy O'Brien threatening to hit Middlesex to victory, W.G. attempted to slow his progress by bowling a succession of extremely wide deliveries, only for the Irishman to respond by thrashing the ball backhanded through the slips, one shot nearly decapitating E.M. An irate W.G. immediately informed the batsman: 'If you do that again, I'll take my men off the field.' But O'Brien was not one to be intimidated by Grace and proceeded to repeat the shot, whereupon Gloucestershire did indeed walk off. A major row erupted, during which W.G. threatened to call the police, before sanity and order were finally restored.

The 'Old Man' (as he had been known perversely since his 30s) made his last first-class appearance in 1908 but continued playing club cricket for a further six years. A week after his 66th birthday, he hit an unbeaten 69 for Eltham at Grove Park in what proved to be his final innings. The colossus who had dominated the game of cricket for nearly half a century and was Britain's best-known sportsman died on 23 October 1915 after suffering a stroke, but such was his value in propaganda terms that the Germans tried to claim him as an air-raid victim. One suspects it would have taken more than the might of the German airforce to silence W.G. Grace.

George Gunn
The Individual Approach

In his *Book of Cricket* Denzil Batchelor wrote: 'The long hop trembled and descended. Another split second and it would have brought immortal ignominy on its author's head by bouncing twice. But when it was three inches from the ground (and not less than 18 off the leg-stump) the batsman solemnly played it up the wicket, as if it contained half-a-dozen mortal traps, successfully foiled. The bowler, heartened by this escape, bowled his best ball of the season – of perfect length, pitching six inches wide of the off-stump and fizzing back on to middle and leg. The batsman square cut it nonchalantly for four. You will not need to be told that the batsman was George Gunn.'

No professional had a more contrary approach to batting than Gunn. He loved to make the most difficult bowlers look easy and the worst ones unplayable. He would walk yards down the wicket to the fastest of bowlers, often chattering to them as he did so, and then play the ball with the deadest of bats when he could have hit it to any part of the ground. Batting almost came too easily for him. If the mood took him, he was capable of making runs against any attack in the world, but on other occasions he seemed to embark on a deliberate go-slow, much to the irritation of spectators. He could switch from one style to the other at the drop of a hat. Batting for Nottinghamshire in difficult conditions at Trent Bridge in 1913, he was taunted by the Yorkshire players after taking six hours to score 132. In the second innings he responded to the criticism with 109 in 85 minutes out of Notts' score of 129 for 3. Wally Hammond said of him: 'He got out dozens of times, perhaps hundreds of times, because he was more concerned deliberately to irritate the bowler than to guard his wicket. I have seen him amuse himself for half an hour on end, apparently deliberately demonstrating batting tricks, careless of his score, and for his own edification – for he never cared a hang what onlookers or anyone else thought of him!' That last point was illustrated when Gunn was heckled by a burly miner for slow scoring against Derbyshire. After half an hour of listening to the abuse, Gunn strolled over to the boundary and, offering his bat and gloves to his critic, said: 'Wouldsta' like a chance?' Nothing more was heard from the vocal spectator.

Gunn was not a man to rile, for although he did not possess the fiery temper of an E.M. Grace or a Botham, he managed to exact revenge by more subtle means. For his Test debut against Australia in 1907–08 he was partnered by Somerset's Len Braund, who had made disparaging remarks about Gunn's batting at breakfast that morning. So Gunn set about teaching him a lesson. He recalled: 'I had strike and I kept taking singles at the end of each over. I reckon I kept him away from the bowling for about the first 45 minutes of his innings. After that, he didn't say much.' The stand with Braund was worth 117, of which Gunn's share was 91. Displaying total contempt for the Australian bowling, he raced from 78 to his century with six boundaries before he was finally out for 119. He later claimed that his concentration had been disturbed – not by the military band but by its solo cornet playing out of tune. He followed up with 74 in the second innings, even though his gloves were filled with blood from the severe blisters he had sustained in the first innings.

Playing against Kent at Catford in 1921, Gunn took exception to remarks made by a Notts committee man, who had told him as opening batsman to knock off the 236 runs needed for victory quickly so that he could get home early. For Gunn, this demand was like a red rag to a bull. Therefore he proceeded to score so slowly that when his captain, Arthur Carr, came in at number four, he asked what the problem was. Gunn replied that he had no intention of taking orders from a committee man and told Carr that he would have to get the runs. Not blessed with Gunn's talent, Carr struggled against Kent spinner 'Tich' Freeman while Gunn leaned disinterestedly on his bat at the non-striker's end. Eventually Gunn sauntered down the wicket to offer much-needed encouragement.

'You've got him worried, skipper,' said Gunn.

'How's that?' asked the perspiring Carr.

'He can't work out what he's doing wrong,' continued Gunn. 'By rights he should have had you out half-a-dozen times.'

Notts did reach their target with a few minutes to spare, but Gunn contributed just 55 not-out to the total of 237 for 2.

Gunn also tried Carr's patience in a fixture against Yorkshire at Headingley. A car crash on the way to Leeds left Nottinghamshire without their key bowlers, so Carr was relieved to win the toss and hopefully give them time to recover. Accordingly he told Gunn to stay in until tea but Gunn protested that at his age it was too much to expect, informing the captain: 'My legs are not what they used to be.' However Carr was adamant and Gunn eventually agreed...on condition that he was paid £1 an hour on top of his usual wages. At 3.30pm he raised his demands, stating that he wanted time-and-a-half for holding out until 5.30. Carr had little option but to agree and the financially-astute Gunn batted comfortably through the entire day.

As Wally Hammond noted, Gunn did not always show such determination to stay at the crease and was perfect capable of throwing away his wicket on a mere whim – never more so than in a match against Hampshire at Southampton. Gunn was at the non-striker's end as the clock reached 1.30pm and, assuming that it was lunch, he headed towards the pavilion, only to be summoned back by the umpire with the words: 'Not yet, George. We're taking lunch at two o'clock today. Back you go.' In stony silence Gunn retraced his steps and prepared to face the next ball. Receiving a straight delivery, he calmly stepped aside and allowed the ball to hit the wicket, whereupon he tucked his bat under his arm and made off once more for the pavilion, informing the startled Hampshire players: 'I take my lunch at one thirty.'

Gunn enjoyed watching matches in the company of his wife. Particularly on a hot day, as soon as he saw her taking her seat in the stands he would land a six near where she was sitting to indicate that he would be joining her shortly. Sure enough, he would then contrive to get himself out. If the prospect of opening the batting held little appeal on a certain day, he would tell Nottinghamshire's number three, Willis Walker: 'Get your pads on, Willis. I'll not be long.'

Gunn scored over 35,000 runs for Nottinghamshire between 1902 and 1932. Yet the feeling persists that he could have made many more and certainly could have appeared in more than just 15 Tests had he not been considered such a maverick. A nephew of William Gunn and younger brother of John Gunn, both of whom played for England, George was born at Hucknall on 13 June 1879. A frail, sickly child, he turned out for Notts Castle from 1896 but his batting was so poor that he was usually the last man in. Two years later, his uncle's influence won him a two-year trial with Nottinghamshire but in 21 matches over a period of two seasons he averaged just 7.43 with the bat and so it was no surprise when he was not retained at the end of the 1899 season. Gunn defiantly told the county they would want him back one day and, after flourishing in club cricket in the south, where he was not burdened by the expectation associated with the family name, he was indeed invited back by Notts in 1902.

With a style built on solid defence, he established himself at county level, although his health continued to give cause for concern, prompting his friends to suggest that he should spend the winter of 1907–08 in Australia. And when illness ironically left the MCC touring team a man short, Gunn was asked to fill the breach and ended up topping the series averages with 462 runs at 51.33. Strangely, he only ever played one home Test, managing just 0 and 1 against Australia at Lord's in 1909.

Gunn always had plenty of time to play his shots – he claimed that he knew precisely where the ball would pitch the moment it left the bowler's hand – and even in his later years played fast bowling well. In 1929 he scored 1,788 runs to help Notts to their first county title since 1907, marking the date of his 50th birthday by hitting 164 not-out against Worcestershire. He was rewarded with selection for that winter's tour to the West Indies, where the crowds warmed to his antics. He would creep up on batsmen holding a mid-wicket conference, his hand cocked to his ear and with a finger to his lips, and on one occasion held out a sun hat in his left hand to catch a steepler but at the last moment, mindful of the rules, cleverly caught it in his right. In 1931, at the age of 52, he scored 183 against Warwickshire, with his son, George Vernon Gunn, scoring 100 not-out in the same innings.

George Gunn died on 29 June 1958 at Cuckfield, Sussex, leaving behind a fund of stories about his idiosyncratic approach to cricket. At Trent Bridge they still speak fondly of the occasion when Gunn was challenged to a single-wicket match by a cocky amateur who proposed a purse of £100. After initially declining, Gunn relented, but only if the stakes were reduced to £5. The match was played each evening on the Trent Bridge practice ground from 5pm to 7.30pm. Gunn batted first and by the end of the second evening had amassed 620 runs, at which his frustrated opponent suggested that Gunn might wish to declare. Gunn thought otherwise but did allow the amateur to bowl at the 6ft-wide heavy roller instead of the stumps. Still Gunn held firm and after a further 90 minutes on the third evening his total had risen to 777. Utterly humiliated, the amateur – whose confident swagger had long since evaporated – decided that he could take no more and, hurling the ball to the ground, stormed off, never to be heard of again. The professional had made his point.

Tony Lock
Best Supporting Artist

It is unfortunate that Tony Lock is perhaps destined to be remembered chiefly for being the supporting act to cricket's greatest Test bowling feat. For while Jim Laker was taking his record-breaking 19 wickets against Australia at Old Trafford in 1956, his Surrey colleague Lock was toiling away at the other end for little reward, his solitary wicket merely serving to spoil Laker's full house.

It was not an experience that Lock enjoyed. A combative individual in contrast to the more laid-back Laker, he became increasingly frustrated with each wicket that fell. Alan Oakman, the lanky Sussex opener who played in that memorable Test, could not help noticing Lock's demeanour. 'At the start,' he said, 'he'd been applauding Jim's wickets but by the end you could see him just folding his arms.'

Bizarrely, just three weeks earlier Lock had enjoyed his own 10-wicket return, taking 10 for 54 against Kent at Blackheath, giving him 16 wickets for the match. But that was the County Championship; England–Australia was on another plane altogether. Lock was consigned to play second fiddle.

Born in Limpsfield, Surrey, in 1929, Lock made his first-class debut for the county a week after his 17th birthday and marked it by taking a spectacular catch at backward short leg against Kent. The acrobatic catch close to the wicket would become a Lock trademark, his 831 career-victims proof that there have been few finer fielders in that area. But he was selected principally as a purveyor of slow left-arm spin and earned his county cap by taking 72 wickets in 1950 to help Surrey to a share of the County Championship with Lancashire. At that stage he had a high-arm action and the classical spin bowler's loop but after two winters working at an indoor school in Croydon, *Wisden* noted that 'he emerged with a lower trajectory that produced vicious spin at around medium-pace. Now the ball spat from leg-stump to hit the top of the off, or spun devilishly and jumped shoulder high.' It was thought that a low beam in the Croydon nets had forced him to drop his arm. From being an orthodox slow left-armer, Lock had become an aggressive, attacking spinner but whilst the new action produced immediate results, there were dark mutterings about the legitimacy of his faster ball.

A week after making his Test debut against India in 1952, Lock was no-balled three times in two overs for throwing his quicker delivery. Despite raising the beam at the Croydon nets in a bid to recreate his old action, he was again called for throwing on the 1953–54 tour of the West Indies and temporarily withdrew the contentious faster ball from his armoury. It had certainly created a furore in the cricket world. When Essex captain Doug Insole was bowled by Lock in gathering gloom, he complained to the square-leg umpire: 'How was I out then – run out?'

Lock had helped England regain the Ashes in 1953 (despite missing the first three Tests with a raw spinning finger) and by the time the Australians visited again three years later, he and Laker had formed a devastating partnership, their complementary styles enabling Surrey to win the County Championship every season between 1952 and 1958. If 1956 was indisputably Laker's summer, Lock truly came into his own two years later on wet English pitches against a modest New Zealand team. He took 34 wickets in that series at just 7.47 apiece.

Shocked by seeing himself on film the following year, he again remodelled his action but went on to achieve the remarkable record of taking 100 wickets every season between 1951 and 1962. Lock was a volatile character, prone to vociferous appeals that made Shane Warne seem like a choirboy, and during the 1960s he utilised his competitive nature to great effect as captain of Western Australia and Leicestershire. He even managed a final Test appearance – his 49th – as replacement for Fred Titmus in the West Indies in 1968, where his belligerent 89 at Georgetown surpassed his previous highest first-class score and enabled England to draw the match and win the series.

After retiring with 2,844 first-class wickets to his name, Lock coached in Perth and London but his later years were overshadowed by two separate charges of sexually abusing young girls. He was cleared on both occasions but he had been forced to sell some of his cricket memorabilia to cover his legal costs and the ordeal, coupled with the death of his wife from a heart attack, left him a broken man. In 1995, shortly after being acquitted of the second charge, Lock died in Perth from cancer.

Shortly before his death he commented bitterly that he would be remembered for the abuse charges rather than his cricket. But, quite apart from his own outstanding career, the events of that July day in Manchester back in 1956 ensured that the name of Tony Lock would never fade away. He may have resented Laker's achievement at the time but some years later, in mellower mood, he confessed to Laker's wife that he wished he hadn't taken that one wicket. For a born competitor such as Lock, that was quite an admission.

Ted Pooley
Gambler Anonymous

Ted Pooley should have gone down in cricket history as the man who kept wicket for England in the very first Test match. Instead he serves as nothing more than a footnote – the man who languished in jail while England lost that historic encounter with Australia in March 1877. His downfall was gambling, the eventual culmination of which was his miserable, penniless death in a London workhouse.

Pooley was born in Chepstow, Monmouthshire, in 1842 and he played briefly for Middlesex before joining Surrey, primarily as a batsman. Ironically, Surrey themselves took something of a gamble by appointing the chirpy youngster as replacement for their injured wicket-keeper Tom Lockyer. Pooley recounted his introduction to wicket-keeping in *Old English Cricketers*: 'Old Tom Lockyer's hands were bad, and the ground being fiery he could not take his usual place behind the sticks. Mr F.P. Miller, the Surrey captain, was in a quandary as to who should relieve him, so I, saucy-like, as usual, went up to him and said, "Mr Miller, let me have a try." "You? What do you know about wicketkeeping? Have you ever kept wicket at all?" was Mr Miller's remark. "No, never, but I should like to try," I replied. "Nonsense," said he, and when just at that moment H.H. Stephenson came up and remarked "Let the young 'un have a go, sir," Mr Miller relented. I donned the gloves, quickly got two or three wickets, and seemed so much at home that Tom Lockyer was delighted, and said I was born to keep wicket and would have to be his successor in the Surrey team.'

By 1866 Pooley was established in the Surrey side, proving particularly effective in keeping to the slow bowling of James Southerton. *Wisden* describing him as 'quick as lightning and with all his brilliancy very safe.' Keeping for Surrey at the Oval against Sussex in 1868 (with Southerton curiously playing for the opposition), Pooley claimed 12 victims – eight caught and four stumped. He further proved his worth to the county by scoring 93 during the Canterbury Week of 1871 while batting with a broken finger. Pooley's bravery – he stood up to all bowlers, slow and fast – saw him break both thumbs and every finger in the course of his career. At

Lord's one day he staggered into the pavilion with three teeth knocked out and bumped into the prizefighter Jem Mace who told him: 'Pooley, I would rather stand up against any man in England for an hour than take your place behind the stumps for five minutes.'

The first indication that Pooley was involved in gambling came when he was suspended by Surrey in 1873 following an incident at Bramall Lane, Sheffield. It appears that he won a bottle of champagne in a bet with a colleague, drank the contents at breakfast and consequently had to be replaced as wicketkeeper after lunch. Although it was reported that money had also changed hands, Surrey listed his suspension as being due to 'insubordination and misconduct'.

Four years later Pooley was selected as a member of James Lillywhite's England side for the trip to Australasia. Betting was commonplace on many of the matches, with odds published in local newspapers, and Pooley was not one to miss out on a wager. Before England's game with a Christchurch XXII in New Zealand, Pooley, who was ruled out of the action because of a leg injury, bet local gambler Ralph Donkin that he could correctly nominate the individual scores of each of the Christchurch players. Donkin offered him odds of 20 to 1, whereupon Pooley bet that every Christchurch batsman would score a duck – a smart move since many teams of 22 contained a fair proportion of no-hopers. For every player that failed to score, Pooley stood to earn £1; for every incorrect prediction he had to pay Donkin a shilling. So when nine players registered ducks, Pooley expected to be almost £9 richer, but Donkin sensed that he had been duped and refused to pay up. The resulting argument descended into a brawl, with Pooley openly threatening Donkin. Pooley was arrested and thrown into jail pending a trial. By the time he was acquitted, his depleted team-mates (Pooley was the only wicketkeeper in the party) had travelled to Australia and lost the First Test by 45 runs. Pooley's only consolation was that on his release the residents of Christchurch, touched by his plight, presented him with £50 and a gold watch.

Pooley arrived back in England a month after the rest of the team and two months after the birth of his second child. By then, at 35, his career was on the slide. He never did play for England and when his Surrey career ended a few years later, his life declined to the point that he finished up bankrupt in a workhouse, dying in Lambeth Infirmary in 1907.

Dermot Reeve
The Improviser

It was not without irony that former England all-rounder Dermot Reeve should reveal in 2005 that he was addicted to cocaine, for he had spent most of his career getting up people's noses. Usually it was the opposition, but as Warwickshire's West Indian star Brian Lara would readily admit, sometimes the sentiment extended to those under his own captaincy.

Whilst in the heat of the contest he could be more abrasive than an entire pack of sandpaper, off-duty Reeve is engaging company, specialising in wickedly accurate impersonations of the likes of Imran Khan and Geoffrey Boycott. But above all, he was an enterprising, inventive captain who led Warwickshire to three trophies in 1994 and another two the following year, occasionally by bending the rules about as far as they would go without actually breaking them.

Reeve was born in Kowloon, Hong Kong, in 1963 and, moving to England, signed for Sussex in 1983. He stayed on the south coast for six seasons, performing ably as a middle-order batsman and a seam bowler whose action resembled an octopus experiencing an epileptic fit. He says he inherited his competitive streak from his mother and remembers going home one evening after getting out cheaply by trying to hit spinner Richard Illingworth over the top. His mother appeared decidedly fidgety and, although talk of cricket was banned in the household, after half an hour she could contain herself no longer and announced: 'I have to get this off my chest: do you think you should have hit over the top so early?' His mother may have been his fiercest critic then but she would soon have plenty of rivals for the post.

In 1988 he moved to Warwickshire where his progress, particularly in one-day matches, led to inevitable comparisons with Ian Botham. He loved to improvise and became one of the most accomplished practitioners of the reverse sweep. He would also go down on one knee to hoist pacemen over mid-wicket – anything to unsettle the bowlers. And when it was his turn with the ball his subtle variations in pace never allowed the opposing batsmen a moment's comfort. He made his first one-day international appearance for England in 1991 and his Test debut in New Zealand the following winter. It has been suggested that he might have enjoyed a longer international career than 29 one-day internationals and three Tests had his attitude not upset some of his England team-mates.

He was appointed captain of Warwickshire in 1993 and, despite his frosty relationship with Lara, led the county to unprecedented success. Yet he was still regarded with suspicion by some, who felt that his win-at-all-costs philosophy was occasionally detrimental to the reputation of the game. In a County Championship match against Hampshire in 1996, he came up with a controversial way of dealing with left-arm spinner Rajesh Maru. During his innings, Reeve threw his bat to the ground 15 times in padding away deliveries from Maru, thereby seeking refuge in a clause in Law 32 which states that a player has to be holding his bat to be caught off the glove. It was legal but was it within the spirit of the game? Reeve was characteristically unrepentant but the incident reveals why Warwickshire were not universally popular champions.

He left Warwickshire in 1997 to coach Somerset and also began commentary work for Channel 4. His views at the microphone were suitably forthright and incisive but his poor timekeeping started to let him down. In 2004 Channel 4 disciplined him for being later than usual for the Lord's Test against New Zealand, his punishment being suspension from the commentary team for the next Test. Then in May 2005 a national newspaper exposé of his cocaine addiction forced him to quit. He revealed that he had commentated under the influence of cocaine during that Lord's Test against New Zealand the previous year. He admitted: 'I have no recollection of seeing the ball on Saturday and Sunday. I had to watch the match video to hear what I said. No one seemed to notice much difference, they just said I was my usual self but more chirpy – and kept doing Imran Khan impressions off-screen.'

He may have suffered an untimely fall from grace but the charismatic Reeve remains a popular after-dinner speaker, drawing on his experiences as a master of motivation, innovation and some-times provocation.

Phil Tufnell
Rebel, Rebel

When someone asked Phil Tufnell why he became a slow bowler, his answer was simple: 'You can't smoke 20 a day and bowl fast.' The remark is vintage Tufnell, one of the great anti-heroes of modern sport, the man nicknamed 'The Cat', not for his supreme athleticism but because, as a result of too much partying, he slept through his 12th-man duties for Middlesex at Headingley in 1988. Throughout his career Tufnell did his utmost to live up to his reputation as the 'bad boy' of English cricket. There were fines, sulks and bust-ups aplenty. And his private life was even more colourful, as he reflected in his autobiography. 'In my time,' he wrote, 'I've been arrested, spent a night in the cells on three separate occasions I can remember, and been hit over the head with a half-brick by a man I sincerely believe wanted to kill me for the treatment of his daughter.' For good measure, he could have added that he was briefly booked into a psychiatric unit and that one of his ex-wives later became a prostitute. The Phil Tufnell Story was rarely dull.

It began at Barnet on 29 April 1966 when Philip Clive Roderick Tufnell entered an unsuspecting world. A teenage punk, he was expelled from school and soon found that the only thing he was good at – apart from drinking, chasing girls and getting into trouble – was playing cricket. In 1984 he joined the MCC groundstaff but when a Middlesex scout came to watch him in a match against Surrey, he blew his chances with a spectacular strop. First, he argued so vehemently with captain Don Wilson over field placings that he was removed from the attack and banished to the deep. Then when he had the opportunity – unlikely as it may seem – to impress with his fielding, he was in such a foul mood that he registered his protest by trapping the ball with his feet and petulantly booting it back 30 yards in Wilson's direction. While Wilson stared at him in disbelief, the scout climbed into his car and made a hasty exit.

Fortunately for Tufnell he created a more favourable impression during a Middlesex second XI fixture and was taken on by the county. He made his first XI debut in 1986 against Worcestershire and was so nervous when he went in to bat against paceman Neal Radford that David Smith, fielding at short leg, inquired: 'Who is this fucking muppet?' Tufnell never did relish facing quick bowlers – even those of Radford's modest pace – his approach to the task being to back away to the extent that by the time the ball reached the stumps he was almost standing alongside the square-leg umpire. Self-preservation came high on Tufnell's list of priorities.

The young rebel found himself in constant trouble at Middlesex and was regularly hauled before the committee and told to buck up his ideas. Despairing of Tufnell's scruffy appearance, his captain, Mike Gatting, kidnapped him during the lunch interval of a game against Yorkshire at Uxbridge and dragged him to a nearby barber's for a short back and sides to replace his ponytail. However, his bowling meant that he was beginning to be noticed for the right reasons. A quirky run-up that consisted of a kick of the back leg, a skip and a jump was the prelude to a catalogue of left-arm subtlety. He would end up taking over 1,000 first-class wickets, many of his victims being deceived in the flight.

He made his Test debut against Australia at Melbourne in 1990 but, in a foretaste of things to come, caused a storm in a teacup by appearing to snub captain Graham Gooch after taking his first Test wicket. In fact, Tufnell was in such a rush to congratulate catcher Eddie Hemmings that he failed to spot Gooch's outstretched hand. Tufnell elaborated: 'The truth is that Elle Macpherson could have been standing in front of me as naked as the day she was born and I wouldn't have noticed.'

It was on the 1990–91 tour of Australia that Tufnell achieved cult status. He was barracked mercilessly by the Australian fans for the standard of his fielding, which combined the lethargic with the incompetent. The lowpoint came in a one-day international in Sydney. Following a horrendous mix-up, both Australian batsmen were at the same end as Tufnell prepared to gather the ball just five yards from the stumps. Steve Waugh had already given it up as a lost cause, tucked his bat under his arm and started to walk from the field, but he had reckoned without Tufnell who, after first fumbling the easy throw, then panicked, took a wild shy at the stumps, missed, and also bypassed all the fielders who were backing up. Waugh, with his gloves off, couldn't believe his luck and turned round to run back 20 yards from the pavilion to the crease and preserve his wicket.

After that episode, the Australian fans baited Tufnell whenever he visited their shores. One heckler famously called out: 'Tufnell! Can I borrow your brain? I'm building an idiot.' On another occasion someone asked for his autograph and then slapped a minced beef and onion pie on his head. He fared little better in New Zealand, where the crowds threw fruit at him. Yet every misfield, every mishap merely served to boost the Tufnell legend. Former England captain Mike Brearley was baffled by it all. 'Why,' he asked, 'is Tufnell the most popular man in the team? Is it the Manuel factor, in which the most helpless member of the cast is most affectionately identified with?'

The only aspect of Tufnell's play that was comparable in ineptitude to his fielding was his batting, his Test average of five speaking volumes – and even that figure was bolstered by a number of not-outs. Predictably he found international fast bowlers even more distasteful than those on the county circuit. After claiming the wicket of Craig McDermott in the 1991 Perth Test, Tufnell heard the Australian paceman snarl: 'You've got to bat on this in a minute. Hospital food suit you?' The answer was an unequivocal 'no', so it was a visibly nervous Tufnell that came out to bat with England's innings in tatters. Almost immediately he received a brutal delivery from Merv Hughes that reared up from a length, caught him on the top of the thumb and went through for a catch. To Tufnell's horror, however, the umpire seemed about to reject the appeal, so, thinking quickly, Tufnell wailed: 'Ow, my thumb! I think you've broken my thumb.' The umpire took the hint and raised his finger, allowing Tufnell to return to the sanctuary of the pavilion 'not a moment too soon.'

His memories of India are scarcely any fonder, prompting his remark after just two weeks on the subcontinent in 1993: 'Done the elephants, done the poverty. Can we go home now?' During a match against the Rest of India at Vishakhapatnam, he once again allowed his frustration to get the better of him, initially at being repeatedly no-balled for overstepping the popping crease and then when wicketkeeper Richard Blakey missed a stumping chance to get rid of Sachin Tendulkar, India's foremost batsman. Tendulkar's escape unleashed a torrent of abuse from the bowler. Tufnell said: 'I was swearing at everyone and everything. It was a blind rage, the kind you see from kids being dragged round supermarkets, the kind which bring down the house and have everyone cringing with embarrassment.' Still seething, at the end of the over he snatched his cap from umpire Jayaprakash, called him a cheat, and kicked the cap all the way back to his fielding position at fine leg. Even a supermodel would have been proud of such a tantrum. Back at the team hotel he hid in Robin Smith's toilet, hoping that the fuss would die down but he paid for his petulance with a £500 fine.

Another fit of pique saw Tufnell sent off by the long-suffering Gatting during a county game against Yorkshire at Sheffield. Already angry at being dropped by England, Tufnell sulked throughout the match, matters finally coming to a head on the third day when he had a row with the captain over a field placing. Tufnell swore and kicked the turf, whereupon Gatting shouted back and ordered him to leave the field. He did bat, however, and ironically his endeavours with the willow helped Middlesex claim a draw. But Gatting still suspended him for the next match.

For all his temperamental outbursts, Tufnell saw no point in taunting the opposition. 'I don't really sledge batsmen,' he said. 'If I beat his outside edge and say, "You're a shit batsman," and then the next ball he hits me for six, who's the prat?' Tufnell was not always associated with such mature reasoning.

His behaviour at the wicket was not helped by his chaotic private life. Facing charges of assaulting his girlfriend, he took to the field for a Middlesex second XI fixture at Uxbridge but his mind was in such a turmoil that he was unable to bowl and walked off dejectedly. He was eventually persuaded to return to the action but his head was still all over the place. On tour to Australia in 1994–95 he actually suffered a breakdown and was booked into a Perth psychiatric unit, although he discharged himself after an hour. He hit the headlines again when denying allegations that he had smoked pot in the disabled toilet of a restaurant in Christchurch, New Zealand. The England management accepted his account but he was later fined £1,000 for failing to turn up for a random drug test after a County Championship match. He laughed off most of the tabloid scandals. 'The next thing you know they will be saying I wear stockings and suspenders under my flannels.'

Tufnell's occasional moments of inspiration – such as his 11 for 93 against Australia at the Oval in 1997 – kept his fan club happy but after 42 Tests he retired from first-class cricket in 2002. He then won a whole new fan base through his appearance on the TV reality show *I'm a Celebrity, Get Me Out of Here!* The Cat had finally landed on his feet.

Shane Warne
Spin Genius

It was a raw April afternoon in the Lancashire town of Ramsbottom and Accrington skipper Andy Barker was trudging back to the pavilion, cursing himself for getting out. He had barely reached the dressing room when he heard a roar behind him. He instinctively hoped that Shane Warne, the overweight but likeable 21-year-old recruit from Australia who was making his Lancashire League debut, had hit a boundary. 'But then,' recalls Barker, 'I looked back and saw the middle stump uprooted and he was walking back and some of the spectators, who he had been buying drinks for the night before, were shouting: "Send him back, he is rubbish."'

The year was 1991 and once he had adjusted to the Lancashire climate Warne never looked back, finishing his season with 73 wickets for Accrington. He also got through three wicketkeepers, two having given up in despair at not knowing which way Warne's deliveries were going to turn – a sentiment that would be shared by countless English batsmen over the next 16 years. For, unbeknown to those huddled together in the stand at Ramsbottom that afternoon, the shy youngster would go on to become one of the greatest cricketers of the 20th century, a man hailed by Richie Benaud as 'the finest leg-spinner the world has ever seen.'

He was the first cricketer to take 700 Test wickets, one of which, his very first delivery against England, was named 'Ball of the Century'. He revived the art of leg-spin, previously thought to be extinct, and introduced a whole new vocabulary of zooters, sliders, flippers and floaters. Before each series it was announced that Warne had devised a new type of delivery; England's batsmen quaked collectively in anticipation. And he did it all on a diet of junk food and against a series of lurid tabloid headlines about women, a bookmaker, diet pills, and more women.

Shane Warne was born in Ferntree Gully, Victoria, on 13 September 1969 yet his was so nearly a talent that went unfulfilled. As a 21-year-old at the Australian Institute of Sport's new Cricket Academy in Adelaide, he was overweight and undisciplined. His attitude and lifestyle – the gambling, the drinking, the smoking, the partying, the reluctance to train – threatened his career before it had even started. Warne seemed happy to be the life and soul of the party until former Australian Test leg-spinner Terry Jenner took him under his wing. Jenner remembers well their first meeting at the Academy: 'Without any real warm-up he bowled this leg break which curved half a metre and spun just as far! It was seemingly effortless, yet a magnificent delivery.'

At the Academy, by practising with a tennis ball in his hotel corridor, Warne soon mastered the flipper – a skidding backspinner that keeps low and straight. It was a ball which Clarrie Grimmett, the famous Australian leg-spinner of the 1930s, had practised for 12 years before bowling it in anger. At the height of his powers, Warne was able to deliver his flipper at 70mph, compared to 45mph for the average leg break. Because he tweaked the ball so hard, he was also able to deceive batsmen by the tremendous amount of drift he obtained. Discussing his art, Warne revealed: 'The advantage I've got over most other leg-spinners is my drift. That's what plays on a batsman's mind as he's playing the shot, the drift...It floats away, and they have to second-guess the shot. They think it's there but it's not.'

However, Warne was still not exactly the Academy's idea of a model pupil and a row with one of the coaches over his perceived lack of effort on a training run led to him being axed from the Academy's January 1991 tour of Sri Lanka. Instead Warne went home to Melbourne and a couple of weeks later made his debut for Victoria against Western Australia. It was an inauspicious start to his first-class career; his first two balls were hit for four, his third for three, and altogether his opening two overs cost 20 runs. Unsurprisingly, he lost his place in the team and come spring decided to head for the sunny climes of Accrington.

His Test debut the following January was scarcely more distinguished as he finished with figures of 1 for 150 against India at Sydney but his career really took off in the First Test at Old Trafford in 1993 with *that* ball, which pitched a foot outside leg before hitting a bemused Mike Gatting's off-stump. The prodigious turn that Warne extracted from the pitch left seasoned observers searching for superlatives. Many years later a philosophical Gatting reflected on the significance of that delivery. 'I suppose I can say that "I was there" at the moment he (Warne) first indicated his potential to the wider world...there or thereabouts, anyway.'

That one ball turned Warne into a global superstar, able to attract huge commercial deals, and also cast a spell over English batsmen for the rest of his career. The England boys were in good company. South African Daryll Cullinan had tried to dish out a few fat-boy jibes but was forced to eat humble pie as he became Warne's personal bunny. So mesmerised was Cullinan by Warne's bowling repertoire that he was forced to seek psychiatric help in a bid to conquer the Australian's hold over him. Warne had no qualms about sledging, saying: 'If I can get a batsman out by saying something that affects his game so much, then why not? That's a chink in his mental armour.' He was certainly not backward in voicing his opinions on the field, his appeals to umpires being of such volume that an inquiry for lbw at the Oval could be heard at Lord's. However, he overstepped the mark when bowling South African opener Andrew Hudson round his legs at Johannesburg in 1994. As Hudson walked, Warne fired off a loud volley of abuse and had to be physically restrained by Australian wicketkeeper Ian Healy from taking matters further. After being heavily fined and widely condemned, Warne tried to explain his actions. 'It is just as important for a spin bowler to be aggressive as it is a fast bowler,' he said. 'We play at a very high level of arousal, on the edge of fury if you like.'

Warne was to become no stranger to controversy. In 1998 he was tricked into accepting £3,000 from an Indian bookmaker for information about pitch conditions against Sri Lanka. In 2003 he was sent home from the World Cup in South Africa and banned for a year after testing positive for a banned drug. He lost a lucrative anti-smoking sponsorship deal by being photographed smoking a cigarette while playing cards outside a dressing room in Wellington, New Zealand, and has been the subject of a number of tabloid 'kiss-and-tell' stories. Fresh allegations of extramarital affairs appeared as Warne was in England preparing for the 2005 Ashes series, prompting his distraught wife Simone to announce that she was leaving him. 'He'd only been alone for eight weeks,' she said. 'Being faithful for eight weeks isn't too much to ask, is it?'

The Australian media was also losing patience with him. 'Warne's failure to accept responsibility, his vanity, insecurity and fragile ego, have made him a liability,' suggested the *Australian*. 'The distraction and destruction of Cyclone Shane may yet prove Australia's greatest Ashes' enemy.' Yet once the series began his personal problems were put aside as, at the age of 36, he produced the performance of his career: 40 wickets and 249 runs, sometimes standing alone in taking the battle to England. Indeed it should not be forgotten that as well as being a magnificent bowler and sharp slip fielder (125 Test catches), Warne is an accomplished batsman whose records also include that of making more Test runs (3,154) than anyone else without reaching a century. The nearest he came was being dismissed for 99 off what was later shown to be a no-ball.

Warne announced his retirement from Test cricket in 2007 following Australia's 5–0 series victory over England and after claiming his 1,000th international wicket (Tests and one-day internationals combined). His final total stood at 708 Test wickets. Another Australian legend, Merv Hughes, spoke for the world of cricket when he said: 'Whatever you say about Shane Warne isn't enough. His performances have not only shaped cricket in Australia but worldwide. Most people go through a purple patch and Shane Warne has had a purple patch for 15 or 16 years.'

UNLIKELY ATHLETES

Warwick Armstrong
The Big Ship

It was said of Warwick Armstrong that any ball he drove and any deckchair he sat upon were never the same again. This is perhaps not surprising in view of the fact that towards the end of his career the former Australian captain nicknamed 'The Big Ship' weighed a colossal 22 stone. He had a temper to match his build and is credited by many as being the first Australian to use intimidatory tactics, both on umpires and opposing batsmen, *Wisden* relating that he 'bore himself in a way likely to cause offence.' He routinely queried umpiring decisions and helped psych out Jack Hobbs at Headingley in 1909 after the umpire had given the batsman the benefit of the doubt regarding a claim for hit-wicket. Hobbs subsequently wrote: 'The Australians made a rare fuss. They gathered together on the field and confabulated. The chief offender was Warwick Armstrong, who got very nasty and unsportsmanlike, refusing to accept the umpire's decision. This upset me. I did not know whether I was standing on my head or my heels, with the consequence that two balls later I let one go, never even attempting to play it, and it bowled me.' Hobbs added that he never forgave Armstrong over the incident.

Armstrong was also one of the pioneers of leg theory, deliberately bowling over after over wide of the leg-stump to a field set accordingly. He was supposedly bowling leg-breaks but any turn was minimal, the effect being to tie the batsmen down until they took foolhardy risks. There was no denying his effectiveness. He captured over 800 wickets and scored more than 16,000 runs in first-class cricket, his batting average a fraction under 47. He played in 50 Tests, captaining Australia in two series against England, which produced a remarkable record of eight straight victories followed by two draws. Small wonder that the English did not always speak fondly of him.

Warwick Windridge Armstrong was born in Kyneton, Victoria, in 1879. As an athletic youth, before his 6ft 2in frame was bloated by his fondness for whisky, he played Australian Rules football for South Melbourne and was a kicker of some repute. In the summer, however, he played cricket for Victoria and, earning a reputation as an aggressive batsman and tidy bowler, was selected for his country against England at Melbourne in 1902. His impact was instant, joining forces with Reg Duff to record the first-ever century partnership for the last wicket in a Test match.

Thereafter he became a permanent fixture in the national side, missing out only when he refused to tour England in 1912 in protest at how the Australian Board of Control had decided that the team would be managed. Even such an open act of defiance failed to dent his standing and not only was he recalled for Australia's next Test, he was also promoted to captain.

By the time he led Australia to a 5–0 whitewash of the 1920–21 MCC tourists, Armstrong's girth had expanded along with his influence. Edmund Blunden wrote that he made the bat look like a teaspoon and the bowling like weak tea. However, tea was by no means Armstrong's favourite drink. At the First test in Sydney he sat, padded up, drinking whisky with friends in the Members' Bar before going out to make 158.

On the voyage to England for the next series in the summer of 1921, he sharpened his fitness by spending the six weeks at sea helping to stoke the ship's boilers. The exercise failed to reduce his weight by a single pound, the *Sportsman* noting that since his last visit to England he was 'so greatly increased in bulk, without becoming the least bit corpulent, that he dwarfs all his neighbours.' Armstrong dismissed the teetotallers in the Australian party as 'the lemonade crowd' and although he ordered his players to be in bed by 11 o'clock, he himself often didn't arrive back at the hotel until the early hours. However there was no doubting his professionalism and will to win. Indeed, in the tourists' match against Kent he was so incensed at being run out by opposing captain Leslie Troughton, a notoriously poor fielder, that he hurled his bat away and stormed off to the pavilion without it. There he ordered one of his team to go back and fetch it.

After Australia had won the first three Tests that summer, rain halted their progress at Old Trafford, where the highlight was a mix-up over the rules. The first day having been washed out, the England captain, the Hon. Lionel Tennyson, decided to declare at 5.50pm on the second evening. The England batsmen left the field but Armstrong stayed put and sat on the turf near the stumps where he had been bowling. He then pointed out to the umpires that the law, amended in 1914, stated that in the event of a lost first day, a declaration could not be made later than an hour and 40 minutes before close of play. After a 20-minute delay, England were forced to resume their innings, the umpires in such a muddle that they allowed Armstrong to bowl the first over on the resumption, meaning that he had bowled two successive overs.

Armstrong firmly believed that all Test matches should be played to a finish, irrespective of time, and when the Fifth Test at the Oval was heading for a certain draw he made his displeasure known by resting his main bowlers and retiring to the outfield where he picked up a discarded newspaper and started reading it to see if he could find any cricket going on anywhere!

That was to be Armstrong's final Test. At the age of 42 he retired and took up journalism, writing about the game with characteristic candour, sometimes to the displeasure of those on the receiving end of his observations. When he died in Sydney in 1947, Australian cricket lost a giant in every respect.

David Boon
The Keg On Legs

For all his 7,422 Test runs at an average of over 43, that is not the record for which pugnacious Tasmanian batsman David Boon is most fondly remembered in Australian circles. That honour goes to the 52 cans of beer he is said to have consumed on the flight from Sydney to London ahead of the 1989 Ashes series.

Boon's feat, which shattered the old record of 46 held by Rod Marsh, was not planned – he simply couldn't stop drinking. Luckily the Qantas staff were keeping count and, as the 47th can was finished to rousing cheers, the captain of the plane came on the PA system and congratulated Boon on his fantastic effort. Amazingly, Boon managed to walk – almost unaided – from the plane at the end of his marathon binge and went on to attend a sponsor's cocktail party, where he downed another three pints. After that he didn't wake up for 36 hours and missed two training sessions. Coach Bob Simpson was not amused but decided against sending Boon home. It proved a wise move. Boon went on to make over 500 runs in the Test series at an average of more than 70 as Australia regained the Ashes. A beer or 50 merely whetted his appetite for battle.

Victory in the First Test at Headingley that year inevitably resulted in another long, hard drinking session, the only problem being that the Australians were due to play Lancashire the following day. Alas, the tourists lost the toss and thus faced the prospect of an arduous day in the field while feeling considerably the worse for wear. Even though several catches were dropped – Boon fell flat on his face in one vain attempt – the Australians somehow won the game.

Boon had previously been suspended by Tasmania following a late-night fracas at a hotel, and in 1988 he vomited on the Adelaide Oval in front of a live national TV audience of millions before going on to make 122 and be named 'Man of the Match'. An escapade in South Africa had a smaller audience but was no less embarrassing. Having celebrated a Test victory with a few drinks, Boon returned to his hotel room and decided to pack as many items as possible that evening so as to give himself an extra half-hour's sleep in the morning. He carefully placed his clothes for the morning next to the bed and, pleased with his foresight, carried his bags towards the foyer, only to be intercepted by a member of the hotel staff who said: 'I can't let you take them any further.' Boon was puzzled until he looked down and saw that he was completely naked. In his drunken state, he had set aside his clothes for the morning but had forgotten to put any on that evening!

With such a stomach for alcohol, it is no surprise that the stocky fellow with the walrus moustache became an Australian cult hero.

David Clarence Boon was born in Launceston, Tasmania, in 1960. As an 18-year-old he played a starring role in Tasmania's historic Gillette Cup win – their first interstate one-day title – and went on to help his country to four Ashes series' wins. He usually batted at number three, adopting an awkward but effective style, his belligerent square cutting and pulling upsetting the rhythm of the world's finest bowlers. He was a tough competitor, making a century against the West Indies in Jamaica in 1991 after being hit in the face by a ball from Patrick Patterson. The wound was later stitched up...without anaesthetic.

Boon was also a fearless fielder at forward short leg. He was hit on the helmet with such ferocity by a pull shot from Robin Smith at Trent Bridge that the helmet shattered and one piece was even found outside the boundary rope. When the Trent Bridge physiotherapist asked him how he felt, Boon complained of an ache high up on the right side of his head. 'When I opened my mouth to demonstrate,' said Boon, 'my entire jaw clicked back into place!'

In spite of the dangers, he was always happy to field there. 'Bat-pad is an excellent vantage point,' he explained. 'First and foremost, you don't have to do as much running as other fieldsmen. Just practise your diving skills, fall over, lie down and watch someone else chase the ball to the boundary.'

He played the last of his 107 Tests in 1996 and the following year led Durham in the County Championship before eventually retiring in 1999. But the legend of the man nicknamed the 'Keg on Legs' for his drinking exploits lives on, in the form of talking Boony dolls marketed by Victoria Bitter. The doll has a range of typical Boon phrases, such as 'Time to get a beer, cricket's about to start.' In Tasmania he is still revered. A stand at the Launceston ground has been named after him and it has even been suggested that the Tasmanian speed limit be lowered to 52kph, the figure chosen as a touching tribute to David Boon's finest achievement. I'll drink to that.

Mike Gatting
The Fat Controller

When former England captain Mike Gatting was awarded the OBE, certain players on the county circuit reckoned it stood for Obese Branston Eater. He certainly managed to get himself into a pickle on more than one occasion, and while his commitment to food never wavered, understandably there were times when he despaired of the England cricketing hierarchy. Having survived the finger-jabbing incident with Pakistan umpire Shakoor Rana, he was stripped of the England captaincy for *not* sleeping with a barmaid. It would have driven most men to drink, but Gatting would probably have settled for a double cheeseburger and large fries. Comments about his weight were the staple diet of county banter, his unambiguous nicknames ranging from 'Fat Gatt' to 'The Fat Controller'. The jokes followed him on to the pitch. When the then England captain David Gower was discussing field placings with bowler Chris Cowdrey, he asked Cowdrey whether he wanted Gatting a foot wider. 'No,' replied Cowdrey instantly, 'he'd burst!'

Mike Gatting worked hard and he ate hard. Squat and portly, he didn't look much like an athlete from a distance and the impression barely changed on closer inspection. But he had muscular arms and a no-nonsense attitude, which enabled him to take on and master most of the world's leading bowlers. He was also a natural leader of men, qualities that were needed time and again, not only at international level but also in controlling a Middlesex dressing room that contained such difficult characters as Phil Edmonds and Phil Tufnell. He epitomised the British bulldog spirit.

Even as a child (he was born in Kingsbury in 1957) Gatting was described as 'a proper little bruiser', yet curiously was considered a promising ballroom dancer. More obviously, he also displayed a talent for football (brother Steve later turned professional with Arsenal and Brighton), but joining Middlesex meant that he had to reject the apprenticeship he had been offered by Watford Football Club. He made his first-class debut in 1975 and at the age of 20 was sent on tour to Pakistan. However, it took him several years to establish himself in the England side and 54 Test innings to convert one of his many 50s into that elusive 100.

On the 1985–86 tour to the West Indies he was badly injured by a bouncer from Malcolm Marshall that smashed his nose. When Marshall picked up the ball and found a piece of Gatting's nose bone embedded in it, he threw the ball down in horror, later admitting: 'I've hit quite a few batsmen, but I can't recall inflicting such a nasty looking injury as that.' On arriving back at Heathrow, his nose squashed, bloodied and bruised, Gatting was asked by a reporter: 'Where exactly did it hit you?'

A popular member of the England set-up and already established as Middlesex captain (a post he would hold for 14 years), Gatting stepped up to become England skipper in 1986 and led the team to a surprise Ashes success in Australia. The tour was not without mishap, the new captain accidentally oversleeping before the match with Victoria at Melbourne. He eventually hurried on to the pitch 20 minutes and five overs late, David Gower having tossed up in his place and lost. As punishment, Gower brought him on as first change bowler and Gatting responded by taking 4 for 31 with his medium-pacers.

After such a promising start, the next 18 months would see Gatting tread on more toes than in his ballroom dancing days. First, there were the disgraceful scenes in Faisalabad after umpire Shakoor Rana wrongly accused Gatting of cheating during the Second Test with Pakistan by moving a fielder behind the batsman's back while Eddie Hemmings was bowling. Gatting lost his cool and stood eyeball-to-eyeball, paunch-to-paunch with Rana in an unseemly confrontation in the middle of the pitch. Rana refused to stand again in the match until Gatting apologised, which he duly did, but only after the third day had been abandoned because the Pakistan players chose to remain in the pavilion in support of Rana.

Gatting managed to ride that particular storm but six months later he was involved in further controversy when two national newspapers reported that on the night before going in to bat against the West Indies at Trent Bridge he had invited a barmaid, Louise Shipman, to his hotel room for a drink to celebrate his 31st birthday. Ian Botham, no stranger to tabloid tales himself, leaped to the captain's defence, pointing out: 'It couldn't have been Gatt. Anything he takes up to his room after nine o'clock, he eats.' Gatting denied any sexual impropriety but while the Test and County Cricket Board accepted his version of events, they decided to sack him as captain anyway. It was thought the board had been looking for an excuse since Faisalabad but had been deterred from action by Gatting's enduring popularity. The *Melbourne Age* headline read: 'Gatting, caught rumour, bowled hypocrisy, 0.'

When Ted Dexter succeeded Peter May as chairman of the selectors in 1989, he pressed for Gatting's reinstatement as captain, only to be overruled by his colleagues. A disappointed Gatting took a rebel team to South Africa instead. Although he never regained the

England captaincy, Gatting kept his place in the team, eventually totalling 79 Tests. It was, of course, his misfortune to be on the receiving end of Shane Warne's wonder ball at Old Trafford. Describing Gatting's stunned expression as he walked off, Graham Gooch said: 'He looked as though someone had just nicked his lunch.' Gooch also offered the thought that if the ball 'had been a cheese roll, it would never have got past him.' Journalist Martin Johnson was almost as perplexed as Gatting, musing: 'How anyone can spin a ball the width of Gatting boggles the mind.'

Gatting made his last Test appearance two years later, and since his retirement as a player has worked as a coach and commentator. Happily, despite the various controversies in which he was embroiled, the cricket authorities have not forgotten his unique qualities and on Bangladesh's 2005 tour of England, Gatting was given the task of finding a curry chef to cater for the players. There could be no finer man for the job.

Inzamam-ul-Haq
Heavyweight Hero

Just as it was Mike Gatting's lot to be the butt of food jokes, so Pakistan's bulky batsman Inzamam-ul-Haq seems to attract animal comparisons. Peter Roebuck described him as appearing to lumber about like a hippo in a wetlands while Inzy's misfortune in falling over his own stumps at Headingley in 2006 prompted Jonathan Agnew to liken his attempt at evasive action to 'an elephant trying to do the pole vault.'

Wildlife similes extend to the fact that Inzy is a big game player, the man on whom Pakistan can rely in a crisis. He ambles to the wicket with an air of casual indifference but once in his stride he can be terrifyingly destructive. As befits someone of his build, he is a ferocious hitter and is particularly strong on the leg side, the pull stroke being probably his most effective shot. Imran Khan has called him 'the best batsman in the world against pace' because 'he seems to have so much time on his hands before the ball reaches him.' Sadly, Inzy's surprisingly nimble footwork at the crease is not matched in the field or in his running between wickets. Although an excellent slip fielder, he is almost immobile in other areas of the field and will only saunter after the ball if no one else is in the vicinity. Meanwhile his running between wickets is little short of catastrophic, as illustrated by the fact that he has been run out more than 40 times for his country. Peter Roebuck wondered: 'Whether he has heard of short singles can only be guessed. It may be that he presumes they are a reference to unmarried gnomes.'

Inzy's aversion to physical exercise is well documented. In 2000, when Pakistan were practising before a Test, he remained in the dressing room while his team-mates went out for their warm-up and fielding drill. As they moved on to the nets, Inzy ventured outside, strolling to a large wicker chair that had kindly been placed for him next to the nets. When it was his turn for batting practice, he hauled himself slowly from the chair, dealt with each delivery with the minimum of effort and returned to the dressing room. The next day he made a century. Ahead of the 2003 World Cup he did actually try to shed some of his 16-and-a-half stones in a bid to become a lean, mean, batting machine. He managed to lose over two-and-a-half stone but was so miserable as a result that he scored just 19 runs in six innings and was dropped. Thereafter he resolved to maintain his ample proportions.

Inzamam was born in Multan, Punjab Province, in 1970 and first made his name in the semi-final of the 1992 World Cup against New Zealand, blasting a match-winning 60 from just 37 balls. His size made him an obvious target for opposition supporters and produced a bizarre incident at the 1997 Sahara Cup in Toronto, Canada. An Indian fan with a megaphone tormented Inzy through-out the game, calling him a 'fat potato' among other choice insults. Eventually Inzy snapped and, after ordering the 12th man to bring out a bat, jumped into the stands with it and began remonstrating with his accuser. One eyewitness claimed: 'If not for the spectators and security staff curbing him, he would have broken the head of that guy.' Canadian police charged Inzy with two counts of assault and one of assault with a deadly weapon, but the charges were later dropped. Nevertheless, he was banned for two one-day inter-nationals by the match referee.

Surprisingly for one with such a languid approach, Inzy has been involved in a number of controversies, mainly for disputing umpiring decisions or appealing in an overly aggressive manner. Appointed captain of Pakistan in 2003, he led by example with the bat but also displayed marked errors of judgement on the leadership front, none more so than in the Fourth Test at the Oval in 2006 when he become the first captain in history to forfeit a Test match. Riled by the decision of umpires Darrell Hair and Billy Doctrove to impose a five-run penalty for alleged ball tampering, Inzamam kept the Pakistan team in the dressing room after tea on the fourth day. Having failed to persuade him to reconsider, the umpires eventually decided that the match could not be resumed and England were later awarded the victory. Some 45 minutes after the scheduled restart, Inzamam finally led the Pakistan players back on to the field – and then straight back into the pavilion as he realised that neither umpires nor England batsmen were present. He was subsequently cleared of ball tampering but was banned for four one-day internationals after being found guilty of bringing the game into disrepute.

Inzy's personal turmoil escalated at the 2007 World Cup. A shock defeat by Ireland saw Pakistan knocked out of the competition but that paled into insignificance next to the mysterious death of the national coach Bob Woolmer. Inzy resigned as Pakistan captain and announced his retirement from one-day internationals. It was an unsatisfactory conclusion to a glittering career that had seen him score over 20,000 runs for his country in all forms of cricket.

In spite of his disciplinary lapses, he was a deceptively witty man. Asked why he won the toss so often, he replied deadpan: 'I practise a lot.' For Inzy, tossing a coin was sometimes about as close as he got to exercise.

Ken 'Slasher' Mackay
An Immovable Object

On the night before the final day of the Fourth Test between Australia and the West Indies at Adelaide in 1961, former West Indies captain Gerry Alexander was invited to the house of Sir Donald Bradman. At the end of a pleasant evening, Alexander, preparing to leave, said: 'Well, it looks like we've got you tomorrow.' All too aware that having been set 460 to win, Australia were teetering precariously on 31 for 3, Bradman sighed, 'Yes it looks that way,' before adding on a more optimistic note, 'but if ever there is a situation for Mackay, it's tomorrow.'

The Mackay in question was Ken Mackay, a dour, gum-chewing, craggy-faced Queenslander, ironically nicknamed 'Slasher' because slashing at a ball was the last thing he would ever dream of doing. Instead, with a crouching style built for defence, the plucky left-hander of the Australian middle order had earned something of a cult following for occupying the crease for hours while grinding out the occasional run, often by virtue of a deflection wide of cover point or a sort of shovel shot past mid wicket. The cap worn at a rakish angle hinted misleadingly at a fluent entertainer. Slasher was anything but; if he could avoid playing a ball, he would, *Wisden* noting that he 'was an uncanny judge of line, often leaving balls that seemed to make the bails quiver.' In his obstinacy and durability, he was Australia's answer to Trevor Bailey.

Bradman's prediction was spot on. When the ninth Australian wicket fell at 207 with 109 minutes of play still remaining, a West Indies victory looked inevitable but Mackay had other ideas. Revelling in the backs-to-the-wall situation, Mackay, joined by Lindsay Kline, frustrated Frank Worrell's men for over after over. As the clock reached six, the fearsome Wes Hall prepared to send down the final delivery of the match to Mackay – a case of an irresistible force meeting an immovable object. Hall gave it all he had but Slasher, rather than offer a shot and risk getting an edge, allowed the ball to crash into his ribcage. Mackay was bruised but unbowed and the match was drawn. Australia had finished on 273 for 9, Mackay's contribution being an undefeated 62 made in 223 minutes – nearly four hours. That night, he was Australia's unlikeliest hero.

John Arlott once said: 'Mackay is the only athlete I have ever known who, as he walked, sagged at ankles, knees and hips.' Far from resembling a professional sportsman, he looked as if he had been hastily assembled by someone who hadn't read the instructions. Yet this gutsy, gritty character played 37 Tests between 1956 and 1963 and although he was rarely a match-winner, he managed to save plenty.

Kenneth Donald Mackay was born at Windsor, Queensland, in 1925 and first played grade cricket in Brisbane at the age of 15. By 1946 he had won a place in the Queensland side and would go on to make 100 appearances for the state. He was appointed captain of Queensland in 1954 but must have thought his chances of Test cricket had passed him by until, at the age of 30, he was selected to tour England with Ian Johnson's side. He made his Test debut at Lord's, batting for a total of seven hours in the match while scoring just 38 and 31. Watching grass grow was considered positively exciting next to Slasher Mackay's batting. Although he struggled for the rest of the tour (even his formidable resilience was no match for the unplayable Jim Laker at Old Trafford, where he bagged a pair), Mackay redeemed himself on the 1957–58 trip to South Africa, hitting five half-centuries in the Tests and finishing the series with an average of 125 thanks to four not-outs.

But there was more to Mackay than slow batting; he was also a useful medium-paced bowler. Although he batted left-handed, he bowled right-arm, capturing the odd vital wicket but, in keeping with his natural style, being used primarily as a defensive, containing bowler. *Wisden* wrote of his bowling: 'He had a steady, almost apologetic approach to the wicket, but the innocuous appearance of his deliveries masked subtle variations of pace and swing.' His finest hour with the ball was in Dacca in 1959–60 when he finished with the remarkable second innings figures of 45–27–42–6 to help Australia to their first Test win in Pakistan. On the same tour he recorded his highest Test score – 89 – against India at Madras, an innings which ended when he was uncharacteristically stumped. One of the few other occasions that Mackay forgot himself and emerged from his shell was when he made a whirlwind 168 against Middlesex at Lord's in 1961.

He played his last Test against England at Adelaide in 1963 and shortly afterwards announced his retirement from first-class cricket. In a display of genuine affection and gratitude, the people of Brisbane contributed some £20,000 to a 'bob in for Slasher' campaign that was organised by the city's morning paper. He became a state selector and later state coach before dying, all-too-young, in 1982 at the age of 56. Sadly, life was one innings that even Slasher Mackay could not prolong.

Colin Milburn
The Jolly Buccaneer

Surveying the generously-built Colin Milburn, Northamptonshire's wicketkeeper and captain, Keith Andrew, advised: 'I know how to help you with your weight problems, Colin. Instead of drinking pints in the bar after play, drink halves.'

Milburn reacted to the suggestion with indignation, replying bluntly: 'My father drank pints, and I'm going to.' The subject was dropped.

A few days later after a hard day in the field, Andrew was buying drinks for the team. 'What'll it be, Col?' he asked.

'Two halves please, skipper,' smiled Milburn.

Colin Milburn was never happier than with either a bat or a pint glass in his hand and could do considerable damage with both. An immensely powerful hitter, he was also the life and soul of any party, a jolly 18-stone giant who was known affectionately as 'Ollie' after the comedian Oliver Hardy. Journalist Ian Wooldridge wrote that Milburn's philosophy was 'not only to burn the candle at both ends, but to cut it in two and set fire to all four ends.'

Unfortunately Milburn's *joie de vivre* did him few favours in terms of his career. He was dropped by England for being overweight and Test selector Alec Bedser was heard to remark disapprovingly: 'Every time I see him he's got a pint in his hand.' Nevertheless, the single factor that ultimately prevented him adding to his nine Test caps was the tragic road crash in 1969, in which he lost the use of his left eye after being thrown through his car windscreen. It was a cruel fate to befall any cricketer, but especially such a warm-hearted, gregarious character whose popularity was commensurate with his bulk. Crowds would go to Northampton just to see Milburn bat and if, opening the innings, he was out cheaply it was not uncommon for disappointed spectators to leave the county ground in the first half-hour of a day's play. He even endeared himself to the most partisan of crowds in the West Indies, who would loudly applaud him to the wicket and react to an early dismissal for their adopted hero with stony silence. His England colleagues could only dream of such affection in the Caribbean, but then few had the charisma of Colin Milburn.

Born in the County Durham mining village of Burnopfield in 1941, Milburn inherited his large build and sporting ability from his father, a useful professional player in northeast league cricket. By the age of 11 young Colin was playing for Burnopfield's second team and within two years had graduated to the first XI. Already a forceful batsman with a penchant for striking the ball out of the ground – 'I've always been a slogger, and my father was a slogger before me' – he joined Chester-le-Street in 1959, where a string of spectacular performances earned him selection for Durham, then still a Minor County. Making his Durham debut against the touring Indians at Sunderland, Milburn struck an impressive 100, an innings which brought him to the attention of Northamptonshire.

He moved to the Midlands county in 1960 and made 1,153 runs for the second XI that season. The training regime at Northants came as something of a shock, however, and on one of his first training runs he was left so far behind that he was forced to hitch a lift on a passing milk float. He was given a spot in the first team the following season but, although he dealt confidently with fast bowlers, spinners frequently proved his downfall. John Arlott observed: 'This was probably less a matter of technique than physique; if, when he played a stroke, his arms passed over his stomach, there was bound to be a wide gate between bat and pads; he had to learn to close it by straddling rather than orbiting his midriff.'

He eventually cemented a regular place with some spectacular knocks. Perhaps because he was not too keen on running unless he really had to, more than 75 per cent of his runs would often come in boundaries. Typically his 123 against Yorkshire was made in just 113 minutes and contained seven sixes and 14 fours. He believed in attacking the bowling from the outset. Keith Andrew once bet him that he couldn't play out the first over of the innings as a maiden but received nothing more than an apologetic smile from the middle as two balls were swiftly despatched to the boundary. Milburn was very much an all-or-nothing batsman, alternating majestic centuries with low scores, but he was being harsh by labelling himself a mere slogger. He had a sound defence when he chose to use it, but his natural instincts were to attack the bowling with powerful shots square on either side of the wicket, his superb eyesight and dashing footwork enabling him to hook as well as any player in the country. He was also a surprisingly agile fielder at short leg and a handy medium-paced bowler, although not of sufficient standard to elevate him to the status of all-rounder.

Described by one writer as having the charisma of a film star, the humour of a stand-up and the power of a small elephant, Milburn was a born entertainer. He would often tell a joke to close fielders, break off the story to hit a boundary, and then deliver the punchline. He also rated himself as a singer and would enliven many an evening with renditions of Elvis or Tom Jones numbers to his team-mates. At one stage he took his singing so seriously that he asked permission from Northants to perform in nightclubs, but when the county discovered this would require him to stay up until 3am they expressed grave reservations, to which Milburn countered: 'I wouldn't be in bed before then in any case!' Yet despite frequently arriving for matches bleary-eyed and at the last minute, his nocturnal excursions never adversely affected his batting.

He was a mainstay of single-wicket competitions, although Fred Titmus, the Middlesex and England off-spinner, irritated him by setting all his fielders deep, thereby forcing Milburn to run a lot. Another year, with defeat staring him in the face against Leicestershire all-rounder Jack van Geloven, Milburn put everything into one fast delivery, but ended up crashing into the turf 'like a steamroller' and had to be carried off by two burly firemen as van Geloven completed victory.

Having been touted for an England place for some time, Milburn finally made the breakthrough in 1966 when he was selected for the First Test versus the West Indies at Old Trafford. Run out for a duck in the first innings, he redeemed himself with 94 in the second against what was then the best bowling attack in the world. Gary

Sobers said: 'We applauded him all the way, for here was a man who could steal a West Indian heart.' When Milburn then hit his maiden Test century – a brilliant effort at Lord's that saved the match for England – fans ran on to the pitch and tried to raise him aloft in celebration, only to discover that the combined efforts of four men were unequal to the task. After such sterling displays, imagine Milburn's dismay when he was dropped for the final Test at the Oval because he was too slow in the outfield – in the words of E.W. Swanton 'a dreadful liability' in the field when there was no need of a short leg. Milburn's response was a thunderous double century for Northants against Essex at Clacton.

That winter he played for Western Australia, where he proceeded to score the fastest first-class century (in 77 minutes) at Adelaide since 1928–29 and the quickest in Australia since the Second World War. His jovial manner made him a huge favourite with the Australian crowds, never more so than when, after a long chase to the boundary, he would go down on one knee to be cooled by a spectator with a fan. They warmed to his unkempt appearance – sometimes underlined by split trousers as the material buckled under the sheer strain of trying to support his body – and to his sportsmanship. If he thought he was out he would walk immediately without waiting for the umpire's verdict. Unfortunately popularity alone could not guarantee a Test place. Originally omitted from the 1968–69 tour of Pakistan, he was called up as an emergency replacement on the back of a whirlwind 243 for Western Australia at Brisbane (he was out in the first over after tea on the first day). The England players formed a guard of honour as he descended from the plane on arrival in Pakistan and he duly obliged with an innings of 139 in the Karachi Test before it was abandoned due to rioting.

Returning to Northamptonshire for the 1969 domestic season, Milburn started in the best possible way with 158 against Leicestershire. Then tragedy struck. On 23 May he was on his way home when his car was involved in a collision with a lorry. The accident cost him the sight of his left eye, the lead eye for a right-handed batsman. At Manchester Eye Hospital doctors decided to fit a false eye. As the nurse opened a drawer and searched for one to match his brown right eye, Milburn joked: 'Better find two – one to match it now and a bloodshot one to match it in the mornings.'

Most people in the game thought Milburn's career was finished but, following the example of the Nawab of Pataudi, who had resumed his career after sustaining eye damage, Milburn did return to the Northants side in 1973. He was even able to make capital out of his injury. Bowling against Derbyshire, he suddenly stopped his run-up and announced that his eye had fallen out. A thorough search took place until one of the umpires found it near the crease. Milburn then rubbed the glass eye with his handkerchief, put it back in and finished the over. However he was a shadow of his former self and managed just one 50 before admitting defeat in 1974 and retiring with a career total of over 13,000 first-class runs (including 100 before lunch on four occasions) and a Test average of more than 46.

He continued to struggle on in league cricket but his life lacked direction. He missed the limelight and, unable to find regular work, hit financial difficulties. On 28 February 1990, aged just 48, he collapsed with a heart attack in Newton Aycliffe and died in the ambulance on the way to hospital. Fittingly, among the pallbearers at his funeral was another robust character from English cricket, Ian Botham.

In truth, Colin Milburn's life ended with the road crash. He had been cut off in his prime. Paying tribute to one of the most flamboyant characters in modern cricket, Geoffrey Boycott said: 'Whatever it says on his death certificate I will always be convinced that Ollie began dying in 1969...I believe he went through a living death knowing his beloved cricket had been taken away from him – he felt cheated.'

Charles Palmer
Master Of The Lob

Charles Palmer was essentially a quiet man. Bespectacled, slightly built and softly spoken, he possessed an easy-going nature that was unlikely ever to cause any ructions, Trevor Bailey once describing him as 'a natural for the role of hen-pecked bank clerk in a farce.' Yet in the course of his career this affable individual managed to find himself at the centre of a controversial England tour to the West Indies and to create mutterings of discontent in some quarters over his propensity to bowl donkey drops that soared as high as a house before dropping with unerring accuracy onto the batsman's stumps.

'They went miles up in the air,' recalled his Leicestershire team-mate Maurice Hallam, 'into orbit. We're talking probably 20 feet. But his strike rate was unbelievable. He hit the top of the stumps or people trod on their wicket.'

Palmer delivered his artful lobs off his standard run-up, with the result that the batsman was invariably taken unawares. Mike Turner, another Leicestershire colleague, who later became county secretary, says: 'They were uncanny. He ran up normally but then the ball went as high as the roof of a house. Jock Livingston of Northamptonshire saw one coming and leaned over the stumps looking to slog it. The ball ran down the face of the bat and he was caught at slip!' Palmer's party piece was particularly effective against the 1957 West Indies tourists, his donkey drops accounting for Rohan Kanhai, Frank Worrell and Nyron Asgarali.

Ordinarily Palmer's bowling was, in keeping with his general demeanour, not calculated to unsettle opponents. Of slow-medium pace, it brought him 365 first-class wickets at an average of 25.15 but he had earned his place in the county side primarily through his batting. However, on one particular day in 1955 he was transformed – albeit temporarily – into a demon bowler and finished with the truly startling figures of 8 for 7, which but for a dropped catch, would have been 9 for 0!

Leicestershire's opponents at Grace Road on 21 May that year were all-conquering Surrey, then in the middle of their run of seven successive County Championship titles. The early weeks of the season had been damp and cold – a few days earlier the entire country had been under a blanket of snow – but that did not prevent Surrey winning their opening five matches. Batting first, Leicestershire were hustled out for 114 (Tony Lock taking 6 for 37) and by tea Surrey had progressed to 42 for 1 in reply, with Peter May striking the ball with ominous ease. Palmer, who was captaining the side, did not intend bowling as he had a bad back, and in any case he never considered himself to be much more than an occasional bowler. In fact, in his five previous matches that summer he had sent down just four overs. However during the tea interval he had decided to switch his spinners round, which meant that somebody had to bowl one over. Sensing that a single over at his pace could not do much damage to his back, Palmer took the task upon himself. 'Go easy on me,' he said to May. 'I haven't bowled this year.'

With his second ball he clean bowled May, the best batsman in England at the time, and not unreasonably decided to extend his spell into a second over, during which he accounted for two more Surrey batsmen. Although the pitch had almost dried out, one wet patch remained and Palmer was able to hit it time and again, making his normally gentle bowling virtually unplayable. Soon Surrey had crumbled to 67 for 9, and Palmer's analysis read 12–12–0–8. All but one of his victims had been bowled. *Wisden* wrote that the crowd, aware that Palmer had bettered Jim Laker's 8 for 2 taken five years earlier, called out, 'Take yourself off, Charlie!'

Ironically, Palmer's world record was to be wrecked by Laker himself, the last Surrey man in. First he slashed the ball high into the covers, where the chance went begging, and then got a fortunate edge down to fine leg. Terry Spencer eventually bowled Laker for 14 and Surrey were all out for 77, Palmer's final figures reading 14–12–7–8. Afterwards, he popped his head around the Surrey dressing room door and grinned: 'Sorry, gentlemen!'

Palmer then top-scored with 64 in Leicestershire's second innings but the pitch grew more docile and Surrey knocked off the 203 needed for victory for the loss of three wickets. Palmer again returned incredible figures, however – 13–12–1–0 – giving him a match return of 27–24–8–8. Not bad for an occasional bowler.

Palmer was born on 15 May 1919 at Old Hill, Staffordshire, of Wesleyan Methodist stock. He read English at Birmingham University but showed such flair for cricket that at 19 he made his senior debut for Worcestershire. Although only 5ft 7in tall and of frail build, he possessed deceptively strong wrists, making him an effective exponent of the cut. He confirmed his potential with three centuries in the summer of 1939, only to lose his best years to the Second World War, most of which he spent in an anti-aircraft battery in Sussex. After the war he became a teacher at Bromsgrove School, continuing to turn out for Worcestershire in the school holidays, and in 1948 he caught the selectors' attention with a hard-hitting 85 against Don Bradman's touring Australians. He was chosen for the England tour of South Africa in 1948–49 but failed to make the Test side.

In 1950 Palmer became captain and secretary of struggling Leicestershire, and soon brought about an improvement in the county's fortunes. He scored 2,071 runs in 1952 – including a fine 127 for the Gentlemen against the Players at Lord's – and helped Leicestershire to a highest-ever Championship finish of sixth. They bettered that with third the following year, and Palmer was rewarded by being appointed player-manager for England's tour to the West Indies that winter. Palmer's hopes of a nice pleasant break in the Caribbean were shattered by the racial and political tensions that clouded the tour, the grim atmosphere not helped by the attitude of the England captain Len Hutton, who was more concerned with victory than diplomacy. It was a tour of riots, umpiring controversy and general discontent, and one that required stronger leadership than Palmer's easy-going approach. He was later criticised for failing to discipline his men, prompting E.W. Swanton to describe his appointment as 'just about the worst decision ever to come out of Lord's.' Palmer made his solitary Test appearance on that tour, but his scores of 22 and 0 in a heavy England defeat did little to lift his spirits.

Having amassed 17,458 first-class runs at an average of thirty-one, Palmer retired in 1957 to work for a steel company. He returned to Leicestershire as chairman in 1964 and oversaw their first County Championship title in 1975. A long-standing MCC committee member, he served as President in 1978–79, when he dealt ably with the fallout from the Kerry Packer affair, although some felt that pitting the inoffensive, lightweight Palmer against the blustering, heavyweight Packer was rather a mismatch. From 1983 to 1985 Palmer was chairman of the Test and County Cricket Board, and also chaired a committee that recommended the introduction of four-day county cricket.

A popular administrator and player (unless you happened to be on the receiving end of one of his donkey drops), Charles Palmer died on 31 March 2005 at the age of 85. At first glance he might not have looked like a natural sportsman, but he certainly left his mark on the game.

Jack Simmons
Flat Jack

Jack Simmons acknowledges that there is every chance he will not be remembered as much for his 12,000 runs and 1,500 wickets for Lancashire as for his legendary consumption of fish and chips. This is a man who, after a hard day's cricket, would go to a fish and chip shop and order two fish, two portions of chips (large) and six pies, all open. And then he'd eat the lot.

He must be the only cricketer to have had a fish supper named after him. He explains: 'There's an amazing fish and chip shop in Great Harwood. I'd come back from a Lancashire game, pop in there and order steak pudding, chips, peas and gravy – with a fish on top. To this day the shop still call it the "Simmo Special".'

His appetite never ceased to amaze his team-mates. 'One day,' he says, 'we got rained off early at Old Trafford and David Lloyd and Graeme Fowler, who both lived in Accrington, had given me a lift home. I asked Bumble (Lloyd) to drop me off at the chippy and I said I'll eat them on the way home because the wife will have the supper on.'

Simmons was in many respects an unusual county cricketer, not only in terms of his diet but also because he was a latecomer to the first-class game. He didn't make his Lancashire debut until he was 27 but then carried on playing for the county until he was nearly 50.

He was born in 1941 in the Lancashire town of Clayton-le-Moors and followed in the footsteps of his father and grandfather by playing club cricket for nearby Enfield. It was there that he first developed a taste for pies, thanks to Bobby Marshall, the club's chairman of selectors. Simmons says: 'Bobby was a baker for the Co-op at Clayton-le-Moors and he used to take me to Blackpool on a Sunday when I was about 15, to get better practice, and so that we didn't have to pay for anything, he would bake a big beef pie. I loved them. Ian Botham said I should have written a book on pie shops and fish and chip shops throughout England because it could have been a best-seller!'

Having picked up invaluable experience from the club's professional, West Indian star Clyde Walcott, Simmons was chosen for Enfield's first team at 14, primarily as a batsman. On leaving school, he became a draughtsman with the Accrington Brick and Tile Company, earning extra money by playing cricket at weekends for Baxenden in the Ribblesdale League and then for Blackpool, where, in 1968, his outstanding form brought him to the attention of Lancashire, for whom he had played a few second XI matches at the start of the decade.

Simmons' belated arrival at Old Trafford coincided with the boom in one-day cricket. All-rounders were much in demand for the limited-overs game and Simmons fitted the bill nicely. As well as being an aggressive lower-order batsman (fortified no doubt by all those fish suppers), he was a tidy off-spinner whose flat bowling trajectory and accuracy made him highly economical. It was his reluctance to give the ball much air in one-day matches that earned him the nickname of 'Flat Jack'. It certainly didn't refer to his stomach as he fought a constant – and often losing – battle with his weight, although it did not prevent him being a sharp fielder close to the wicket.

Simmons' influence helped Lancashire become the kings of one-day cricket in the early 1970s, during which time they won the Gillette Cup on four occasions. The most memorable encounter was the 1971 semi-final against Gloucestershire, which finished in near-darkness at Old Trafford. Simmons remembers: 'Dickie Bird was clucking about like an old mother hen, going, "We can't play first-class cricket in this light." Eventually senior umpire Arthur Jepson went over to him, pointed to the moon and said, "What's that in the sky, Dickie?" "It's the moon," said Dickie. "That's right," said Jepson. "You can see the moon. How far do you want to see?"' Thanks to some inspired hitting by David Hughes in the gloom, Lancashire finally clinched victory at 8.50pm.

In winter, Simmons worked wonders as player-coach of Tasmania, leading the state into full first-class status, nurturing the talent of a young David Boon and capturing the Gillette Cup in 1979. Simmons contributed to that shock success – 'the greatest thrill of my career' – with a typically robust 55 from 78 balls.

Having once thought he would never get the chance to play county cricket, Simmons was determined to extend the dream for as long as possible. An immensely popular figure at Old Trafford – his 1980 benefit raised £128,000 – he kept himself in reasonable shape and was a shrewd enough bowler to take 63 wickets at the age of 47. He wanted to continue until he was 50 but Lancashire had decided on a policy of bringing through younger players, and therefore Simmons decided to retire from the first-class game in September 1989. He returned to Baxenden and made a century in the Ribblesdale League at 51. However, he paid the price for his exertions. 'The following morning I could hardly walk down the stairs. I had to walk down sideways.'

He later became chairman of Lancashire but the man who scarcely missed a match – or a meal – over 20 years as a player with the club doubts that he would have been able to cope with the pasta that today's players have to eat. 'I don't know what I'd make of dietitians and fitness trainers,' he admits. 'I did manage to get fish and chips and black pudding on the menu at one Test match in the guests' room at Old Trafford, though, and they loved it.'

David Steele
The Bank Clerk

Following a string of poor results, English cricket was in turmoil. A crushing defeat to Australia in the First Test of 1975 had led to the resignation of captain Mike Denness, and now new skipper Tony Greig was in desperate need of a player who could stand up to Australia's ferocious pace duo of Jeff Thomson and Dennis Lillee. So he rang round a couple of dozen county bowlers and asked them which batsmen they found the most difficult to get out. Time and again he received the same answer: Geoffrey Boycott and David Steele. With Boycott on his self-imposed exile (see p. 15), that left Steele.

Thirty-three-year-old Steele had been a county cricketer since 1963, but had scored only 16 centuries in that time and boasted a modest average of 31. Prematurely grey and wearing metal-rimmed spectacles, the mild-mannered Northamptonshire batsman was hardly a sight to strike fear into the Australians, but cometh the hour, cometh the man. Described by the *Sun*'s Clive Taylor as 'the bank clerk who went to war', Steele courageously defied the hostile Australian new ball attack throughout that summer to become one of Britain's unlikeliest-ever sporting heroes.

Born in Bradeley, Staffordshire, in 1941, Steele made his name on the county circuit as a right-hand bat and slow left-arm bowler, a peculiar trait that he shared with his younger brother, Leicestershire's John. With his hunched stance, David built a reputation as a dogged, unspectacular player who put the emphasis firmly on a sound defence, probably little realising that these were the very qualities that would bring him England recognition towards the twilight of his career. To say the least, the call-up came as a surprise but the only indication of nerves was when he went out to bat on his debut in the Second Test at Lord's with England already struggling at 10 for 1. Trotting down the stairs after leaving the dressing room, he went down one flight too many and found himself in the basement toilets. Not expecting to be confronted by a man in pads, gloves and holding a bat, the doorman asked him where he was going. 'To the wicket,' said Steele hopefully. Informed of his mistake, he quickly retraced his footsteps and managed to make the field of play without becoming the first Test batsman to be timed out.

Once in the middle, the welcome was pure Australian. Eyeing Steele's glasses and bushy black eyebrows, Thomson snorted: 'Who the fuck is this, Groucho Marx?' But the Australians weren't laughing for long. Whereas some of his team-mates' footwork and judgement was dubious, Steele concentrated on getting himself directly behind the line of every ball. As he faced each delivery from Lillee or Thomson, he said to himself: 'Watch the ball, watch the ball.' This mantra, allied to a long stride and a firm defensive forward stroke, frustrated the Australians for innings after innings. He resisted Thomson and Lillee for a total of 19 hours over three Tests, in the process accumulating 365 runs – 45 and 50 at Lord's, 73 and 92 at Headingley, and 39 and 66 at the Oval. England didn't win the series (it was drawn, enabling Australia to retain the Ashes) but Steele's doughty defiance in refusing to be bullied or browbeaten by the Aussies' intimidation – while batting in spectacles and without a helmet – greatly endeared him to the folk of Middle England. Here was a British Steele they could be proud of. His newfound popularity was confirmed when he was named BBC 'Sports Personality of the Year'.

Harking back to Lillee and Thomson, Steele remembers: 'I got to them all right. The thing is, it's a long way to run in and if you're keeping them out they soon get frustrated.'

Not only did Steele look like a bank clerk, but he possessed similar financial acumen. Following his debut at Lord's, he struck a deal with a Northampton butcher who said he would give Steele a lamb chop for every run up to 50 that he scored in each of his remaining Ashes innings, and a steak for every run over 50. 'When I got 73 in the first innings at Headingley,' said Steele, 'the butcher sent me a telegram saying, "Go easy in the second innings, I'm running out of lamb."' At the end of the series, Steele asked statistician Bill Frindall to check how many runs he had scored. When given the answer, Steele grumbled: 'I thought so. He's done me out of two chops!' Nevertheless he had won so much lamb that he never had to go to a butcher's shop for another two years.

This sponsorship had a bizarre aftermath when the Inland Revenue contacted Steele to inquire about the value of the meat he had been given. Indignantly, he offered to meet his tax liability in chops but expressed the view that it was a poor way to treat someone who had bravely stood up to the Australians all summer. He never heard another thing. Although a well-liked member of the county circuit, Steele was allegedly careful with money, particularly in the bar after a game, earning him the nickname of 'Crime', because crime never pays.

Having topped the England averages against Australia, the following summer he scored another 308 runs against the equally deadly West Indian pace attack of Andy Roberts, Michael Holding, Wayne Daniel and Vanburn Holder, including his maiden Test century at Trent Bridge. Then after just eight Test appearances and with an average of more than 42, he was sent back to the relative anonymity of county cricket as quickly as he had been plucked from it two years earlier. The decision to drop him still rankles to this day. 'I was badly, badly let down,' he says.

He played on in county cricket until 1984 – latterly with

Derbyshire – and has coached regularly at Oakham School, where his protégés included young England paceman Stuart Broad. After all, David Steele knew a thing or two about fast bowling.

THE JOKERS

William Buttress
The Ventriloquist

Described by some observers as England's most difficult bowler of the 19th century, William Buttress also had the knack of being able to throw his voice as accurately as he bowled a ball. A noted prankster, he enjoyed nothing more than using his skill as a ventriloquist to cause chaos and confusion on a train. Sitting quietly in the corner, apparently dozing peacefully, he could convince his fellow passengers that there was a kitten hiding somewhere in the compartment, mewing pitifully. Ladies would start searching frantically under the seats and behind the racks in their urgency to locate the non-existent feline. Sometimes he would add a barking puppy and invent a chase scene between the two to heighten his amusement. When the fuss eventually died down, it is not known whether the ruse was ever uncovered or, even if it was, whether suspicion fell on the cunning Buttress.

He may not have needed any props to carry out his ventriloquist's routine but he was a veritable dummy with a cricket bat in his hand. The same writers who lauded his ability with the ball expressed the opinion that he was the worst batsman who ever lived. Buttress himself did not disagree with the judgement and saw little reason in trying to improve his technique. He once remarked: 'If you bowls 'em straight, I misses 'em and I'm bowled, and if you bowls 'em crooked, I hits 'em and gets caught. Either way I'm out, so what's the use?' He played in 17 first-class matches between 1849 and 1861 and the highest score he managed in that 12-year period was 9 not-out. In 27 innings, he totalled a mere 65 runs and finished with a career average of 3.82.

He even managed to cause confusion when called upon to act as a runner. In 1854 – shortly after the MCC had introduced a new rule permitting injured batsmen to have a runner – Julius Caesar was playing for England against Nottinghamshire at Lord's when, possibly suffering from gout, he asked for a substitute. Buttress came out to perform the role but was soon involved in a desperate mix-up. Caesar drove a ball from William Clarke and, forgetting all about his runner, set off to the opposite wicket, his batting partner, John Wisden, also swapping ends. Buttress meanwhile did not move a muscle. Clarke broke the wicket at the bowler's end (where Caesar now was) but the umpire gave Wisden out on the grounds that Wisden and Buttress had not crossed. However Clarke disagreed and insisted that Caesar should go, and when the umpire refused, Clarke and the other Nottinghamshire players walked off. *Bell's Life* reported that 'after a long argument at the pavilion, it was decided that Caesar should go out. Neither the striker nor the substitute being off their ground, we are of the opinion (according to the law) that Wisden ought to have been given out, although the case would have been very hard indeed.'

Buttress was born in Cambridge on 25 November 1827 and went on to play for Cambridge Town, Cambridgeshire and both regional and national representative XIs. To compensate for his batting, he was a fiendishly accurate right-arm slow bowler whose reward was 83 first-class wickets at an average of 15. *Wisden* wrote: 'Buttress's sovereign gift was the power of bowling a deadly leg-break with a real control over his pitch. He got so much spin on the ball that, according to Mr Henry Perkins, the man who tried to play him without gloves on was almost certain to have the skin knocked off his knuckles.' Indeed he put such spin on the ball that at the end of a match it was, in the words of one MCC witness, 'all cut about with the imprints of his nails.'

Above all, Buttress was an intelligent bowler who used to play on a batsman's weaknesses. He could pin opponents down but he was also quite happy to 'buy' wickets, tempting the batsman to hit out irresponsibly and offer a catch in the deep. Sadly his influence on the game was limited because of the problems in keeping him sober. Playing for a United All England XI against the All England XI at Lord's, he bowled out Thomas Hayward, Richard Daft and George Parr – the three finest batsmen of their time – in the same over. He was so pleased with himself that he overdid the celebrations and for the next 48 hours was described as being 'in a state of hopeless imbecility.'

William Buttress died on 25 August 1866, aged just 38. The ventriloquist who could make a cricket ball talk would surely have achieved much greater fame had he been able to say 'no' to yet another gottle o' geer.

Ray East
The Essex Jester

Batting for Essex one afternoon against Gloucestershire, Ray East was given out lbw in the last over before tea. After the interval, the new batsman came out to face the remaining couple of balls from the unfinished over. Umpire Jack van Geloven, who had given East out, was about to take his place behind the stumps at the bowler's end when he noticed something strangely familiar about the newcomer. 'Hey, haven't I seen you somewhere before?' he cried. It was East, cunningly disguised under a helmet, but padded up and ready to continue. The ruse exposed, as he knew it surely would be, East scurried back to the pavilion, happy in the knowledge that he had brought a little merriment into a sport that was, at the time, in danger of becoming too serious.

East could never resist an opportunity to play the fool on the cricket pitch. Regardless of the state of the match, if a car backfired near the ground while he was bowling he would instinctively fall to the floor as if he had been shot. He was a natural clown. People told the slow left-armer that if he had cut out the funny stuff he could have played for England, but that was not his style. Anyway he never accepted that the criticism was valid. 'I can switch on and off at will,' he said, 'and so my effectiveness as a cricketer is in no way impaired when I crack a joke between balls.'

For East, cricket was a game to be enjoyed – even if his personal safety was at risk. Going out to bat against Lancashire on a fiery pitch, he decided to have a quiet word with fast bowler Ken Shuttleworth on his way to the crease. As a number nine batsman who was occasionally promoted to nightwatchman in the event of the fall of a late wicket, East made no great pretence about his ability with the willow and indicated to Shuttleworth that he had little desire to be roughed up on this occasion. In fact, he told the England man that if he pitched the next ball up and kept it straight, the bat would not prevent it hitting the stumps. Sensing a cheap wicket, Shuttleworth duly bowled a half-volley on middle and leg. Perhaps to look convincing, East gave an agricultural heave but instead of missing the ball, as arranged, he sent it sailing over the ropes for six. Steam was coming from Shuttleworth's nostrils. He was livid and East was 100 per cent certain that the next delivery would be a bouncer. Shuttleworth did not disappoint but barely had the ball left the bowler's hand than East threw his bat away and dived out towards point, with his hands on his head. He recalled: 'I landed, flat out, well in time to look up and see the ball bouncing at great pace some six feet above me.'

His antics did not always go down well with Lancashire. When Lancashire opener Barry Wood was doubled up in pain by a ball from Essex's Norbert Phillip, East, wrongly as it turned out, thought he was overacting. 'Consequently,' said East, 'when the 12th man appeared on the field to bring him a glass of water I met him at the edge of the square, supposedly to carry it to the injured batsman. Instead, I drank the water in one go, thanked the 12th man profusely and went back to my position in the field. Woody was not highly amused.'

East was born at Manningtree, Essex, in 1947 and appeared in his first village match at the age of 11 when Suffolk team East Bergholt, for whom his father and uncle also played, were a man short. It was a baptism of fire. East Bergholt were routed for 11 by Ipswich Greyhounds and the youngster was last man in. The experience did not put him off, however, and within two years he had taken 8 for 21 in a village match. He was subsequently invited to join Essex and give up his career as an electrician. He made his first-class debut in 1965 and was a stalwart of the Essex side for the next 19 years, during which time he took over 1,000 wickets, scored more than 8,000 runs (including an improbable century), held 374 catches and ate 'so many salads there was a danger of contracting myxomatosis.' In 1973 he played in a Test trial at Taunton and took the only hat-trick of his career. He thought he had made a good impression until the following morning one of the selectors greeted him: 'Good morning, Roy.' He never did play for his country.

His bowling action was described as looking like a puppet with a drunken operator and, fielding out on the boundary, he used to amuse the crowd by acting like a stringless puppet. He would also tell spectators that they should be ready to stop the next ball because he was dizzy from being moved around so much by his captain. Banter with the crowd was all part of the fun and, after making a good stop or delivering an accurate throw, he would acknowledge their cheers by doffing his cap. Audience numbers were thin on the ground when Essex played Cambridge University in April 1981 but the few that did brave the bitter cold were treated to a display of vintage East, who kept warm by borrowing an overcoat from the scoreboard operator and wearing it while fielding at deep fine leg. He was eventually put out of his misery when play was suspended due to the chill factor.

East was in his element when bowling to a fellow clown, such as Nottinghamshire's Derek Randall. Hearing Randall whistling loudly between deliveries, East started whistling in response as he came in to bowl. Before long the field of play sounded like a Roger Whittaker concert.

Not even his own team-mates were safe from East's jokes. One day East and fellow slow bowler David Acfield were driving down to Glamorgan with the county's new recruit, Barbadian Keith Boyce. As they reached the Severn Bridge, East casually asked the others whether they had their passports ready. Acfield was in on the prank but Boyce had no idea what was going on.

'What do you mean?' he asked. 'You don't need a passport for Wales, do you?'

'Course you do, Boycie,' said East convincingly. 'Don't say you've forgotten it!' Pulling the car over to the side of the road, East went on: 'There's only one thing for it. We can't go all the way back to Essex – you'll have to be smuggled through in the boot.'

So it was that the gullible Boyce squeezed his fast bowler's frame into the boot of East's car and made an ignominious entry into Wales.

In the summer of 1980 Essex played the West Indies tourists in a friendly match at Stamford Bridge to pioneer the concept of floodlit cricket. The non-competitive nature of the game presented East with an extra excuse for clowning and when Graham Gooch was hit on the foot by a yorker, East ran on with a bucket and pretended to re-chalk his toecap. In the same year several Essex players were struck down by a flu virus, prompting East to parade back and forth outside the dressing room, carrying a placard saying 'Unclean'.

His humour was highly contagious and spread to some of his team-mates. After one drinks interval, fast bowler John Lever, pretending that his orange juice had been laced with alcohol, began his run-up for the next over first by tottering unsteadily on his feet and then by running in the direction of mid wicket. And in a match against Cambridge University, Lever bowled a delicious half-volley with an orange, which disintegrated as it hit the bat. Keith Pont also took a leaf out of East's book when, exhausted through having to field at third man from both ends, he borrowed a child's bicycle from the crowd at the end of the over and pedalled around the boundary to his new position.

Although there were a number of outstanding players in the Essex side, there was a feeling in some circles that, rather like errant school-boys, they would never amount to much. Ray Illingworth, in his most headmasterly tone, warned: 'That load of madmen will never win anything until they learn some self-discipline.' So Essex derived tremendous satisfaction from winning their first-ever County Championship title in 1979, the Benson & Hedges Cup in the same year, and the John Player League in 1981 – all with the assistance of their joker-in-chief, Ray East. Indeed, East's gutsy innings of 48 against Hampshire – compiled while facing Malcolm Marshall at his most hostile – helped secure that first elusive county title. Asked afterwards by a journalist what it had been like in the middle, East replied: 'At one end I felt like Donald Bradman, at the other Donald Duck!'

His bowling proved particularly effective in one-day games. In the John Player League he took five wickets in an innings on four occasions, although he did also bowl what was then the most expensive spell in the competition – 1 for 79 off his eight overs.

There was only one instance when East can recall that his clowning got him into trouble. The defending county champions were battling to hold on for a draw against Northamptonshire in 1980 on a pitch of uneven bounce. The ball was keeping so low that East made a point of exaggeratedly going down on one knee to play a forward defensive stroke to off-spinner Richard Williams. That raised a smile or two but nobody was laughing a few overs later when Jim Griffiths bowled him. Back in the dressing room East was lambasted by captain Keith Fletcher, who accused him of not trying and of setting a bad example. East was dropped as a result and eventually had to apologise.

Not all of East's comic moments were intentional. Towards the end of his career, he acted as coach to the Essex second XI and was sitting in the dressing room one day watching his team batting when the phone rang. The call was for one of the fielders patrolling the boundary. Leaning out of the window, East mimed that the fielder was wanted on the phone. Moments later, the two Essex batsmen arrived in the dressing room. 'Lunch already, lads?' inquired East. 'No,' said one, 'we've declared, haven't we? Wasn't that you waving us in?'

On his retirement from the game, Ray East ran a pub in East Bergholt. He certainly never had any shortage of material on which to draw for funny stories.

'Chuck' Fleetwood-Smith
The Bird Impersonator

Australian left-arm spinner Leslie O'Brien Fleetwood-Smith – known to his friends as 'Chuck' – appears in most cricket books for one reason only: his figures of 87–11–298–1 against England at the Oval in 1938 are the worst in Test history. Yet there was so much more to this delightfully eccentric character who specialised in doing bird impressions as he came into bowl and performing songs from the shows while he was fielding out on the boundary.

He evidently had a low boredom threshold, so perhaps cricket wasn't the ideal game for him anyway. Faced with the prospect of another long day in the field, he used to liven up proceedings with his ornithological repertoire. As he ambled in to bowl, he would distract the batsman by making the loud cacking noise of a magpie or the whoop of the whipbird, the latter accompanied by Fleetwood-Smith dramatically raising his head skywards for added authenticity. Although these impressions were designed largely for his own amusement, they did occasionally help to defuse tension. On

Australia's 1938 tour of England there was an awkward moment at Northampton following the contentious dismissal of one of the county's batsmen. As matters threatened to turn distinctly ugly, Fleetwood-Smith lightened the mood by treating all present to an impromptu impression of a kookaburra on heat, complete with flapping wings and frenzied hops. It was hard to pursue a feud in the face of such top-class entertainment.

When he wasn't doing bird impressions in the field, he was strolling along the boundary singing *I'm In The Mood For Love* and other romantic numbers, always playing to the gallery. On other occasions he would suddenly start practising his golf swing, miming his joy at getting an imaginary hole-in-one, or start chuckling away to himself inexplicably. On that 1938 tour at Worcester the crowd were bemused to hear him chant 'Lord Hawke, Lord Hawke' for no apparent reason. He was also liable to cry out 'Up Port Melbourne, Go Port Melbourne' in honour of his favourite football team.

Fellow Australian Test player Bill O'Reilly attributed Chuck's strange behaviour to the phases of the moon. 'When the moon was high,' said O'Reilly, 'Chuck would go crazy, calling out various stupid chants...God had given him everything required of a bowler, except a brain-box. He was definitely a screw loose.'

Fleetwood-Smith was born into a journalistic family at Stawell, Victoria, on 30 March 1908, his father being a newspaper manager while his mother at one time edited the *Pleasant Creek News and Stawell Chronicle*. Even as a young cricketer he was unconventional. He had always bowled right-armed until, convalescing at home following a bout of flu, he began bowling with his left arm in the family backyard after the right grew weary. To his surprise, he found that he actually preferred bowling left-armed and in school matches would sometimes mix right- and left-arm deliveries in the same over, no doubt to the bewilderment of the batsmen. He remained ambidextrous, and even in his first-class career continued to bat and throw right-handed while bowling with his left.

A success in Melbourne college cricket, he recorded his first appearance for Victoria against Tasmania in 1931 and made his Sheffield Shield debut against South Australia the following year. On his first visit as a player to the Sydney Cricket Ground he was dismayed to see that his nameplate on the famous scoreboard had been reduced, for reasons of space, to 'F-Smith'. He quickly sought out the scoreboard attendants and demanded that his name either appear in full or not at all. The attendants reluctantly agreed to repaint his nameplate, somehow managing to squeeze in all the letters. His double-barrelled surname was something of an affectation anyway; his father's name was Fleetwood Smith and young Leslie decided to incorporate it in full into his own name.

A Clark Gable lookalike with a moustache and thick black hair, Fleetwood-Smith actively pursued and was pursued by a number of women. After the war he was cited as co-respondent in a divorce case, the impact of which resulted in the break-up of his own marriage. He revelled in a movie star image and would sometimes take to the field sporting a fat Havana cigar in his mouth, only stubbing it out when the ball came in his direction. A dapper dresser, on one England tour he joined forces with Arthur Mailey and Bill Ponsford to go fishing one night off Brighton Pier – all three men still wearing their dinner jackets. He always liked to look the part, the only exception to the rule being his lucky singlet. He had worn it when taking six wickets in an innings for Victoria against the 1931–32 South African tourists and, in the belief that it had brought him good fortune, he insisted on wearing it for every other major match of his career. When setting off on tour, it was always the first thing he packed, even though by the late 1930s it was virtually threadbare. His other lucky charm was a threepenny bit (given to him by his first wife), which he always kept in his right pocket while bowling.

Although he toured England in 1934 and took 119 wickets (including three in four deliveries against Oxford University), he was unable to force his way into the Test side at the expense of O'Reilly and Clarrie Grimmett. However, his chance came against South Africa at Durban in 1935 – the first of 10 Test appearances. His natural delivery was the leg-break but he could also bowl a well-disguised googly and developed considerable powers of spin, strengthening his arm and hand by squeezing a squash ball. In the Fourth Test at Adelaide in 1937 he bowled an unplayable ball to dismiss Wally Hammond and effectively retained the Ashes for Australia. He had also returned impressive match figures of 10 for 239 in the previous Test at Melbourne. Alas, his batting never scaled such heights, the *Australian Dictionary of Biography* noting that 'he would often ignore his side's or his partner's needs.' His first-class career average of 7.34 supports Fleetwood-Smith's own claim to have been the worst batsman in the world at the time.

Before the 1937–38 season he decided to tackle the problem of his expanding waistline by taking up wrestling. Dressed in bright yellow tights, he toured gymnasiums and clubs in the Melbourne area looking for suitable opponents. After one particularly strenuous bout, he was hardly able to move his neck when he turned up for a training session with the Victoria cricket team. As well as being one of the few wrestling cricketers in history, he was also a golfer of some repute, although, as with his chosen profession, he would have fared considerably better had he taken the game more seriously. His favourite ploy was to tee the ball up, step back a few paces, trot in and hit the ball on the run!

He played in four Tests on the 1938 tour of England but, always in search of something to break the monotony, upset the Australian Board of Control by sneaking off one Sunday morning to go for a glider ride over the Peak District. He simply shrugged off the subsequent reprimand and went on to take seven wickets in Australia's victory in the Fourth Test at Headingley, which ensured that they again kept the Ashes. However, it was a different story in the final Test at the Oval when Fleetwood-Smith entered the record books for all the wrong reasons by producing the worst bowling figures in Test history and England achieved a total of 903. Len Hutton was his chief tormentor with 364, prospering after he had been missed off the hapless Fleetwood-Smith on 40. Recalling that long, fruitless bowling spell, Fleetwood-Smith said: 'You woke up in the night-time and your arm was still going round.'

Arthur Mailey reckoned that Fleetwood-Smith was the only man he knew who genuinely applauded a six hit off his own bowling. When congratulating the batsman, 'Chuck' would put on an aristocratic English accent and gush: 'Great shot, old man.' He certainly had plenty of opportunity to practice the accent at the Oval.

His figures in that Test match may have been sufficient to end his international career on their own but Hitler's intervention put the matter beyond doubt. By the end of the Second World War Fleetwood-Smith was 37 and after one more season in club cricket, he announced his retirement. Unfortunately this coincided with his divorce and, as a consequence, the loss of his job as a salesman with the soft-drinks company owned by his former father-in-law. He remarried but struggled to adapt to living in reduced circumstances and his life spiralled into an alarming decline. He began drinking heavily, sustaining his habit with short-lived jobs, begging on the streets of Melbourne and ultimately theft, for which he was charged – along with vagrancy – in March 1969. By then he was living and sleeping in the derelicts' community on the banks of the Yarra River. The charge of theft was dropped and that of vagrancy adjourned for a year as old friends, among them former Prime Minister Sir Robert Menzies, rallied to his aid. Fleetwood-Smith gave up drinking, was reconciled with his wife and found more regular employment, but the years of dissipation had wrecked his health and he died of cancer on 16 March 1971 – a sad end for a cricketer who had created such a good impression.

Patsy Hendren
Alias Elias

Patsy Hendren was a whimsical character. He made a duck in his opening first-class match and a duck in his last, the perfect symmetry of the statistic apparently giving him as much pleasure as the 170 centuries he hit in between. It appealed to the impish sense of humour of a man who was not only a splendid batsman for county and country but also an accomplished wit, mimic and practical joker.

He invariably played the game with a smile on his face – Neville Cardus wrote that he was always liable to be given out smile before wicket – one of his trademark routines being to charge down the wicket to spinners and if he missed the ball, to carry on walking towards the pavilion without so much as a backward glance. Once he was at the non-striker's end when his Middlesex captain, Walter Robins, decided to copy him. Robins was about halfway down the pitch when Hendren yelled: 'Look out, he's missed it!' Robins instinctively turned and hurled himself headlong on the muddy pitch in a bid to regain his ground, little realising that it was one of Hendren's jokes: the wicketkeeper hadn't missed the ball at all. The crowd roared with laughter as Robins picked himself up, brushed himself down, and turned to see his wicket broken and both Hendren and the keeper grinning broadly.

He also pulled a neat trick the first time he faced Surrey's new fast bowler, Alf Gover, in 1929. By then Hendren was 40, and before beginning his innings he confided to Gover that he no longer relished facing really fast bowling. So Gover, relishing the prospect of claiming an illustrious scalp, immediately sent down a bouncer, which Hendren hooked imperiously into the stand for six. Convinced that the shot was a fluke, Gover tried two more bouncers, which were swiftly despatched for four and six respectively. At the end of the over Surrey team-mate Jack Hobbs asked Gover why he was persisting in bowling bouncers at Hendren.

'Because he doesn't like fast bowling,' said Gover.

'Who on earth told you that?' demanded an incredulous Hobbs.

'He did,' came the reply.

'Well, I'm telling you,' said Hobbs firmly, 'that Pat is still as good a player of fast bowling as anyone I know.'

The young bowler had been well and truly outfoxed by the old hand.

Elias Henry Hendren was born at Turnham Green, Middlesex, on 5 February 1889 but was popularly known as 'Patsy' on account of his Irish ancestry. He joined the Lord's groundstaff at 16 as a match-card seller and made his first-class debut for Middlesex in 1907, only to be denied the chance to bat when the match was abandoned after the first day because spectators had caused damage to the pitch. He gradually established himself in the side, making his first century in 1911, but it was not until the resumption of cricket after the First World War that he truly blossomed.

Short and stocky, it was said that he 'stood at the wicket with a slight crouch, a sharply protruding rump proclaiming his resolution.' The speedy footwork that made him a lively winger with Brentford, QPR, Manchester City and Coventry City early in his career was used to great effect against slow bowlers, but, as Alf Gover was to discover, it was Hendren's ability to deal with fast bowling that made him such an exceptional player. With his strong forearms, he was rated as the finest hooker of the day and was also a magnificent driver and cutter, his career total of 57,611 first-class runs bettered by just two men – Sir Jack Hobbs (61,237) and Frank Woolley (58,969). He averaged over 50 in a first-class career spanning 30 years.

Hendren's highest innings in first-class cricket was an undefeated 301 against Worcestershire in 1933 and he reached three figures for Middlesex against every other first-class county. His best season was 1928 when he hit 3,311 runs, including 13 centuries, at an average of over 70. He played in 51 Tests for England (average 47.63), his highest score being 205 not-out against the West Indies at Port of Spain in 1930. His aggregate of 1,766 runs at an average of 126.14 on that tour remains a record for a season in the West Indies. In 1933 be created a stir at Lord's by batting against the West Indies' fast bowlers wearing a special protective cap. Designed by his wife, it had three peaks, two of which covered the ears and temples, and was lined with sponge rubber. He explained that he needed the extra protection after being struck on the head two years earlier by the persistent bouncers that had recently become fashionable among fast bowlers.

Hendren's value on England tours stretched way beyond his batting. With a permanent twinkle in his eye and a cheeky grin, he contributed hugely to team spirit, ensuring that there was never a dull moment. One evening during the Third Test at Melbourne on the 1928–29 tour of Australia he spotted a passing brewer's cart, pulled by two big horses. He immediately dragged his England team-mates on to the cart and, surrounded by crates of beer, conducted the players in a riotous rendition of anti-temperance songs through the streets of the city. As Jack Hobbs said: 'Patsy was a great cricketer and great companion. He was the life and soul of the party on all our tours.'

He enjoyed a wonderful rapport with crowds all over the world. He was the idol of the Lord's Tavern, Neville Cardus claiming: 'I have seen men leave their drinks at the bar of the Tavern when Patsy has just come in to bat.' He was almost as popular with the Hill at Sydney, where his quick wit enabled him to give as good as he got. Once, when Hendren dropped a difficult catch, a voice from the Hill shouted: 'I could have caught that in my mouth.' To which Hendren answered: 'So could I, if I had a mouth as big as yours!'

There was one catch in Australia that he says he did regret taking. Stationed in the deep as usual, on an undulating country ground in Queensland, Hendren found himself fielding on the lower side of a ridge that completely hid the rest of the field from view. For hours he saw no action whatsoever until suddenly a ball emerged from the sky towards him. He dived forward and, breasting the slope, took a magnificent catch. 'Only one thing against it,' said Hendren. 'I'd caught my own captain!' His story may just have to be taken with a large pinch of salt.

A dropped catch was a rarity for Hendren – he took 759 in total and saved countless runs not only by his superb fielding but also because he developed an artful dodge to fool the batsmen. Chasing a ball in the outfield, he would bend down as if to pick it up when he was still 10 yards away from it. Batsmen fell for the trick time and time again, settling for two runs when a perfectly safe third was available. It was just another of the jokes that made spectators warm to him.

He played his last Test match in 1935 – against the West Indies at Kingston – but continued in first-class cricket until 1938. In his final match, for England Past and Present against Sir Pelham Warner's XI at Folkestone, he was caught by 20-year-old Denis Compton for a duck. After serving as coach at Harrow School and then Sussex, Hendren became scorer for Middlesex from 1952 until 1960, when ill-health forced him to retire. He died two years later, on 4 October 1962, aged 73. Former MCC secretary Billy Griffith paid tribute to Hendren's effervescent personality. 'Apart from being a great cricketer, and perhaps more importantly, he brought a tremendous amount of fun and happiness to everything associated with the game. We at Lord's shall miss him terribly.'

Allan Lamb
Dickie's Nemesis

It is an episode umpire Dickie Bird will never forget. He was standing at square leg during the Trent Bridge Test in the 1990 series against New Zealand when Allan Lamb came out to bat at number four for England. Instead of walking to the crease, Lamb headed straight for Bird and, explaining that he had forgotten to remove his mobile phone from his pocket, asked the umpire to look after it. As a parting shot to the flustered Bird, Lamb added: 'Oh, and if it rings answer it.'

About 10 minutes later, the phone did indeed ring. Reluctantly Bird answered it and whispered: 'Hello, this is Dickie Bird speaking on Allan Lamb's phone. Who's there?' The voice on the other end boomed: 'This is Ian Botham ringing from the dressing room. Tell that fellow Lamb either to play a few shots or get out.'

Dickie had been well and truly set up by Lamb – and not for the first time either. In the middle of the 1983 Trent Bridge Test against New Zealand, Lamb dropped firecrackers on Bob Willis's run-up, and as his fellow conspirator Botham recalled: 'When Bob's lumbering strides set them off one by one, Dickie almost had a heart attack because he was convinced he was under attack from crazed gunmen.'

Bird was singled out again when Northamptonshire travelled to Old Trafford for a county match in 1987. First Lamb pushed burning waste paper under the umpires' locked dressing room door, causing smoke to billow into the room and necessitating the swift intervention of a Lancashire official with a fire extinguisher. Then at the close of play when Bird went to his car ready to drive home, he noticed to his horror that all the wheels had been removed. Instead the vehicle had been left standing on bricks with a message on the car reading: 'Have a good journey home, Dickie.' There was no doubt about the culprit – it was the same Allan Lamb who had once crept up on Bird and set fire to the newspaper he was reading in a hotel bar in Bristol. And the same Lamb who chose an unusual method of cheering Dickie up during the 1987 World Cup in India and Pakistan. With Dickie lying ill in bed in his hotel room, Lamb recruited half a dozen of the armed guards who were acting as hotel security and led them to Bird's room. When a pale and weak Bird answered the door, Lamb marched the guards in, lined them up at the foot of the bed and ordered: 'Right! Put the poor bugger out of his misery. Ready! Aim! Fire!' Mercifully, Bird quickly realised it was another of Lamb's pranks.

If Dickie Bird was a predictable choice of stooge for Lamb, Eddie Barlow was definitely not. The South African had a reputation for being a hard taskmaster and very little about his general demeanour ever suggested that he might be mistaken for one of the Chuckle Brothers. He was a domineering captain of Western Province, but that did not prevent a young Lamb risking his wrath during a match against Rhodesia in Salisbury. As punishment for a previous prank, Barlow made Lamb walk from one third man position to the other at the end of each over. After making the trek for the umpteenth time, Lamb was still cursing Barlow when he noticed a guy with a bicycle watching the game. So at the end of the over, he asked the puzzled spectator whether he could borrow his bike and then proceeded to ride across the pitch to his next fielding position. Apparently even Barlow saw the funny side.

Having been born in Langebaanweg, South Africa, in 1954, Lamb made his mark in first-class cricket under Barlow at Western Province. In 1978 Lamb signed as an overseas player for Northamptonshire and, with South Africa still banned from Test cricket because of the apartheid regime, Northants secretary Ken Turner advised him to take advantage of his English-born parents and play for England. He went on to play 79 Tests between 1982 and 1992, hitting 14 centuries and averaging 36.09. A pugnacious little batsman and one of the few not be intimidated by the West Indies pace attack of the 1980s, he also captained England on three occasions. His finest hour probably came in a one-day international against Australia at Sydney in 1987 when he smashed 18 runs off Bruce Reid's final over to secure a dramatic victory with one ball to spare.

In total, he scored more than 32,000 runs in first-class cricket and as captain almost led Northants to a first-ever County Championship in 1995 with his customary brashness and confidence, Matthew Engel describing him as 'strutting round the county grounds like Napoleon.' That turned out to be his final season but his image lived on for a while in TV adverts for British meat in which he and Ian Botham appeared as cartoon characters 'Lamby' and 'Beefy'. Allan Lamb is remembered chiefly as a reliable and aggressive member of England's middle-order batsmen, and also as someone whose wicked sense of humour has helped keep Dickie Bird in after-dinner stories.

Arthur Mailey
The Art Of Self-Deprecation

'The great spin bowlers,' wrote Arthur Mailey, 'were personalities and men of character – not always pleasant but invariably interesting. They may have lacked the charm and friendliness of their faster confederates; they may have been more temperamental and less self-disciplined; but there seemed to be an absence of orthodoxy about them and they were able to meander through life as individuals not as civil servants.'

Mailey himself was certainly an individual. The slightly built Australian leg-spinner was also an eminent cartoonist, painter and journalist who flatly refused to take himself or the game too seriously. Even in his darkest hour with the ball, he showed himself to be a master of self-deprecating humour. When he finished with figures of 4 for 362 from 64 eight-ball overs (no maidens) as Victoria compiled their record-breaking total of 1,107 against New South Wales in 1926, he observed dryly: 'It was rather a pity Ellis got run out at 1,107, because I was just striking a length.' He also revealed deadpan that his figures would have been much better if a man in a trilby hat hadn't dropped a couple of easy catches in the back of one of the stands. Incidentally, New South Wales gained a modicum of revenge five weeks later by bowling out Victoria for just 35.

But figures never meant much to Mailey anyway. He was described as 'the millionaire bowler' because he was willing to 'buy' a wicket at any price. He maintained that if ever he happened to bowl a maiden, it was not his fault. Wilfred Rhodes said of him: 'He never gave up. He would have 0 for 100 and might finish with 6 for 130.'

Writing in the *Cricketer*, the esteemed journalist R.C. Robertson-Glasgow recounted how, as a young tail-ender for Oxford University, he faced Mailey in a game against the 1921 Australian tourists. 'He smiled as I came in, a wide and sympathetic smile. He has always, I fancy, regarded batting as a necessary but inferior part of cricket. He had reason this time. I knew, and he guessed that I knew, nothing at all about the art of playing leg-spin bowling of quality. No discernment. So he smiled; and bowled three high and harmless non-spinners just outside the off-stump. I swished at them, and three times connected. Mailey had deliberately presented me with 12 runs. Then he had me stumped by a wide margin of space and time. "Enjoyed yourself?" he said as we walked in. That was Arthur Mailey; the giver of good things, especially to the young and ignorant.'

Alfred Arthur Mailey was born on 3 January 1886 in South Sydney. He left school at 13 and three years later became a glassblower, a job that helped to strengthen his lungs and fingers. He later worked as a labourer for the Metropolitan Board of Water Supply and Sewerage. However, even the joys of sewerage could not compete with his real love, cricket, and, after perfecting the art of bowling leg-breaks and googlies, he entered grade cricket. It was there that he bowled for the first time against his idol, Victor Trumper, and had the great man stumped off his third ball. Most young bowlers would have been ecstatic at claiming the wicket of a Test star, but Mailey was different. 'There was no triumph in me,' he wrote, 'as I watched the receding figure. I felt like a boy who had killed a dove.'

Having established himself in the New South Wales side, Mailey made his Test debut against England at Sydney in December 1920. He went on to take 36 wickets in the series (despite playing in only four matches), a record for an Ashes series that stood for 57 years. In the second innings of the Fourth Test at Melbourne he finished with figures of 9 for 121 in 47 overs, his victims including Jack Hobbs, Wilfred Rhodes and Frank Woolley. Like many wrist spinners, his length was sometimes erratic, making him expensive, but his strong fingers imparted such spin to the ball that he was always dangerous and he loved experimenting with flight. And despite his slim physique, he was able to bowl long spells, exemplified by his 10 for 66 in the second innings against Gloucestershire at Cheltenham in 1921, a feat that inspired the title of his 1958 autobiography: *Ten for 66 And All That.*

One of his colleagues called Mailey's bowling a mixture of 'spin, flight and sheer fun.' He would have appreciated the description, noting the contrast with some of his more disciplined, serious-minded contemporaries such as fellow Australian leg-spinner Clarrie Grimmett, of whom Mailey once remarked: 'Clarrie Grimmett thought that a full toss was the worst form of cricket vandalism and the long-hop a legacy from prehistoric days when barbarians rolled boulders towards the enemy.' Mailey operated under no such restrictions.

He was extremely modest about his bowling and was horrified when a semi-jocular remark to a journalist friend appeared in print the next day. On the eve of a charity match in Sydney, Mailey had confided that his googlies might trouble Donald Bradman, so when he saw the headline 'MAILEY TO DEFEAT BRADMAN', he feared the worst. 'I know what's going to happen when the little fellow reads this,' groaned Mailey. Sure enough Bradman scored a century in 39 minutes, reserving his fiercest punishment for Mailey.

Mailey played in 21 Tests, claiming a total of 99 wickets at an average of 33.91. With the bat he was a confirmed number 11, although against England at Sydney in 1924 he did contribute an unbeaten 46 in a last-wicket stand of 127. For years afterwards he laughed disbelievingly whenever that innings was mentioned.

Running parallel with his cricketing career was that of cartoonist and journalist. He drew sporting cartoons for the Sydney *Sun* in the 1920s, invariably making his own face the centre of ridicule, and later became a cricket writer, covering the infamous 'Bodyline' tour of 1932–33. He also toured England painting watercolours of the countryside, sleeping in his car as he went.

Arthur Mailey died in Sydney on 31 December 1967. Unassuming to the end, he wrote his own mock epitaph when he opened a butcher's shop after retiring from journalism. On the window he wrote: 'I bowled tripe, I wrote tripe, and now I am selling it.'

Cecil Parkin
The Mad Magician

Whether bowling, fielding, or entertaining his team-mates, Lancashire's Cecil Parkin was famed for his sleight of hand. A slim figure with a wry sense of humour, he sometimes gave the impression of playing the game purely for laughs but he took his cunning spin bowling seriously enough to appear in 10 Tests for England. And when a stubborn batsman needed removing, the captain would invariably turn to Parkin who, as befits any conjuror, always had something up his sleeve.

An over from Parkin was an exercise in guesswork for the batsman, who could never know what was coming next. In the space of six balls Parkin happily mixed up fast-medium away swingers, leg-breaks, off-breaks and high, slow full tosses. The last mentioned were delivered from some three yards behind the bowling crease, one seemingly innocuous 'donkey drop' trapping a bemused George Hirst lbw in the 1919 Roses match, to the undisguised delight of the Old Trafford crowd. On occasions Parkin would even bring his right hand over empty and instead bowl a lob with his left hand. If all this wasn't enough to leave batsmen pulling their hair out, Parkin would sometimes burst into song as he ran into bowl, a favourite line being 'The sky is blue and I love you', accentuating the 'you' at the moment of delivery.

Author A.A. Thomson wrote of Parkin's inimitable style: 'He was a genuine master of pace and length and had a colossal range of spin. He had, too, a kind of comedian's slow ball which the batsmen would step out to and miss, then step back to and miss. The victim would then pause for an appreciable moment, watching the ball as a nervous dog watches an angry cat. After that, still as earthbound as though he were shackled, he would stand stock-still while the ball bowled him round his legs.'

Parkin was equally artful in the field. He would pretend to have made a great slip catch, accepting the crowd's applause until they realised that the ball had gone to the boundary. Conversely, he would react as if the ball had flown past him for four until magically producing it from behind his back, the result of a smart catch. Disgruntled batsmen would glare at him as they headed for the pavilion, whereupon Parkin would smile back innocently. Fielding in the covers, he would amble towards a gently rolling ball and without bending down or breaking stride, flick the ball up into his hand with the toe of his boot. Another of his party pieces was to celebrate a wicket by throwing the ball high over his head and catch it one-handed behind his back without looking. His magician's dexterity was again in evidence on the occasion when he substituted an orange for the ball. With the fruit concealed in the palm of his hand, he pretended to make an impossible pick-up and splattered the orange into the gloves of wicketkeeper George Duckworth.

His batting style was said to alternate between agricultural heaves and textbook strokes. He would play a seemingly immaculate stroke and miss the ball completely but then score runs with an appalling shot. The crowd roared with laughter and when Parkin was tired of the routine, he would deliberately run himself out. A run-out always seemed to be on the cards with Parkin at the wicket but often it was one of his tricks for he liked to torment the opposition fielders into taking wild shies at the stumps. Attempting what appeared a suicidal run, he used his long reach to ground his bat in the nick of time, just as the ball whistled past him for overthrows. He was batting once with Richard Tyldesley when the pair found themselves running alongside each other, Parkin having lapped his portly partner. As the ball went for yet more overthrows, Parkin slung his bat over his shoulder and marched back to the crease whistling *The British Grenadier.*

Off the field, he revelled in demonstrating his magical skills to a captive audience during the lengthy voyage to Australia for the 1920–21 England tour and proved the star turn at many a concert party on board ship. Even when attending what was supposed to be a serious cricket debate, he turned the evening into a magic show. Although billed as the opposing speaker, he decided after all that he agreed entirely with the first speaker and, instead of a powerfully persuasive oration, performed a range of card tricks. Cec Parkin was a card himself.

He was born Cecil Harry Parkin on 18 February 1886 at Eaglescliffe and his place of birth was to have a profound effect on his career. He played one first-class match for Yorkshire in 1906 before it was discovered that he had been born 20 yards beyond the county boundary, in County Durham. Yorkshire would only employ natives at the time and so when investigations revealed that Parkin had been born at the 'wrong' end of his house, he was released to play for Staffordshire. He started out as a fast bowler but turned to spin with more than a little help from his wife, on whom he practised his new art in the nets. He recalled: 'At Tunstall she came to the ground with me every morning and afternoon. I asked her to come there to bat at the nets so that I could practise my spin bowling. Day after day for two solid seasons she helped me in this way, and many's the time she's gone home with her fingernails turned black and blue by blows from my bowling. Scores of times I have seen her crying with pain through these blows as she stood there patiently holding the bat and trying to defend herself against my spinners, but she never gave up.'

He remained in minor county and League cricket for eight years, not playing his first game for Lancashire until 1914 by which time he was 28. Making up for lost time, he took 14 wickets on his debut against Leicestershire at Liverpool but the First World War nipped his progress in the bud. When cricket resumed, he again took 14 wickets in that Roses match of 1919 (including the lob that fooled George Hirst) at just 10 runs apiece and, in the first innings of the Gentlemen versus Players match of 1920, he dismissed nine Gentlemen, six of them clean bowled.

This performance earned him a place in Johnny Douglas's England party for the disastrous winter tour of Australia, where he finished as leading wicket-taker, although in truth it was as the best of a bad bunch. Parkin's constant desire to experiment did not always endear him to his captains, who struggled to set fields to his requirements. While the bowler naturally wanted an attacking field, his flights of fancy could prove expensive against an aggressive strokemaker. It did nothing to dent his confidence, however. Parkin used to say to Douglas, only half-jokingly: 'All right, Mr Douglas, thee bowl 'em in and I'll go on after tea and bowl 'em out.' With an innocent look on his face, he also tried to persuade Douglas, who, in company with the other England bowlers on that tour suffered terribly at the hands of the Australians, to bowl from the scoreboard end because 'you can see your analysis from there.' Parkin finished with 16 wickets in the Tests and 73 on the tour, enabling to keep his place when the all-conquering Australians visited in the summer of 1921.

The first three Tests were lost but in the fourth, on his home ground of Old Trafford, Parkin took 5 for 38 and might have bowled England to an improbable victory had it not been for the stubborn resistance of 'Horseshoe' Collins, who stayed at the crease for seven hours in making 40. During this dour rearguard action, a spectator called out to the England captain, the Hon. Lionel Tennyson: 'Hey, Tennyson, read him some of thi Grandad's poems.' To which Parkin shouted back: 'He has done. The beggar's been asleep for hours!'

With the match petering out to a draw, Tennyson asked Parkin to open England's second innings, making him one of a select few to have opened both the bowling and the batting for England against Australia. He proceeded to hit a lively 20-odd, providing a little compensation for the fact that he never once finished on the winning side against the Aussies.

Parkin had only become a full-time cricketer in 1921 but his Test career was curtailed following a newspaper article in which he criticised new England captain Arthur Gilligan. Two years later, in 1926, his county career finished in equally acrimonious circumstances after a public spat with the Lancashire committee. With more than 1,000 first-class wickets to his name, he returned to League cricket where his guile and subtle change of pace continued to reap rewards for years to come.

This delightful oddball died in a Manchester hospital on 15 June 1943. His ashes were scattered on the pitch at Old Trafford, the place where he weaved his own peculiar brand of magic.

Derek Randall
Rags To Riches

There can be no disputing Derek Randall's finest hour. In the 1977 Centenary Test at Melbourne the unlikely lad from Nottinghamshire defied the full wrath of Dennis Lillee at his most awesome in an unforgettable innings of 174 that combined class, bravery and eccentricity. He fidgeted, he fiddled, but he never froze in the face of the Australian demon, and despite England's eventual defeat, earned the praise of his team-mates, the grudging admiration of the Australians and 174 pork chops from Nottinghamshire butcher Steve James.

If ever England were in need of a heroic innings, this was it. Humiliated by the West Indies the previous summer, Tony Greig's men were up against an Australian team at the peak of their powers. After two low-scoring first innings, a century from wicketkeeper Rod Marsh had put Australia into a seemingly unassailable position, 462 ahead, and when Randall came out to bat second time around, England were already struggling at 28 for 1. Making his way to the wicket in front of 110,000 people, he sang cheerily, 'The sun has got his hat on, hip-hip-hip hooray…' It was to be a taste of what was to follow.

Randall had already irked Lillee during his brief first innings by doffing his cap to the bowler after a vicious bouncer. 'No good hitting me there, mate,' he called out, indicating his head. 'Nothing to damage!' In the second innings Lillee let rip with another brutal, short-pitched delivery, momentarily flooring the helmetless Randall, who, in one acrobatic movement, sprang back to his feet and saluted his assailant. Describing his gymnastics, Randall said: 'The ball caught me a glancing blow and helped me on the way down, so I completed the movement with a backward somersault and bounced up like a boxer, ready for the next ball.' Throughout the innings Randall gave Lillee a running commentary. 'That were a good one, Mr Lillee,' he would shout, laughing as he staggered back to the crease after yet another bouncer. Lillee later described Randall as a 'bloody pain in the arse', which, for an Australian, is akin to a compliment.

When Randall was finally out, he was so moved by the standing ovation he received that – head down and bat raised – he walked through the wrong gate. He looked up to find himself at the door to the royal box rather than the dressing room and came face to face with Prince Philip instead of his captain. All in all, it was just a typical day on Planet Randall.

The man who called himself 'Rags' because of his habitual untidiness but became known to cricket fans as 'Arkle' for the way he ate up the ground while fielding, was born in Retford in 1951. Even in his early years of club cricket he could fidget for England. As an 18-year-old playing for Retford in the Bassetlaw League, he became so restless watching a tight finish that team-mate John Cook, a policeman, dragged him to the toilet and handcuffed him to the cistern so as to be able to watch the rest of the match in peace. When Randall turned professional, the Nottinghamshire players bet him a pint of bitter that he couldn't stand still for half an hour. He gave up after 30 seconds, announcing that he wasn't thirsty. He was no better at the crease, shuffling and twitching nervously, talking to himself, whistling Simon and Garfunkel tunes or going for a wander between deliveries. Before virtually every ball, he went through a little routine of tweaking his cap and the top of his left pad, followed by that familiar shuffle across off-stump at the moment of release – no wonder Lillee complained that he hated bowling at Randall because

'I'm not as good at hitting a moving target.' Randall himself claimed that the movement was largely to compensate for the relatively short reach that made him vulnerable outside off-stump, particularly early in an innings when he was also at his most nervous. One Australian described Randall's batting style as being 'like an octopus with piles.'

He was certainly unorthodox but the cricket world – with the possible exception of Lillee – warmed to his boyish enthusiasm, infectious grin and endearing gaucheness. Journalist Christopher Martin-Jenkins remembers interviewing Randall at Lord's early in his career. 'He was modest to the point of self-deprecation during the interview and left the commentary box by walking backwards, as if departing from royalty. I ushered him outside where he immediately put his foot through a large hole in the floor of the stand. His boot stuck there and he moved out of my sight with one boot still on, the other in his right hand, muttering embarrassed apologies. Charlie Chaplin could not have done it better.'

His life could be gloriously haphazard. On the 1982–83 tour of Australia he was rooming with Norman Cowans. On the night before flying from Brisbane to Melbourne, Randall realised that he had packed all his shoes and so had none to wear for going out that evening. As Cowans was planning on a quiet evening in the room, he offered Randall the pair that he had left out, provided that Randall retrieved his shoes later that night. Randall remembered but also packed Cowans's shoes in his case, with the result that England's latest fast-bowling hopeful was forced to make a long plane journey in his socks.

As a youngster on his first MCC tour in the winter of 1976–77, Randall enlivened a pompous official reception in India by suddenly turning a cartwheel, a gesture that provoked a reaction of amusement and amazement from his hosts. When handed caviar on the same tour, he remarked to captain Greig: 'The blackcurrant jam tastes of fish to me.' He danced with umpires and amused the crowd by flicking his sunhat in the air and catching it on his head. On other occasions in the field he would do somersaults and cartwheels or stumble into a swaggering walk, all with the approval of Greig who knew that it paid to keep the volatile Indian crowds onside. Greig recalled: 'I told him to act the fool as he pleased because the crowd would love him for it – if they were in good humour there would be little chance of any trouble.'

Randall made his Test debut in that series but it was that innings in the 1977 Centenary Test at Melbourne a couple of months later which truly heralded his arrival on the world stage. Yet despite his popularity with the crowds, he never achieved quite the same rapport with the England selectors, who feared that his approach was sometimes too cavalier. He seemed to reserve his best for the Australians. In the Fourth Test at Sydney in 1979 he compiled an unusually patient match-winning 150 in over nine hours and in temperatures exceeding 100 degrees. He chatted away to himself throughout the innings: 'Come on, Rags. Concentrate. England needs you.' He did play 47 Tests but his final average of 33.37 indicates that he never realised his full potential.

There is a suggestion that he wasn't always the sharpest tool in the box. Aware of his fondness for the hook shot, Middlesex captain Mike Brearley instructed Simon Hughes to bowl short to Randall in a county game, and in both innings Randall was out cheaply after hooking to a fielder in the deep. Furthermore, Brearley had told Randall of his plan over dinner the previous evening!

However, Randall's modest batting average was offset by his ability as a fielder in the covers where it was reckoned his speed saved at least 20 runs per innings. A bundle of boundless energy, he could swoop and throw in one rapid movement and ran out some of the best batsmen in the world, among them West Indies' Gordon Greenidge in the 1979 World Cup final. Whereas other fielders walked in as the ball was bowled, Randall would trot in from the covers and claimed many of his victims by this ploy. He was usually gracefulness personified except when he ran out Barry Richards with an underarm throw, which was delivered as he slid along the ground on his bottom, and ended up straddling the broken stumps with his legs in a most ungainly fashion. He took his fielding deadly seriously, although just occasionally he could not resist playing to the crowd. During a tight match against Yorkshire he was fielding in the deep when John Hampshire lofted a ball from Notts spinner Bob White towards him. Randall positioned himself beneath the ball but at the very last minute he appeared to bow his head and allow the ball to fall behind him. The umpire duly signalled a six and White was on his way to remonstrate with the fielder when Randall mischievously produced the ball from behind his back. He had thought it would be a neat trick to try and catch the ball with his hands behind his back. Luckily on that occasion at least, it worked.

Randall's last Test appearance was in 1984 but he continued playing with Nottinghamshire for another nine years. He scored over 28,000 runs in first-class cricket, making 1,000 runs in a season on eight occasions. More surprisingly, he took 13 wickets, his strike rate of one wicket per 31 balls comparing favourably to the county's illustrious New Zealander Sir Richard Hadlee, whose strike rate was 45. One of Nottinghamshire's favourite sons, Randall went on to play Minor Counties cricket for Suffolk, turning out in the NatWest Trophy at the age of 49.

Derek Randall brought a welcome ray of sunshine into the world of international cricket. He was always game for a laugh, even if it wasn't always intentional or if he happened to be on the receiving end. On tour in India he fell foul of the local food and was suddenly caught short while playing golf. Interrupting his swing, he dived into some bushes, from where he was heard to ask his playing partner for some toilet paper. 'Don't be silly,' came the reply. 'Who carries loo paper on a golf course?' Randall digested this for a second before asking plaintively: 'Has anyone got change for a hundred-rupee note?'

Bryan 'Bomber' Wells
A Leisurely Approach

Perhaps it was because of his ample girth that Bryan 'Bomber' Wells did not believe in exerting himself unnecessarily on the field of play. He bowled off a one-pace run-up, was regarded as the slowest and most reluctant fielder on the county circuit and as a batsman was notorious for his indecisive running between wickets. In an average day's play the sightscreen probably moved more than Bomber.

Yet here was a man who loved the game and who played as a professional with first Gloucestershire and then Nottinghamshire with the same carefree spirit that he had shown as a club cricketer. A natural clown and raconteur, he had, in the words of Michael Parkinson, 'a summer's day in his face and laughter in his soul.'

The son of a blacklisted trade unionist, Wells was born in Gloucester on 27 July 1930. His approach to the game upset authority from the very start. He recalls the very first ball he received at junior school was from a teacher who had been wreaking havoc with his medium pacers – that is, until young Wells came in and promptly hit him out of the playground, over the top of the school and into the street. The teacher gave him a clip around the ear, called him a stupid idiot and flatly refused to pick him for the school team.

Fortunately, others were less petulant and Wells began to make a name for himself in club circles with his clever off-spinners and the occasional well-disguised leg-break tossed in for good measure, all delivered with the minimum of fuss. David Green, in his history of Gloucestershire County Cricket Club, wrote: 'Bomber did not really need a run-up at all, save for a couple of hops. He might extend this as the spirit moved him, or even reduce it, but the batsman was conscious that he might be ready to bowl at any time.' Occasionally his almost unique one-pace run-up did take the batsman by surprise. After the Second World War he played for the Gloucester Nondescripts for a couple of years, a team who, because they played only away games, did not like to upset the opposition. So when Bomber bowled Oxfordshire's Len Hemming in a match at Witney, the umpire said to the Nondescripts' captain: 'I don't think he was looking when Bomber bowled him. I'll get him to come back.' Hemming returned somewhat sheepishly and the next ball Bomber bowled him again. Once more the umpire turned to the Gloucester captain but before he could say a word, Hemming announced: 'If you think I'm staying here for him to get his bloody hat-trick, you've got another think coming.' And off he went.

In 1951 Wells joined Gloucestershire and on his second XI debut took 6 for 51 in each innings. His first-team call-up against Sussex followed 10 days later under Sir Derrick Bailey, Gloucestershire's amateur captain. Wells recalls: 'I was put in the gully, and there wasn't a third man. The ball went past me and I thought, "That's gone, there's no need to run for that." Jack Crapp was in the slips. "If I were you, son," he said, "I'd go after that." I think they ran five.' Bomber's sloth in the field never deserted him and even at his most energetic it was said that he would gently accompany the ball from short third man to the boundary. His lack of enthusiasm for a chase did little to impress his captain and it was as a last resort that Bailey brought him on to bowl against Sussex, but he responded by taking 6 for 47 in 25 overs, all delivered from just a two- or three-pace run. The story goes that Sir Derrick, fielding at mid-off and unaware of Wells's style, saw only three balls of Bomber's first over. Apparently he turned round and walked back to his mark after the first ball and by the time he turned round Bomber was bowling the third one. After sending down another 36 overs in the second innings, Wells returned to the dressing room and announced: 'I can see that if I'm going to play for this side, I'm going to have to do a lot of bowling. I shall have to cut my run down!'

The length of his run became another source of irritation to Sir Derrick. 'At Worcester I bowled an over to Roly Jenkins,' says Wells. 'We started as the cathedral clock was beginning to chime twelve. It was all arranged. I bowled it, and Jenks pushed every one down the wicket. I finished it before the chimes were done, and Sir Derrick came across. "What do you think you're doing?" he said. "You're making the game look ridiculous." He insisted that I take a run-up, so I began by stepping out a couple of paces, then it went to three and finished up at six yards. With a smile of satisfaction on his face he told me to bowl it from there, so I did! And it pitched right on a length. Sir Derrick went berserk. He dropped me for two matches, but it was worth it.'

Playing against Essex, Wells lost patience with a young amateur batsman who kept stepping away whenever he was about to bowl. 'To teach him a lesson, I ran all the way round the square, past mid-on, square leg, behind the keeper, back to mid-off, and I shouted out, "Are you ready now?" And I bowled him first ball.'

Wells reckoned he could bowl standing still – and often did – but the speed with which he got through his overs meant that the bowler at the other end enjoyed little respite from the action. More often than not this was his fellow Gloucestershire spinner Sam Cook, who lamented: 'Bomber was a very good bowler indeed but boy was it hard work bowling at the other end. I always thought I was bowling without a break. And when asked what end he wanted, it was always with the wind as he said the wind blowing in his face made his eyes run.'

Cook also featured in many of Bomber's most memorable mishaps in running between the wickets. As a tail-end batsman – 'he used to bat at number 11,' said Dickie Bird, 'since one couldn't bat any lower' – Bomber's aim was to hit the ball higher than it had ever been hit before, but his career average of 7.47 is testimony to the fact that he rarely succeeded. His average was not helped by the number of times he was run out. After one mix-up, Cook begged him: 'For God's sake, call!' To which Wells replied: 'Heads.' On another occasion a frustrated Cook reprimanded his silent partner: 'For crying out loud, say something, Bomber, if it's only goodbye!' Eventually Gloucestershire took decisive action – and threatened Wells with a half-crown fine for each time he was run out.

Wells was a great favourite at Gloucestershire and while waiting to bat would happily chat to spectators, even enjoying a cup of tea with them and, if he was lucky, a slice of cake. Apart from cricket, eating was his favourite pastime, which was why he used to sit next to Sam Cook at lunch and tea. Cook didn't like to eat much during a game and Bomber was happy to relieve him of the burden of unwanted cake and sandwiches. Just when it looked as though he would become a permanent fixture in the Gloucestershire side, Wells found his place under threat from two other off-spinners, David Allen and John Mortimore, both of whom would go on to play for England. Although Wells was their equal with the ball, they were better batsmen and fielders (which, in truth, was hardly difficult), so in 1960 Bomber moved to Notts. He stayed at Trent Bridge for five years until, having been told that he had reached a first-class career total of 999 wickets, with customary quirkiness he decided to retire in the belief that nobody else had taken that number of wickets. 'They offered me the game against Gloucester at Bristol,' he remembers. 'They said, "Somebody down there will give you their wicket." But I said, "No. Plenty of people have got a thousand wickets. I bet no one's got 999."' Sadly, three months later the statisticians informed him that he had only taken 998.

Thus the first-class game lost one of its great characters, a man of simple pleasures who played for fun. 'I entered the game completely uncoached in July 1951,' he once said with some pride, 'and left it altogether in 1966 still uncoached.' You simply couldn't teach anyone to play cricket quite like Bomber Wells.

MEN OF SUBSTANCE

Denis Compton
Father Of Invention

Journalist Basil Easterbrook once wrote of Denis Compton: 'He could do all the right things superbly, but when he broke all the rules the ball still ended up at the fence.' Compton was a master of improvisation and is, of course, credited with inventing the sweep shot. In the course of his innings of 210 for Middlesex against The Rest at the Oval in 1947 – the golden summer in which he scored a record-breaking 3,816 runs – Compton charged down the wicket to the Gloucestershire off-spinner Tom Goddard, contrived to spike one boot with the other, fell over, but still managed a sweep that sent the ball off the middle of the bat to the square leg boundary. That was Compton: he could end up in an unholy mess but somehow through charm and style he invariably came up smelling of roses.

Many of his scrapes were caused by his absent-mindedness. As a 16-year-old he was selected to play for the MCC against Suffolk but on arriving at the ground at Felixstowe, he realised that he had left his cricket bag at Lord's. George Brown, the former Hampshire player, generously offered Compton his flannels and boots, the only problem being that Brown was seven inches taller and wore boots that were two-and-a-half sizes larger. Thus Compton waddled awkwardly on to the field for his all-important MCC debut, wearing boots stuffed with paper and trousers that had room for his batting partner. Scarcely able to move around the batting crease, it was little surprise that he failed to trouble the scorer.

Compton remained a slave to the chaos theory throughout his life. He turned up for the Old Trafford Test against South Africa in 1955 without his kitbag, having left it in London, but undaunted, he wandered into the museum and, borrowing an antique bat off the display, went on to score 158 and 71. On another occasion Compton, leaving his arrival to the last minute as usual, was driving across Vauxhall Bridge on his way to the final day's play at an Oval Test when he switched on the radio for a time check. As the clock struck 11am, he heard John Arlott say: 'Well, now that Bill Edrich is out, we'll be seeing Denis Compton next.' For once Arlott was mistaken, Compton having completely forgotten that on the last day of a Test, play started half an hour earlier.

When his old Middlesex and England colleague John Warr retired from his job in the City of London, Compton arrived at the Stock Exchange at 5.30 on a Tuesday afternoon to discover that the farewell party had actually been arranged for 4.30 at the Royal Exchange the following day. Operating a diary that would have done credit to Mr Bean, Compton once managed to get himself billed to appear in two charity matches, miles apart, on the same day. In the event he appeared at neither, turning up instead for a pro-am golf tournament to which he hadn't been officially invited. Naturally whenever his blunders came to light he offered profuse apologies, which were almost always accepted unreservedly. In fact his lack of organisation contributed enormously to Compton's appeal and has formed the basis of many stories. Peter Parfitt, the former Middlesex and England batsman, was among the speakers at a major celebration in London to mark Compton's 70th birthday. He claimed that at one point the chief guest was informed there was a telephone call for him from a lady who had heard about the dinner. Eventually Compton agreed to take the call. 'Denis,' said the voice on the other end, 'it's me, your mother. You're not 70, you're only 69'

Compton liked to enjoy life to the full. Married three times, he was fond of a drink and was even known to arrive for the start of play wearing last night's dinner jacket. Occasionally his mind would wander in the course of a game, as when he advanced down the ground at the height of a Test match to inquire after the result of the 2.30 race at Ascot.

His relaxed approach to life manifested itself most noticeably in his haphazard running between the wickets. Compton himself estimated that he had been involved in no fewer than 275 run-outs, although in one or two instances he may well have been the innocent party. This was certainly not the case when, at his brother Leslie's benefit match in 1955, Denis managed to run him out for a duck before he had faced a single ball. A number of those who had the misfortune to bat with him have recounted their experiences in print. John Warr claimed that Compton was the only batsman in history who called his partner for a single and wished him good luck at the same time. Warr added that Compton's first call was always an opening bid – a tentative statement of policy – and the second merely a basis for negotiation. Only after that did the serious business start. Trevor Bailey remembered batting with Compton in the 1954 Old Trafford Test against Pakistan: 'I set off for a run when Denis called me, and I was a third of the way down the pitch when he yelled "Wait!" Then he said "No" as we passed each other. So you might say I was a victim of the three-call trick.' Middlesex team-mate Ian Peebles attempted to get to the root of Compton's running: 'Whereas the methodical runner is like a traveller who consults weather, routes and timetables, Denis was more akin to the lover of nature who, seeing a glimpse of sunshine, snatches up his hat and sets out just for the joy of life.'

That joyous life began on 23 May 1918 when Denis Charles Scott Compton was born at Hendon, Middlesex, the second son of Harry and Jessie Compton. His father was a self-employed decorator who became a lorry driver when his business hit hard times. Harry Compton was also a keen cricketer, as was Leslie, Denis's elder brother. The brothers practised against street lamp-posts and Denis became so adept that by the age of 12 he was playing for his father's team and North London Schools. He joined the MCC groundstaff at Lord's in 1933 and three years later made his Middlesex debut, batting at number 11 against Sussex. He made 14 in an important last-wicket stand with Gubby Allen that enabled Middlesex to claim first innings points and was only given out lbw because the umpire was desperate for a pee. He was soon promoted to number seven and ended up passing 1,000 runs for the season, to be labelled England's best young batting prospect since Wally Hammond.

However Compton's sporting year did not end there. In September he made his Football League debut on the left-wing for Arsenal, scoring the opening goal in a 2–2 draw with Derby County, and for the next few years he continued to juggle the two sports admirably. He made his Test debut against New Zealand at the Oval in 1937, scoring 65 before being unluckily run out while backing up. For once it wasn't his fault. His first Test century came against Don Bradman's Australia the following summer, and in 1939 he scored over 2,000 runs. When the Second World War intervened, he served with the army as an unlikely sergeant major in India, where he formed a lasting friendship with the Australian all-rounder Keith Miller. They were on opposite sides in a match between East Zone and the Australian Services, which was interrupted by rioting, with Compton on 94. One of the rioters ran up to Compton and said, 'Mr Compton, you very good player, but the match must stop now', a phrase which Miller gleefully repeated whenever Compton subsequently came to the crease. Compton also appeared in a number of wartime soccer internationals for England but these did not count as official caps.

Post-war Britain was in desperate need of a dashing sporting hero and it found one in Compton, whose magnificent form during that halcyon summer of 1947 made the population forget the hardships of the bitterly cold, fuel-rationed winter a few months earlier. He scored 18 centuries that summer and slammed a total of 753 runs in the Tests against the touring South Africans. His strength was his audacity. He dared to be different and was always willing to take risks, even standing outside the crease to fast bowlers. Keith Miller said: 'He could play every damn thing, but more than that, he contrived shots that weren't in the book so you never knew what he was going to do next.' Foremost among these was the sweep, a shot now considered decidedly risky but one to which Compton was out only twice in his entire career. Compton himself pointed out: 'But I swept quite differently from the way they sweep today. I never hit it to square leg. I used to let it come on a long way and help it on its way. I can honestly say that nobody taught me the sweep. It seemed to be something that was an instant reaction to a ball that pitched middle and leg or middle stump.'

Compton was also a useful slow left-arm spinner, taking 622 first-class wickets, mostly with his chinamen, although he never really treated his bowling with the seriousness it merited.

Another free-scoring series against the formidable Australian side of 1948 further enhanced his public standing and led to numerous opportunities to cash in on his popularity. Wisely, he decided to employ an agent to sort out his ramshackle affairs, the result being the famous deal with Brylcreem that saw Compton receive £1,000 annually for nine years. The only cloud on the horizon was a knee injury sustained in a collision with the Charlton goalkeeper but even that could not prevent him gaining an FA Cup winner's medal with Arsenal in 1950.

Although the Wembley appearance virtually marked the end of his football career, fears that the injury might cause the 'Brylcreem Boy' to lose a little of his shine on the cricket field proved unfounded as he continued to maul the world's finest bowlers, hitting the runs that won the Ashes in 1953 and a year later making his highest Test score, 278 against Pakistan at Trent Bridge. In 1955 he had his right kneecap removed, his surgeon keeping it as a souvenir before giving it to the MCC as part of the Lord's archive. The operation enabled him to carry on playing for another two years. He played his final match as a professional for Middlesex in 1957 but made sporadic appearances as an amateur until 1964. He finished with over 38,000 first-class runs and a Test average of 50 from 78 eight matches.

Thereafter, he became a cricket journalist for the *Sunday Express* and a member of the BBC commentary team, his florid face at the close of play summary brightening up many a day's inaction. He maintained his zest and enthusiasm for life until the end, which came when he died in hospital at Windsor on 23 April 1997 following complications from a hip operation. It was somehow fitting that a man who was a hero to so many Englishmen should die on St George's Day.

Learie Constantine
The First West Indian Superstar

Learie Constantine was the first West Indian cricketer to make a real impact on the world stage. The complete all-rounder, he was a penetrating fast bowler, an attacking batsman and, perhaps above all, a brilliant fielder. *Wisden* observed: 'His batting could win a match in an hour; his bowling in a couple of overs, his catching in a few scattered moments.' Yet his contribution to West Indian history extended way beyond his favourite sport. He became a member of the British Race Relations Board and was created a life peer in recognition of his lifelong battle against racial inequality, in the process becoming the first black man to sit in the House of Lords. As C.L.R. James wrote: 'He revolted against the revolting contrast between his first-class status as a cricketer and his third-class status as a man.'

Learie Nicholas Constantine was born in Diego Martin, Trinidad, on 21 September 1901. His love of cricket stemmed from his father Lebrun, a plantation foreman, who had first toured England with the West Indies team of 1900 – but only after a last-minute dash. On the day the boat sailed, Constantine senior was seen wandering aimlessly downtown because he could not afford the fare. A public subscription was opened on the spot and a fast boat was chartered to enable him to reach the tourists' ship shortly before it was due to depart the Gulf of Paria. Lebrun scrambled on board and repaid his countrymen's generosity by becoming the first West Indian to score a century in England. Learie played with his father for Trinidad against British Guiana at Georgetown in 1923 and, after just three first-class matches, was selected for H.B.G. Austin's West Indies team to tour England that year.

Five years later he was back in England as a member of the first West Indies side to play in a Test series, but it was in a county game that he captured the public's imagination, defeating a powerful Middlesex side almost single-handedly at the home of cricket, Lord's. Struggling with a torn muscle and defying medical advice to play, Constantine first hit a whirlwind 86 to save the follow-on, reaching his 50 in 18 minutes. Then he tore through the Middlesex second innings, taking 7 for 57, five of his victims being clean bowled. Then with the tourists floundering towards their victory target of 259, Constantine came to the rescue, smashing 103 out of 133 in 40 minutes with two sixes and 12 fours to see the West Indies home by three wickets. For the third time in the match he received a standing ovation. Although, as expected, the West Indies were hopelessly outclassed in the Test series – losing all three matches by an innings – Constantine earned plaudits for his superbly athletic fielding. Neville Cardus once wrote of him: 'There are no bones in his body, only great charges and flows of energy. He can catch anything. Constantine ought to have first refusal of all chances hit to any part of the field.' He loved to demonstrate his party piece when walking back to his bowling mark. A fielder would throw the ball at his back and Constantine, without breaking stride or even appearing to look, would catch the ball one-handed between his shoulder blades. No one ever saw him miss. When a game in India was rained off, he treated the crowd to a fielding masterclass, hurling flat, fast throws with deadly accuracy to the wicketkeeper and then throwing the ball high into the sky and catching it behind his back.

Constantine's form in that summer of 1928 won him a contract with Nelson in the Lancashire League, making him the first West Indian to play professional cricket in England. In his 10 seasons there, the club won the championship eight times and were runners-up twice. He packed in the crowds, scoring over 6,000 runs and taking 776 wickets at an average of only 9.52, and was later made a Freeman of the Borough. His League engagements restricted him to just 119 first-class matches, in which he took 439 wickets and averaged 24 with the bat. He professed to be more interested in entertaining strokeplay than making big scores and never hit a Test century. 'I never wanted to make a hundred,' he said. 'Who wants to make a hundred anyway? When I first went in, my immediate objective was to hit the ball to each of the four corners of the field. After that I tried not to be repetitive.' He played in 18 Tests, taking eight wickets at Georgetown in 1930 when the West Indies gained their first victory over England. His last Test was at the Oval in 1939 when, even at the age of 37, he picked up five wickets in the first innings and hit a typically fiery 78. Like so many bowlers, as he grew older he replaced outright pace with guile, developing a cleverly concealed slower ball. Indeed when called upon, he could bowl slow spin most effectively. He continued playing in charity matches well into his 50s.

Off the field his dignity in the face of racial discrimination earned him widespread admiration. In 1944, in a benchmark case, he successfully sued London's Imperial Hotel for refusing him accommodation but with typical grace pushed for only nominal damages. He was profoundly moved when his fellow cricketers – all white-skinned – elected him as captain of the Dominions team that played England in 1946 as part of the end-of-war celebrations.

After years of studying law, he gained entrance to the English bar in 1954 but returned to Trinidad, where he was elected an MP in his country's first democratic parliament. In 1962, the year in which he was knighted, he was appointed High Commissioner for Trinidad and Tobago in London. He was also a much-respected cricket broadcaster and later a governor of the BBC.

On 1 July 1971 – two years after becoming Lord Constantine – he died in London. Trinidad posthumously awarded him the Trinity Cross, the country's highest honour – a fitting tribute to a man who had worked so tirelessly on behalf of black people everywhere.

C.B. Fry
A Man For All Seasons

Searching for a fresh sporting challenge in his early 70s, that consummate all-rounder C.B. Fry wandered into his club one day and confided to his friend, the writer Denzil Batchelor, that he was planning to involve himself in the world of racing. 'What as, Charles?' asked Batchelor dryly. 'Trainer, jockey, or horse?'

To a generation of wide-eyed schoolboys there seemed to be no limit to the talents of the man hailed by one publication as the 'greatest living Englishman'. He represented England at both cricket and soccer, held the world long-jump record for 21 years and would undoubtedly have gained a blue at rugby but for injury. He was also an accomplished boxer, golfer, swimmer, rower, tennis player and javelin thrower. A brilliant academic, he founded his own magazine, was so impossibly handsome that he considered a career on the silver screen, and was even in line for the vacant post of King of Albania. As if these achievements were not enough, he could also spring backwards without a run-up from the floor on to a mantelpiece well into his 70s!

Yet not every aspect of Fry's life came from the pages of a *Boys' Own* adventure. He suffered depression, endured a miserable marriage, became wildly eccentric and developed an alarming affection for Hitler. That the book (Fry's autobiography, *Life Worth Living*) containing his praise for the Fuhrer should be published in 1939 on the eve of war severely damaged his reputation. However, this lapse of judgement, reprehensible as it may be in hindsight, should not be allowed to overshadow what was a truly glittering sporting career, one unsurpassed in terms of excellence and diversity.

Charles Burgess Fry was born in West Croydon, Surrey, on 25 April 1872. He attended Repton School, winning a top scholarship to Oxford, where he captained the cricket team to victory in the Varsity match, scoring an undefeated century in the process. In 1892 he broke the world long-jump record with a leap of 23ft 5in and would have gone to Athens for the 1896 Olympics had he known they were taking place. He earned an England soccer cap in 1901 and a year later played in the FA Cup Final for Southampton, but by then he was devoting most of his energies to cricket.

In 1894 he joined Sussex and, by playing on-side shots off the back foot at a time when front-foot and off-side strokes were the norm, he was able to exploit gaps in the field and score heavily. He later wrote: 'In my school days the peculiar term the "hook" had not been invented. If one hit a ball in an unexpected direction to the on-side, intentionally or otherwise, one apologised to the bowler. Being by nature a rebel, I used to heave a short ball round to the on-boundary on slow wickets, even if it was straight...An advantage was that the opposing captain never by any chance put a fieldsman there; he expected you to drive on the off-side like a gentleman.'

He made his Test debut in 1896 against South Africa and went on to play for his country on 26 occasions, boasting the distinction that England never lost a match under his captaincy. He scored over 30,000 runs in first-class cricket, many in partnership with his great friend, K.S. Ranjitsinhji, who described Fry as 'the greatest of all batsmen of his time on all wickets and against every type of bowling.' His batting never matched the elegance of his general demeanour but it was undoubtedly effective, bringing him centuries in six successive innings in 1901. And when in 1905 the Australians came to the conclusion that Fry could only make runs in front of the wicket, mainly to the on-side, and set the field for him accordingly, he adapted his game beautifully, producing a series of exquisite cuts in an innings of 144. He countered comments about his limited strokeplay by saying: 'I had only one stroke maybe, but it went to 10 different parts of the field.' Alternatively he could point to his first-class average of 50.22.

Fry could be an aloof character – his Oxford nickname of 'Almighty' was not solely a product of his sporting and academic prowess – and did not take kindly to criticism. He saw himself as superior to ordinary mortals, who were condescendingly referred to by his close circle of acquaintances as 'small fry'. Bordering on the regal, as a footballer he even had his own dressing room and bath! Rather like the Graces, he sought to impose his authority on the cricket field and was hugely aggrieved when the legality of his fast bowling action was called into question by heavyweight Australian umpire Jim Phillips, who no-balled him nine times in a match at Hove for throwing. Back in the pavilion, Fry tied his bowling arm in a splint and concealed the apparatus by buttoning down the sleeve of his shirt, daring Phillips to no-ball him again. It was only when his captain put a stop to the straight-arm experiment that a sense of normality returned. In the wake of the incident, a limerick began doing the rounds of the county circuit:

> There was a young batsman named Fry
> Who at bowling oft thought he would try
> Till an umpire named Jim
> Who was looking at him
> Said: 'Good heavens, I call that a shy!'

Fry's action may have been considered suspect in some quarters – he only bowled 10 balls in Test matches – but it did not stop him taking 166 first-class wickets, including two hat-tricks at Lord's.

Despite – or perhaps because of – his standing in the game, Fry also managed to antagonise spectators, receiving a hostile welcome on more than one occasion when playing for Sussex at Canterbury. He was barracked mercilessly during one match for reasons, according to cricket writer William Pollock, that were a combination of two mis-fields, his 'rather swaggering walk' and his unconventional appearance – 'a most voluminous pair of trousers' and 'a funny white linen hat, with the front of the brim turned up, so that – if the hat had been black – he would have looked like a coalman.' Fry was so incensed at his treatment that he threatened to take his side off the field and the Kent captain had to warn the spectators that the game would be abandoned unless their behaviour improved. The Canterbury crowd booed Fry again in 1911, as a result of which he reportedly challenged one particularly vocal critic to a boxing match behind the pavilion. The following year he led England to victory against Australia at the Oval, but in the course of the match he had been booed by a section of the crowd for refusing to restart play after a break for rain because he thought it would hand the advantage to the Australians. The result vindicated Fry's decision and as England celebrated victory – one that also clinched the rubber – the crowd's jeers turned to cheers. However, Fry stubbornly refused to step forward and acknowledge them, despite Ranjitsinhji pleading with him: 'Be your noble self.' To which Fry replied loftily: 'This is not one of my noble days.'

Towards the end of his playing career he moved to Hampshire, where he continued to bat with distinction, finally calling it a day in 1922. There he demanded to be listed on scorecards as 'Commander C.B. Fry', even though he had actually done precious little to warrant that naval rank during the First World War. His feelings of self-importance were further illustrated by his repeated attempts to enter Parliament, but three times in the 1920s his campaign met with failure, something to which he was singularly unaccustomed. Meanwhile a more exotic opportunity presented itself – the throne of Albania. This came about in 1920 through his association with Ranjitsinhji, who by then was a member of the Indian delegation to the League of Nations and had appointed Fry as his personal adviser. An Albanian bishop approached Ranji and Fry and hinted that if someone, preferably an Englishman, were to be found who was prepared to spend £10,000 a year in Albania, the crown would be his. Fry's old Oxford friend, the poet Hilaire Belloc, strongly advised against acceptance, urging Fry to 'be content with a cellar of wine and the society of those who love you.' Nevertheless Fry was apparently seriously tempted, but the money proved a stumbling block. In spite of his aristocratic air, he was frequently short of money and at one point in his youth had even resorted to nude modelling in order to make ends meet. Although he boosted his finances at the height of his fame by endorsing cigars, chocolate and cricketing equipment, he was in no position to meet the Albanians' demands and the business came to nothing.

One venture that did succeed was the launch of his own monthly magazine, which he himself edited. He imposed a rule that no sentence should exceed 25 words but broke it on such a regular basis that the contributors rebelled. He resolved the dispute by offering a dispensation to those who had shared a classical education, because they 'understood how to frame subordinate clauses'.

Jealous of his Oxford contemporaries' political successes and struggling to face the fact that, with his sporting career finished, he was no longer in the public eye, Fry suffered a prolonged bout of mental illness in the late 1920s. He had suffered a nervous breakdown years earlier while at Oxford and his state of mind was not helped by his marriage in 1898 to Beatrice Sumner, a cruel and domineering woman, 10 years his senior. For England's most eligible bachelor she was a curious choice, particularly as she had a distinctly chequered past. Her appeal seemed confined to the fact that her long-term lover, Charles Hoare, was wealthy enough to finance the three of them. Now, with an unhappy marriage and having failed, so he believed, to realise the full potential of his genius, Fry became paranoid, started dressing strangely and behaving in an increasingly eccentric manner.

He remained out of the spotlight for six years, re-emerging in 1934 to accept an invitation to visit Nazi Germany to discuss youth issues, Fry having played a pioneering role in Britain's scouting movement. He had an hour-long audience with Hitler and was extremely impressed by him and by the standard of the nation's young people. Fry tried to persuade the Nazis to play Test cricket, reasoning that they might be able to produce a blond W.G. Grace, but, unbeknown to Fry at the time, they envisaged conquering wider fields than Lord's and Old Trafford. He was still expressing enthusiasm for the Germans as late as 1938 and, unfortunately, in print a year later.

Meanwhile Fry had returned to public prominence as a journalist, chiefly through his sports column 'C.B. Fry Says' in the *Evening Standard*. His eccentricity remained undiminished. He would sometimes fall asleep between writing his columns for the paper's first and final editions, so he carried an alarm clock, which could be heard ticking in his coat pocket or, occasionally, under his hat. His attire became ever more outlandish, notably when he was sent to cover England's 1936–37 tour to Australia. Fellow scribe Neville Cardus said that the only time Fry dressed 'in tolerably reasonable guise' was at a fancy dress ball. Otherwise his outfits resembled everything from a 'deep-sea monster' to someone 'dressed for a South Polar expedition' or one who 'was about to trace the source of the Amazon'. Fry was in his element demonstrating batting strokes to his disciples, borrowing any implement that came to hand. Pokers, rolled-up newspapers and canes were all pressed into service and at a Sussex

County Cricket Club dance he used an umbrella to instruct Maurice Tate and Tom Cook on how to play swing bowling. On a visit to Queen's College, Oxford, he went so far as to snatch a spear from the wall to use as a makeshift bat in order to demonstrate how his old friend Ranji played the famous leg-glide.

The grand old man of sport died in Hampstead on 7 September 1956, aged 84, having at least achieved the satisfaction of outliving his wife by 10 years. For all the eccentricity of his later life, he had the rare ability for a top-class sportsman of being able to convey in print what he had practised on the field of play. He thought long and hard about how players could improve their technique and was always willing to impart advice. Frank Woolley, the former Kent and England cricketer, said: 'I remember once bowling to him on a "sticky" when the ball was turning a lot. I beat him several times in one over without getting his wicket. Next over, to my surprise, he demonstrated that I was not pitching the ball on the right spot and it was going over the stumps. That was typical of him. He was a great theorist.'

Colin Ingleby-Mackenzie
Cavalier Captain

When Hampshire won their first-ever County Championship title in 1961 after 66 years of trying, their captain, Colin Ingleby-Mackenzie, was interviewed by an earnest television reporter on *Junior Sportsview*.

'Mr Ingleby-Mackenzie,' began the reporter, 'to what do you attribute Hampshire's success?'

'Oh, wine, women and song, I should say,' replied Ingleby-Mackenzie jovially.

'But,' persisted his inquisitor, 'don't you have certain rules, discipline, helpful hints for the younger viewer?'

Ingleby-Mackenzie gave the question a moment's thought before answering straight-faced: 'I absolutely insist that all my boys should be in bed before breakfast.'

His answers may have been flippant, but as the saying goes, many a true word is spoken in jest. In truth, they fairly accurately summed up Ingleby-Mackenzie's philosophy to life in general and cricket in particular. Play hard and, if absolutely necessary, work hard too, but try not to let it get in the way of having a good time. After all, here was a man who once persuaded umpire Harry Baldwin to bring a radio on to the pitch.

Despite the succession of attractive women seen on his arm, it would be wrong to dismiss Ingleby-Mackenzie, Hampshire's last amateur captain, as a mere fun-loving playboy. His apparent indifference, merry quips and easy-going manner masked a quiet determination. He wanted to win, but not at all costs, any success having to be achieved with style, panache and no little daring. It was the Ingleby-Mackenzie way.

The son of a surgeon vice-admiral, Ingleby-Mackenzie was born at Dartmouth, Devon, on 15 September 1933. His father was a fine all-round games player and the boy was playing cricket by the age of three, batting to the bowling of his mother and nanny, and screaming when the tea interval arrived. He was educated at Ludgrove and Eton, where he was hauled before the headmaster for gambling. Academic activity – one tutor at least gave him credit for being 'discreet in his slumbers' – took second place to sporting pursuits as he excelled at football, tennis and cricket. A swashbuckling left-handed batsman, he established himself in the Eton team at just 15 with a sparkling century against the MCC and two years later hit 81 out of 97 in 70 minutes against Harrow at Lord's. His form came to the attention of Hampshire, for whom he made his debut in 1951, only to be bowled for a duck.

After doing his National Service with the Royal Navy – surviving a harrowing ordeal when his submarine became trapped in an uncharted wreck – he played regularly for Hampshire but performed so disappointingly in 1954 that he offered to be dropped. Two years later he toured the West Indies with a team organised by venerable journalist E.W. Swanton. When Swanton demanded that the players should be in bed by 11 o'clock, Ingleby-Mackenzie protested: 'But surely the match starts at eleven-thirty?'

That summer he topped Hampshire's batting averages and, after sharing the county captaincy with Desmond Eagar in 1957, he as appointed sole captain the following year. He immediately announced his credo: 'Win or lose, let's entertain or perish.'

He quickly realised that success for such an unfashionable county was most likely to be achieved with a happy dressing room. He was fortunate to inherit two world-class players in West Indian opening batsman Roy Marshall and veteran England seamer Derek Shackleton, the latter possessing the ability to land the ball on a postage stamp and the stamina to bowl all day. 'Shack will bowl till he drops dead,' said Harold Gimblett, 'and then he'll drop on a length.' Shackleton himself used to grumble good-humouredly: 'Skipper makes one bowling change a day – he switches me to the other end.'

Ingleby-Mackenzie professed little knowledge of tactics, claiming that he left strategy to others, but curiously it was his flair for gambling that played such a key role in the Hampshire success story. His love of horse racing was legendary, more than one cynic noting that any injury he suffered seemed to coincide with Royal Ascot week. And during a match between the MCC and Yorkshire at Lord's he succeeded in stopping play for three minutes while he moved to the boundary fence and listened to radio commentary of the St. Leger. In that summer of 1961 his gambling instincts paid off as, in an experimental season when the follow-on was not permitted, he repeatedly profited from bold declarations after quickly weighing up the odds. No fewer than 10 of Hampshire's 19 victories were attributable to daring declarations on the final day, journalist Ian Wooldridge, an old friend and drinking companion of the captain, observing that the championship was won with 'two great players, nine old lags and outrageous declarations.' Ingleby-Mackenzie himself played no small part in these run chases, batting aggressively in the middle order to hurry along the run rate, his unbeaten 132 in 140 minutes against Essex at Cowes – his highest first-class score – securing a vital victory. Although his first-class career average was only a modest 24.35, the figure was compromised by his attacking approach and willingness to sacrifice his wicket for the greater good. Purely in terms of statistics, Ingleby-Mackenzie's contribution to the Hampshire cause may pale in comparison to others' but his leadership qualities and the team spirit he fostered made him irreplaceable.

The triumph of 1961 was not matched in the following seasons and in 1965 the dashing Old Etonian retired from first-class cricket with 12,421 runs to his name. He became a highly successful businessman, effortlessly combining the world of high finance with trips to his favourite West End club or to the races, where he socialised with two other renowned cricketing punters, Denis Compton and Keith Miller. He was also reputedly one of the last people to see Lord Lucan before his disappearance.

From 1996 to 1998 he served as President of the MCC and, in a move dear to his heart, was instrumental in women being allowed membership for the first time. His untimely death from a brain tumour on 9 March 2006 saddened the world of cricket that had lost one of its most engaging personalities.

In his playing days he used to travel to matches with Hampshire wicketkeeper Leo Harrison and always told him: 'Bring your dinner jacket with you in case we get lucky.' Hampshire cricket could count itself lucky to have been associated with Colin Ingleby-Mackenzie.

Imran Khan
Role Model

It was former Middlesex player Simon Hughes who wrote in his excellent book *A Lot of Hard Yakka*: 'The sight of Imran tearing fearsomely down the hill and the baying of the excited crowd made me realise for the first time that adrenalin was sometimes brown.' Hughes may have been tangibly intimidated by the approaching Imran but that lithe, bounding run-up with the pace and grace of a cheetah served as an inspiration to thousands of young Pakistanis. He was their country's finest-ever cricketer, probably the greatest all-rounder in history, a devastating fast bowler and explosive batsman who led Pakistan to historic first series victories in England and India and to glory at the 1992 World Cup. More than that, he was handsome, suave, intelligent and was invariably seen with a beautiful woman on his arm. What was there not to admire?

Yet perhaps his greatest achievement lay in his powers of leadership. Captaining the Pakistan cricket team has never been a straightforward task; the players' talent was rarely in question but their discipline sometimes was. However, Imran succeeded in moulding them into a cohesive unit, willing to play and fight for each other, as a result of which, under his stewardship, the Pakistan team finally reached its full potential.

Ironically Imran himself was viewed as a wayward youth and was dismissed early in his career as being unlikely to make the grade as a Test cricketer. He was born in Lahore in 1952, the only boy in a well-educated family of seven, and showed sufficient promise at school to be picked for his first-class debut for Lahore at the age of 16. It may also have helped that the chairman of selectors was his uncle and the captain and senior player were his cousins. 'Some called this nepotism,' wrote Imran later. 'I, of course, preferred to regard it as pure coincidence.' He was meant to open the batting but because it was raining, rather than wait around the ground, he decided to go back to where he was staying and catch up with some sleep. After a good rest he returned to find, to his horror, that the game was under way and that another player had been forced to open the innings in his place. His captain – cousin or not – was furious.

However, he knuckled under and two years later, following some impressive performances, he was selected for Pakistan's tour of England, but his privileged background, his youthful exuberance, the hints of nepotism, all combined to make some of the senior players suspicious of him. He was frequently in trouble on the tour for sneaking out to discos and breaking curfews, and was very nearly sent home in disgrace after apparently being set up by his room-mate Saeed Ahmed, the party's most senior player. According to Imran's version of events, Saeed encouraged him to go to a disco in Swansea instead of having an early night as he had originally intended. Saeed, apparently motivated by a desire for a single room, subsequently complained to the tour management about Imran's nocturnal habits and the effect it was having on his own form. Imran also incurred Saeed's wrath for giggling after Saeed had burst into tears during a match because a succession of catches had been dropped off his bowling. Once again Imran was hauled before captain Intikhab Alam and warned as to his future behaviour. Although he made his Test debut on that tour, his form was indifferent and by the end of the series a number of the party had already written him off.

Instead of returning to Pakistan after the tour, Imran studied for his A levels at the Royal Grammar School, Worcester, and played second XI cricket for that county. There he was advised by senior players to concentrate on his batting as they felt he was unlikely to make it as a fast bowler. The turning point in his career came in 1973 when he was admitted to Oxford University and made captain of the cricket team, the opportunity to play regular domestic cricket improving both his batting and his bowling. Within three years he had become a regular in the national side and, in the Test series against New Zealand, he took great pleasure in demonstrating his newfound hostility to John Parker and Glenn Turner, two of the Worcestershire players who had earlier been dismissive of his bowling talent. In 1977 he joined Sussex before signing up for two years of Kerry Packer's World Series. Under the guidance of John Snow and Mike Procter, his bowling action changed and he perfected the fast inswinger that he had been developing after injuring his back when he was 16. He explained: 'When I came back, I found that I had lost the outswinger, and was now bowling inswingers. I think I'd been putting too much pressure on my back trying to bowl outswingers, and without knowing it I had become more chest-on, encouraging the inswinger.'

In 1982 he was named Pakistan captain and, with his mastery of reverse swing, became one of the world's most potent bowlers. Far from affecting his play, the responsibility of the captaincy spurred him on and in that year's Test series against England he topped both the bowling and batting averages. He had little time for the 'old pros', as he called them, who 'tended to enjoy horse racing and the suspension of play due to rain'. Instead Imran brought a dynamic, fresh approach to the art of cricket captaincy, although a few dissenters claimed he was too authoritarian. However, a stress fracture of the shin sidelined him for two years and in 1987 he announced his retirement but was persuaded to return following a personal request from the President of Pakistan. Even when he finally retired in 1992, on the back of the World Cup triumph, the President asked him to reconsider but this time Imran was adamant: he wanted to bow out at the height of his popularity. He finished with 3,807 Test runs (average 37.69) and 362 Test wickets (average 22.81) and, unlike contemporaries such as Ian Botham, he actually got better with age, averaging 50 with the bat and 19 with the ball in his last 10 years of international cricket.

Before he left Pakistan for England on that initial tour back in 1971, his mother's last words to him were: 'Don't bring back a foreign wife.' Given the length of time spent away on tour, Imran had always believed that marriage and cricket were incompatible but that didn't stop him enjoying the company of numerous glamorous women. Then in 1995, free from the constraints of touring, he married Jemima Goldsmith, although the couple subsequently announced their divorce in 2004. He has also immersed himself in the challenging world of Pakistan's politics. Maybe the charismatic, inspirational figure who united a cricket team will one day unite a nation.

Keith Miller
Matinee Idol

'Pressure?' mused Keith Miller, pondering the stresses of the modern game. 'I'll tell you what pressure is. Pressure is a Messerschmitt up your arse. Playing cricket is not.'

Miller should know. He was a Second World War flying ace who, after duelling with Messerschmitts over Germany one night, made an unauthorised detour over Bonn because it was Beethoven's birthplace and he loved classical music. As Michael Parkinson said, on being told the story: 'How cool was that?'

Keith Miller was the epitome of cool. He possessed the dark, wavy hair of a matinee idol, frequented the most exclusive clubs and wined and dined with the famous. He enjoyed dinner with Aristotle Onassis and Maria Callas on the tycoon's yacht and had a close friendship (speculation has always been rife as to precisely how close) with Princess Margaret. It is said that Don Bradman answered a knock on his door one night to be met by a dinner-suited Miller, who was doing his captain the courtesy of affirming that he had been in bed, as ordered, at curfew but was now going out. An inveterate partygoer, he once arrived to captain New South Wales against South Australia still wearing his tuxedo from the night before, and set the field with a single command of 'Scatter.' He then took 7 for 12 as the opposition was routed for 27. The only time he occasionally lost his cool was with a cricket ball in his hand when, perhaps bored by a batsman's stubborn resistance or nursing a sore head from the previous night's partying, he would unleash a venomous bouncer or beamer. Even then he could show commendable restraint. Refusing Bradman's instructions to bowl short at England's Bill Edrich in the 1946–47 Brisbane Test, Miller said: 'I'd just fought a war with this bloke. I wasn't going to take his head off.' Instead he bowled off-cutters off a shortened run and took his career-best Test figures of 7 for 60.

English fans weren't quite sure what to make of the man who was nicknamed 'Nugget' because he possessed the golden touch. On the one hand they wanted to boo him for his aggression, his posturing and for being Australian; on the other, they couldn't help but admire his verve. As proof of his popularity in Britain, Miller became one of only three Australians – along with Bradman and Victor Trumper – to have his portrait hung in the pavilion at Lord's.

Keith Ross Miller was born in Melbourne on 28 November 1919 and named after the Australian aviator brothers Keith and Ross Smith, who at the time were taking part in a historic, 27-hour flight from England to Australia. His maths and cricket master at high school was former Australian captain Bill Woodfull, from whom he learned so quickly that by his early teens he was playing district cricket for South Melbourne. His club coach, Hughie Carroll, remembered: 'He was so small that you had to be careful not to tread on him, but he seemed to gain about 10 inches between seasons, and became a commanding batsman.' He had originally wanted to be a jockey but his growth spurt meant that he had to become a lifelong punter instead.

At 18 he made his Sheffield Shield debut for Victoria against Tasmania, scoring 181, and at that stage was nothing more than an occasional bowler. Then in 1941, by which time he was also playing Australian Rules football, he was asked to open the bowling for a Bradman XI in a match at Melbourne and created quite a stir with his pace and bounce. The advent of war put his career on hold. He flew hundreds of missions for the RAF but a crash-landing on his return to England one night left him with a sore back that affected him for the rest of his life. Not that Miller was one to dwell on his misfortune; in view of what had happened to so many of his friends, he was just glad to emerge from the war alive.

The War over, he starred in the five unofficial Victory Tests of 1945, making a tremendous impact on the cricket-starved British public with a quick-fire 185 at Lord's. As one who never had the slightest interest in averages or records, it is typical that his abiding memory of the day was not his own innings but of a South Australian team-mate, recently released from a prisoner-of-war camp, walking out at the headquarters of English cricket to a thunderous ovation.

Miller soon established himself as Australian's premier all-rounder – a dashing batsman, brilliant slip fielder and devastating bowler. He had the ability to be equally quick off a run-up of two paces as 15 and would switch from a fast bouncer to a leg-break and back again in the space of three balls as the mood took him. This quick-change routine was usually accompanied by a broad grin but it was no laughing matter for some of the batsmen on the receiving end of his most hostile deliveries. As a member of Bradman's famous 'Invincibles' of 1948, he was roundly booed for delivering a spate of bouncers during the 1948 Trent Bridge Test, whereupon he sat down in the middle of the pitch until the barracking had stopped. He sometimes had an uneasy relationship with Bradman, whose win-at-all-costs attitude clashed with Miller's carefree approach. Bradman liked his life to be ordered whereas Miller thrived on spontaneity. On that 1948 tour the Australians hammered the Essex attack for 721 runs in a day at Southend but Miller wanted no part in the slaughter. Arriving at the crease with the score at 364 for 2 he shouldered arms to the first ball he received and allowed himself to be bowled by Trevor Bailey. 'Thank God that's over,' he was heard to say as he returned to the pavilion. While Bradman muttered darkly, Miller headed off to the nearest racecourse.

Horse racing always played an important part in Miller's life. After the brother of umpire Frank Lee had come up with a duff tip, Miller playfully shook his fist when he returned to the crease at Lee's end. Unfortunately one newspaper misinterpreted the gesture and the next day carried the headline: 'Miller Loses Temper Over LBW Decision – Threatens Umpire'.

Possibly because of his relaxed attitude to the game, Miller was never chosen to captain his country, although he did skipper New South Wales, which he joined from Victoria after the War. On one occasion he took to the field with 12 men. When the error was pointed out, Miller asked loudly: 'Right, which one of you is going to bugger off?' Eventually he decided that the youngest should leave, only to discover that was the wicketkeeper. No worries: Miller himself went behind the stumps. Such a disorganised approach would undoubtedly have alarmed the national selection board but nevertheless Richie Benaud called him 'the best captain never to lead Australia'.

He had been tipped to lead Australia on their inaugural tour of the West Indies in 1954–55 but Bradman's influence saw Ian Johnson land the job instead, with Miller as his vice-captain. Miller was deeply hurt by the decision and as tension mounted on the tour, he told Johnson that he wasn't fit to captain a schoolboy team. The pair almost came to blows before the other players intervened. Relations between the two men were equally strained on the 1956 tour of England. With Australia in deep trouble 375 runs behind on first innings in the Old Trafford Test (where Jim Laker would go on to take 19 wickets), Johnson desperately tried to rally his troops. 'We can fight our way back,' he told them in Churchillian tones. 'We need guts and determination. We can still save the match.' At this, Miller, sitting in a corner of the room, lifted his head from the racing pages and said: 'Bet you six to four we can't.' He was right: Australia lost by an innings.

With a knee injury to add to his back problems, Miller played the last of his 55 Tests in India the following winter. He scored nearly 3,000 Test runs at an average of 36.97, including seven centuries, and took 170 Test wickets at 22.97 apiece, but his influence on a sporting generation stretched far beyond mere statistics. When he died on 11 October 2004 aged 84, thousands attended his state funeral to pay respects to a man Benaud said had 'more charisma than any other cricketer or sportsman I've seen'.

Keith Miller also invented Australian cricket's best-known hoodoo – the belief that 87 is an unlucky number. It is typical of the man that he derived as much pleasure from that as from any of his achievements with bat or ball.

K.S. Ranjitsinhji
A Prince Among Men

As with Hobbs and Sutcliffe, Compton and Edrich, Thomson and Lillee, Tufnell and Rothman, so the name of K.S. Ranjitsinhji is inexorably linked with that of C.B. Fry. Sussex team-mates, Fry and Ranji provided a marked contrast in styles – the power and determination of the Englishman next to the grace and elegance of the Indian prince. Ranji's batting was said to have possessed an almost mystical quality and was so widely admired that it made Fry's own style look decidedly basic. Yet the two men became firm friends and formed a mutual appreciation society. While Ranji praised Fry's ability to cope with the most difficult of pitches, C.B. said of Ranji: 'He moves as if he has no bones. One would not be surprised to see brown curves burning the grass where one of his cuts travelled, or blue flame shimmering round his bat as he makes one of his strokes.'

Ranji certainly brought something different to English cricket. Always immaculately dressed with his silk shirt buttoned at the wrists, he revolutionised batting in this country. Whereas previously batsmen had concentrated on playing forward, Ranji took advantage of the improving pitches of the time to play attacking strokes off the back foot. He excelled at the late cut and is credited with inventing, or at least popularising, the leg-glance. These two strokes formed a sizeable proportion of his 24,692 first-class runs, scored at an average of 56.37. He made 15 appearances for England – becoming the first Indian to play Test cricket – and finished with a Test average of a fraction under 45. And he achieved all this while struggling to cope with the English climate, for not only did he suffer from hay fever in warm, dry summers but cold weather affected him terribly. The summer of 1912 was particularly cold and wet, with the result that the Scarborough Festival of that year was only a place for the hardy. The wind whipped off the North Sea with such force that each day Ranji, who had only just returned from a visit to India, had to go shopping to buy another layer of clothing. As each additional vest or waistcoat was applied to keep out the chill, spectators became convinced that he was putting on weight at an alarming rate.

The Times wrote: 'Had the cold lasted, he certainly would not have been able to pass out of the dressing room door.'

Kumar Shri Ranjitsinhji's journey into the hearts of English cricket lovers began on 10 September 1872, when he was born into a wealthy Indian family of princely status in Sarodar, a small village in present-day Gujarat. At 16 he came to England to be educated at Harrow and Trinity College, Cambridge. Prior to his arrival at Cambridge in 1891, he had never played an organised game of cricket and understandably he struggled at first to break into the university team. This was partly due to an inability to keep his right leg still, a problem that he overcame by practising with his leg pegged to the ground. He won his cricket blue in his final year and achieved the remarkable feat of scoring three centuries in a single day – in three different matches. He began by hitting 128 for Cassandra before lunch on the second morning of a two-day match against Saffron Walden on Parker's Piece. After lunch, he wandered over to a game on an adjoining pitch featuring the Basinelles Club. Discovering that they were a man short, he immediately offered his services and struck a rapid 132. He then returned to his original match to find that his side were still batting, steadily building on the foundations that he had provided. Spotting him at a loose end, the Long Vacation team grabbed the opportunity to strengthen their batting line-up for the game with Christ's and Emmanuel. Ranji did not disappoint, hitting 150 to round off a magical day.

Although he would later become known as the 'Black Prince of Cricketers', Ranji's nickname at Cambridge was simply 'Smith', presumably in an attempt to anglicise him.

After graduating, Ranji played county cricket for Sussex, supplementing his sublime batting with occasional change bowling and fine slip fielding. He passed the 1,000-run mark in 10 successive domestic seasons between 1895 and 1904 and in 1899 became the first man to score over 3,000 runs in an English season – a feat he repeated the following year. Like Fry, he could bat on the most treacherous of pitches and in 1896, with echoes of his Cambridge achievement, he hit two first-class centuries in the same day for Sussex against Yorkshire at Hove. One observer described him as 'graceful as a panther in action with lean but steely muscles under his smooth brown skin.' He captained the county from 1899 to 1903 and built up a considerable fan base on the south coast. During one match at Hove he was walking around the ground when he casually tossed aside a small piece of rag that had been protecting an injured finger. Immediately several girls rushed to grab it as a souvenir and nearly came to blows over who had claimed it.

His outstanding form for Sussex prompted calls for him to be selected for England against the visiting Australians in 1896 but he was overlooked for the First Test because MCC chairman Lord Harris felt that only those born in England should be eligible to represent the country. However, for the Second Test at Old Trafford selection rested with the Lancashire committee and they disagreed with the MCC and drafted Ranji into the team. He responded with scores of 62 and 154 not-out, becoming only the second batsman after W.G. Grace to score a century on his England debut and the first to score 100 before lunch. In his first overseas Test innings – against Australia in 1897 – he made 175, which at the time was the highest individual score for England in a Test match. *Wisden* wrote: 'If the word genius can with any propriety be employed in connection with cricket, it surely applies to the young Indian's batting.'

Sometimes batting almost came too easily to him. Partnering Percy Fender for Sussex against Australia at Hove in 1912, he suggested between overs that it might be 'interesting' to nominate in advance which strokes he intended to play. He told Fender: 'I'll send the first ball down to Kellaway's left hand at long leg and the third ball to his right – he's always slow to get back. We'll run two each time.' Sure enough, two of Ranji's famous leg-glances carried out the plan to the letter and each time as they crossed, Ranji reminded Fender to run two. In another over, late cuts to Bardsley at deep third man brought two runs to the fielder's left, then two more to his right. Throughout the innings, Ranji was always as good as his word.

Ranji played his final Test in 1902 and two years later returned to India where, in 1907, he inherited the title of Maharaja Jam Sahib of Nawanagar. An extravagant but kindly ruler, he worked hard to improve living conditions for his people. He did complete two further seasons in English cricket but his career was effectively ended in 1915 when he lost his right eye in a shooting accident in Yorkshire, ironically while home from the War on sick leave. It did not stop him shooting, however, and, using his left shoulder, he once boasted to a friend that he had hit 10 birds from 12 shots. Even with a glass eye he attempted to make a comeback with Sussex in 1920 but, handicapped further by his ballooning weight (which this time was not the result of extra clothing), he failed to recapture past glories and played only three matches for the county.

Ranji died in India on 2 April 1933. His legacy is that he inspired a generation of young Indian cricketers, including his nephew K.S. Duleepsinhji. India's major cricket tournament, the Ranji Trophy, is named in his honour, while his memory still lives on in Sussex, where the Brighton and Hove Bus and Coach Company have named one of their buses K. S. Ranjitsinhji. No cricketer could wish for a finer accolade.

Vivian Richards
Master Blaster

The eyes had it. One moment they allowed Viv Richards to see the ball that split second faster than anyone else and send it crashing off the middle of his bat to the boundary, the next they could stare down the pitch with such intensity that bowlers shrivelled in his presence. 'Staring at bowlers and mouthy fielders was one of my hobbies,' he says. 'I loved to stare, and I could glare for the world. When you stand and glare back, you cannot lose as a batsman because you are in your ground. The bowler is always the one who has to break eye-contact, turn his back and walk back to the start of his run-up.'

A number of fast bowlers could intimidate in the 1970s and 1980s but Richards was the only batsman of that period who put fear into opponents as soon as he entered the arena. His arrival would invariably be slightly delayed – like an actor waiting to make his grand entrance – but when he eventually appeared it was with that familiar languid swagger, arms windmilling slowly. Reaching the wicket, he took guard and then, head tilted back slightly and chewing an ever-present wad of gum, strolled a few paces down the pitch to tap it while looking the bowler straight in the eye. It was enough to unsettle the most competitive of pace bowlers, so imagine what it did to a mild-mannered spinner. As Essex's David Acfield once said: 'When you're an off-spinner there's not much point glaring at a batsman. If I glared at Vivian Richards he'd just hit me even further.'

The contempt in which Richards held bowlers can be gauged by the fact that he was the only batsman of that time who wore a cap instead of a helmet. 'I felt I was good enough to deal with the bowlers without using a helmet,' he says. 'I just didn't want to give them any encouragement. To my way of thinking, I was going into battle for my country. It was a war, and if I was going to die for the cause then so be it. The fear of failure and losing was much stronger than the fear of being hurt. As for the gum, for me going out to bat without chewing gum was like going out without a box.'

The West Indian's aura was such that few experienced bowlers risked his wrath by sledging him. They knew that the payback would be too awful to contemplate, as one naïve youngster discovered to his cost. Playing for Somerset against Glamorgan in 1986, Richards appeared strangely out-of-sorts against promising fast bowler Greg Thomas, who beat the bat with three successive deliveries. As a fourth whistled past the outside edge of Richards's bat, Thomas followed through and mocked: 'Viv, you seem to be having a little trouble negotiating the seed today. For your information, it is red, it's round and it weighs five-and-a-half ounces.' Richards promptly belted Thomas's next ball straight past the bowler's head and into the river. He then turned to Thomas and said: 'As you know what it looks like, you had better go and find it.' Richards went on to make a century and Thomas limped forlornly out of the attack.

Isaac Vivian Alexander Richards was born in St John's, Antigua, in 1952. He showed tremendous promise as a boy but his prison officer father took care not to place too much pressure on his shoulders. 'He used to hide behind a tree when he came to watch me as a kid,' remembers Richards, 'just in case his presence put me off. But then sometimes I would hear his voice from behind the tree booming with some advice.'

The youngster's talent became the talk of the island's cricketing fraternity but his debut at 17 could hardly have been less auspicious. He was given out first ball, contentiously caught bat and pad. 'There was no wood on the ball,' recalled Richards in his autobiography, 'but I knew that I was in trouble from the moment the umpire joined the bowler in his appeal.' When Richards refused to walk and aimed a volley of verbal abuse at the umpire, the spectators, who had been expecting so much from the young prodigy, poured on to the pitch. To prevent the disturbance escalating into a full-scale riot, Richards was amazingly reinstated, only to be stumped without scoring. Then in the second innings – his third – he was caught for a duck. 'It was all very humiliating,' conceded Richards who paid for his petulance with a two-year ban by Antigua from all representative cricket.

The year 1974 proved key to Richards's development into a world-class batsman. Not only did he make his Test debut for the West Indies in India but he also joined Somerset, where he came under the influence of combative captain Brian Close and veteran player-coach Tom Cartwright. 'My first captain was an inspiration to me,' says Richards. 'I think I was pretty tough as a youngster, but Closey was tougher still. He reinforced the message that you yield to no one. At first I kept getting quick 30s and 40s and he drummed into me the need to keep going and to watch the ball for longer on English pitches.' Cartwright was impressed with the way Richards used to keep his head still at the crease. He once remarked: 'You could have put a pint of bitter on his head and he wouldn't have spilled a drop.'

There was no obvious weakness in Richards's game, not a shot that he couldn't play. A superb cover driver, he was also a powerful hooker and had the ability to score quickly as well as stylishly, hence his nickname of the 'Master Blaster'. He holds the record for hitting the fastest-ever Test century, from just 56 balls against England in 1986, and altogether struck 84 sixes in Test cricket. He played in a total of 121 Tests, scoring 8,540 runs at an average of 50.23, his finest year being 1976 when he averaged 90.00 and hit seven centuries in 11 Tests, including a career-best 291 at the Oval. His total of 1,710 Test runs for that single calendar year set a record that remained unbroken for another 30 years.

He was also a man for the big occasion. He ran out three Australians to help the West Indies win the inaugural World Cup in 1975 and hit a century in the 1979 final at Lord's to enable his country to retain the trophy. He captained the West Indies in 50 Tests between 1980 and 1991, during which time he never lost a series. He was also a deceptively dangerous off-break bowler, taking 32 Test and 118 one-day international wickets. In 1986–87 against New Zealand at Dunedin he became the first man to score a century and take five wickets in the same one-day international. Among his career scalps was his great friend Ian Botham in the First Test at Trinidad in the 1980–81 series, a dismissal that prompted an overjoyed Richards to perform a couple of cartwheels right in front of the departing batsman. He explained later: 'He [Botham] had promised me that if I ever got him out with my pup bowling he would buy me drinks for the rest of my life.'

Richards's laid-back demeanour belied a fierce competitive streak, which, thankfully, rarely manifested itself in unsavoury incidents, although he did overstep the mark in the Barbados Test of 1990 with a finger-flapping appeal that led to the incorrect dismissal of England's Rob Bailey. *Wisden* described the gesture as 'undignified and unsightly. At worst, it was calculated gamesmanship.' Richards also became embroiled in an argument with Australian captain Allan Border during a 1984 tour match in New South Wales. An appeal for Richards to be given out caught behind was rejected, sparking an angry altercation, which ended with Richards offering to sort it out at the end of play. Never one to be intimidated, Richards duly stormed into the Australian dressing room ready for a fight, only to be greeted by a bunch of pressmen who had been alerted by Border, presumably in the hope that their presence would deter the West Indian from physical action. Richards wisely decided that discretion was indeed the better part of valour but was still booed and jeered by the Australian crowds for the rest of the tour.

For the most part, however, spectators recognised him for his batting genius, his stock increasing yet further when he refused vast sums of money to play for a rebel West Indies side in apartheid South Africa. In 2000 he was named one of *Wisden*'s five 'Cricketers of the Century', along with Donald Bradman, Garfield Sobers, Jack Hobbs and Shane Warne. In the same year he was knighted for services to cricket.

Naturally Viv Richards is particularly revered in Antigua, where he was honoured by being depicted on a postage stamp back in 1975. It is a little-known fact that he also played football for the island in qualifying matches for the 1974 World Cup. Bowlers the world over must deeply regret that he decided against pursuing a career in football and that the dreaded Richards glare was not directed at referees instead.

C. Aubrey Smith
From Hove To Hollywood

As the only England captain to have appeared in a film with Elizabeth Taylor (the 1949 remake of *Little Women*), Sir Charles Aubrey Smith is assured of a place in cricketing folklore. To film buffs he is best known as the crusty English aristocrat in a succession of 1930s and 1940s movies but to cricket lovers he is remembered as a notable all-rounder for Sussex with a peculiar bowling style and later as the founder of the star-studded Hollywood Cricket Club.

The son of a Brighton doctor, he was born in London in 1863 and educated at Charterhouse, where he was coached by former Surrey and All England cricketer Julius Caesar. He then won a place at Cambridge and furthered his cricketing career by joining Sussex in 1882. He served the county nobly for the next 14 years, acting as captain for two seasons from 1887, and generally performing with distinction in what was otherwise a fairly ordinary side. He averaged 32 in first-class matches with the bat and, using his 6ft 4in frame to full effect, had a knack of plucking slip catches out of thin air. But it was his fast-medium bowling – particularly his approach to the wicket – that set him apart. His curious curved run-up began either from behind the umpire or, if the fancy took him, from an area around deep mid-off, earning him the nickname of 'Round the Corner' Smith. W.G. Grace wrote of the phenomenon: 'When Smith begins his run he is behind the umpire and out of sight of the batsman; and I can assure you it is rather startling when he suddenly appears at the bowling crease.' In spite of – or maybe because of – this peculiarity he gathered 346 first-class wickets at 22.34 apiece and was selected for England on their first tour of South Africa in 1888–89. He picked up 134 wickets on the tour – at 7.61 each – but played only one Test, at Port Elizabeth, where, as captain, he took 5 for 19 in the first innings and 2 for 42 in the second as England won by eight wickets in a low-scoring affair played on matting. Despite these impressive figures, he never captained or even played for England again.

In fact, his life nearly ended in South Africa that October when he was taken so seriously ill that doctors pronounced him dead. A local newspaper duly printed a fulsome tribute, announcing that he had 'succumbed to that fell disease, inflammation of the lungs.' It went on: 'Much regret will be felt at his decease – he made many friends by his kindly disposition.' Happily Smith was in the almost unique position of being able to read his own obituary.

Fully recovered, he resumed his cricket career before branching out into acting, making his debut on the West End stage in 1896 as the villain in *The Prisoner of Zenda*, the film version of which he would star in 41 years later opposite Raymond Massey and Ronald Colman. He made the transition from stage to film in the 1920s and at the age of 63 moved to Hollywood where he played the archetypal Englishman both on and off screen, insisting on the Union Jack being raised every day at his home near Mulholland Drive.

Throughout his film career he retained his love of cricket and, while the 'bodyline' series raged in Australia, he set about recreating the English village green in a corner of southern California. He bought five cartloads of English grass seed to plant a wicket and in 1933 officially opened the Hollywood Cricket Club in Griffith Park, Los Angeles. He immediately launched a recruitment drive among major Hollywood celebrities, using a mixture of charm and bullying. When a young Laurence Olivier booked into the Chateau Marmont Hotel to start his first day in Hollywood, he found a note from Smith waiting for him: 'There will be nets tomorrow at 9am. I trust I shall see you there.' Olivier dutifully turned up in size 13 boots borrowed from Boris Karloff, who was himself a capable wicketkeeper. It was surely a test of any batsman's nerve to stay cool with Frankenstein's monster breathing down his neck. Similarly, David Niven recalled being press-ganged into net practice on an evening that he had set aside for 'chasing some skirt'. Aubrey was not an easy man to refuse.

Others who appeared in the regular Sunday afternoon fixtures included Errol Flynn, Basil Rathbone, P.G. Wodehouse and George Coulouris.

Smith remained an active member of the side in his 70s, his eccentricity endearing him to all and sundry. In one match he was fielding in the slips as usual when he spilled a catch. He immediately stopped the proceedings and demanded that his butler be brought on to the pitch. 'Fetch me my glasses,' he bellowed. Several minutes later, with play still halted, the butler returned to the middle carrying the spectacles on a silver tray. A few balls later, Smith fumbled another slip catch and yelled at his butler: 'Damn fool, you brought me my reading glasses!'

The very Englishness of Sir Aubrey (he was knighted in 1944 for improving Anglo-American relations) attracted visiting international cricketers such as Gubby Allen, Denis Compton, Godfrey Evans and Len Hutton to the club. There was never any doubting his priorities. At the club's AGM of May 1945 he spoke at length, not about victory in Europe, but of the more pressing concern of moles damaging the wicket.

Sir Charles Aubrey Smith died of pneumonia in Beverly Hills in 1948. On one of his last trips back to England, by which time he had long been a famous face on the silver screen, he was spotted in the pavilion at Lord's. 'That man over there seems familiar,' remarked one member to another. 'Yes,' said the second, clearly oblivious to Hollywood stardom. 'Chap called Smith. Used to play for Sussex.'

Lionel Tennyson
The Aristocratic Touch

Lionel, Lord Tennyson, grandson of the poet, was responsible for one of the most remarkable innings in Test match history. As an inspirational leader of men and a free-flowing batsman, the noble lord had already made a considerable impact as captain of Hampshire when he was chosen to lead England against the visiting Australians in 1921. The news came as such a surprise that, on receiving the telegram, he read it, rolled it into a ball, threw it at the ceiling, caught the rebound and exclaimed: 'Good heavens, they've asked me to captain England!' But in the Third Test at Headingley disaster struck when he badly injured his left hand while fielding. Determined not to let the side down, he resolved to bat one-handed and bought a young man's cricket bat in a shop at Leeds in the belief that it would be better suited to the purpose. With his injured hand encased in a wire basket, he took to the crease with England eight wickets down and needing another 92 runs to avoid the follow-on. Wielding the bat like a tennis racket, he proceeded to hammer the redoubtable Australian fast bowling pair of Jack Gregory and Ted McDonald to all parts of the ground, even though every contact of bat and ball caused him pain. He smashed 63 in just over an hour, including 10 fours, to avert the follow-on. The Australians had never seen anything like it.

Neville Cardus wrote in the *Manchester Guardian*: 'Tennyson showed us that a man can drive one-handed if he will get quickly into the right position for driving. He rose high on his toes to the fast bowler's bumpers and played them down with a left elbow beautifully up. Tennyson returned to the pavilion at the end of his fine adventure to the wildest cheering one has heard on a cricket ground for many a long day.'

Although still incapacitated, he hit another 36 in the second innings (including a six) and took a fine catch, but sadly his heroics could not prevent England losing by 219 runs. Even so, he had left his highly individual stamp on Test match cricket.

Tennyson was the most unconventional of county captains, not least because his personal butler, Walter Livsey, often acted as Hampshire's wicketkeeper. Tennyson's instructions to his man-servant when the latter was packing his cricket bags summed up his philosophy to the game – make sure there were enough bottles of champagne to celebrate victory or drown sorrows. Livsey was incredibly loyal to his captain and master. After Tennyson had appealed unsuccessfully against the light in one match, Livsey, the next man in, called out on approaching the wicket: 'Where are you, my lord? I can hear you but I cannot see you.' Whether or not the umpires took the hint is unrecorded.

On another occasion Tennyson was batting in a charity match in which Livsey was standing as umpire. When a confident appeal went up for Tennyson's dismissal, Livsey was reluctant to raise the finger of fate to his master but instead repeated the message which Tennyson had always asked him to relay to unwelcome visitors: 'His Lordship is not in, I regret to say.'

Tennyson was very much a hands-on captain and, watching from the pavilion, invariably had a piece of advice that he wished to pass on to his batsmen. When umpires objected to the constant flow of messages to the men in the middle, Tennyson decided to send his instructions by telegram. Struggling to lay bat on ball, Hampshire's young amateur batsman Harold Day was nevertheless surprised to see a boy in blue uniform trotting out holding a small orange envelope. The contents revealed a terse inquiry from his captain: 'What do you think your bat is for?' With the run-rate sagging during another game, Hampshire batsman Philip Mead also received the telegram treatment, his message reading: 'Too slow. Get out at once. Tennyson.'

Tennyson could well have served as a role model for a later Hampshire captain, Colin Ingleby-Mackenzie. He spent much of his time enjoying the London high life and thought nothing of asking his chauffeur to drive him 80 yards from his flat to one of his clubs. The chauffeur would then wait patiently outside until around three in the morning before driving Tennyson the short distance back home. Tennyson justified the extravagance on the grounds that he found physical exercise tiring unless it was for cricket, golf or dancing. Sometimes he arrived at the ground unkempt and still in his dinner jacket following a night in the West End clubs. One morning, finding himself stranded in London when his services as county captain were required in Southampton, he took a taxi to the ground and ordered the Hampshire secretary to pay the fare, which he did by going around the turnstiles and collecting the admission money.

For the game with Warwickshire at Edgbaston in 1922, Tennyson travelled up from Southampton in the company of Harold Day. As was his custom, his Lordship stopped for refreshment at a number of inns en route, with the result that the pair did not get to bed until dawn. 'Don't worry,' said Tennyson reassuringly, 'I'll win the toss.' Sure enough he did, and put the opposition in. Warwickshire were bowled out for 223 but Tennyson's plan backfired when, in reply, Hampshire were skittled for just 15 in half an hour. At the end of that first day, the Warwickshire captain, the Hon. Freddie Calthorpe, was naturally in bullish mood and suggested to Tennyson that since the match was bound to finish early, they should have a game of golf. Tennyson took exception to this proposal and, apparently in language not appropriate to his social standing, bet Calthorpe £10 that Hampshire would win the cricket match. Other bets on Hampshire were placed at long odds as Tennyson confidently predicted that his men would score 500 in the second innings. This optimism was rewarded when their total of 521 (Livsey at number 10 hitting an unbeaten century) was followed by a Warwickshire collapse to 158 all-out, giving the visitors an unlikely 155-run victory. The Hampshire players returned south considerably wealthier.

As befitted a man who in his younger days gambled away £12,000 on the horses in one week, Tennyson was fond of a flutter. Appearing for the Gentlemen against the Players in 1932, he wagered a bottle of champagne that he would make a century. He had hit 73 by lunch when, unable to contain his thirst any longer, he demanded – and consumed – his bottle of champagne. He then doubled the stakes and went on to make 112, whereupon he drank the second bottle while still wearing his pads. They don't make them like Lionel Tennyson anymore.

He was born in Westminster on 7 November 1889 and spent his childhood in England and Australia, courtesy of his father's appointment as Governor of South Australia. On returning to England, he was educated at Eton and Cambridge but left the latter without taking his degree, having found the lure of London parties and the Newmarket racecourse too great to resist. In 1911 he joined the army and created such a favourable impression in forces' cricket that two years later he was invited to play for the MCC against Oxford University, marking the occasion by hitting a century in better than even time. Within two weeks he had made his first appearance for Hampshire.

Despite his 100 on his first-class debut, Tennyson was primarily regarded as a fast bowler in those days. However, his absurdly long run, coupled with an ungainly delivery that was all arms and legs, understandably sapped his stamina, meaning that after just a couple of overs he was usually a spent force and alarmingly expensive, his 55 first-class wickets costing more than 50 runs apiece. Even so, Tennyson had supreme confidence in his own ability and would introduce himself into the attack as a lesson to his underperforming strike bowlers, who therefore had to stifle giggles on the occasion when he paced out his long run, roared into the wicket and promptly pulled a hamstring.

Tennyson's batting was fearless rather than reliable. As he so bravely demonstrated against Gregory and McDonald, he coped admirably with fast bowling but the spinners were liable to expose his rasher instincts. Nevertheless, on his day he was a fine striker of the ball, scoring an unbeaten century in 55 minutes against Gloucestershire in 1927. In all he hit 19 first-class centuries and scored 16,828 runs at an average of 23.33. He made the first of his nine Test appearances against South Africa in 1913, his last coming at the Oval in 1921, just two matches after his heroic deeds at Headingley.

Tennyson was appointed Hampshire captain in 1919, a post he held for 14 years. In truth, he was just happy to be alive, having been wounded three times in the First World War and erroneously reported dead twice. His man-management skills at cricket were unorthodox, as can be seen from the way he dealt with a rare show of dissent, at Trent Bridge in September 1922. His bowler Jack Newman had deliberated long and hard over field placings before switching to bowling around the wicket, a delay that had incurred the displeasure of a section of the crowd. When he again took his time setting his field at the start of his next over, the crowd reacted angrily and he responded by hurling the ball to the ground. Tennyson told him to pick up the ball and, when Newman refused, he ordered him from the field for what was later described as the use of 'objectionable language'. To compound the felony, Newman petulantly kicked down the stumps on his way back to the pavilion. Dictating the contents, Tennyson subsequently forced the errant bowler to write three identical letters of apology – one to the president of Nottinghamshire, a second to their captain, and a third to Tennyson himself. He then handed Newman £5. Even by Tennyson's standards, this was curious behaviour.

Although his Test career was over, Tennyson continued to lead touring parties to the West Indies, South Africa and India in his usual exuberant style, and from 1928 was able to do so as the third Baron Tennyson, having inherited the title on the death of his father. On a trip to the West Indies he formed an orchestra (with himself as drummer) to counteract the monotony of the long voyage and on his final tour, to India in 1937–38, he went on a panther shoot but only succeeded in bagging a goat that had been left in a clearing as bait. He joked afterwards that the goat was a man-eater.

Lionel Tennyson died in a Bexhill hotel on 6 June 1951, according to one obituary notice, 'like an English gentleman, sitting up in bed smoking a cigar and reading *The Times*.' On hearing of his former captain's death, Jack Newman spoke for the whole Hampshire team when he said: 'What a wonderful man. We loved him, every bone in his body.'

BIG HITTERS

George Bonnor
The Colonial Hercules

Standing 6ft 6in tall and weighing 17 stone, George Bonnor swung his heavy bat like a battleaxe to club opposing bowlers into pavilion and oblivion. The most fearsome hitter of his day, the Australian Hercules once drove the ball back over the bowler's head with such force during a match at Portsmouth that it splintered the sightscreen. He was capable of sending a ball in excess of 160 yards with barely a twitch of his broad shoulders and during the Oval Test of 1880 he was caught for two off a ball he had hit so high that by the time Fred Grace took the catch on the boundary, Bonnor and his partner had run three. 'My heart stopped beating as I went on waiting (for the ball to drop),' said Grace later. Bonnor simply moaned: 'I should have *hit* the perisher!'

With his golden hair and flowing beard, Bonnor was likened to a reincarnation of a Greek god. An English peer who visited him in Australia declared him to be the most perfect physical human specimen he had ever known. Bonnor never married, although a wealthy widow, on whom he had clearly made a deep impression during one tour of England, doggedly pursued him all the way back to Australia.

The son of a merchant, George John Bonnor was born in Bathurst, New South Wales, on 25 February 1855. As a youngster he played for Victoria (later joining New South Wales in 1885) and came to England with Australian teams on five occasions, all during the 1880s. At Melbourne he once drove a ball through the pavilion clock and his reputation as a mighty hitter preceded him to England. Wherever he played, crowds would flock to see him in action.

He did not disappoint. At Bradford in 1882 his innings of 35 included five sixes – one over the pavilion, one over the stand and three on to the road (in those days a ball had to go out of the ground to be worth six). At Scarborough he made 122 out of 167, including 20 off one four-ball over: 6, 4, 4, 6. In 1884 he hit the fastest Test century to date – 128 in 114 minutes.

Although he disliked being termed a mere slogger, Bonnor was quite happy to play up to the crowds. On one voyage to England he made a £100 wager with a fellow passenger that his first throw with a cricket ball upon landing would carry more than 100 yards. Bonnor duly won the bet by burling the ball 119 yards – without even bothering to remove his coat. In Yorkshire he entertained onlookers by throwing a ball over a railway viaduct, and in practice he regularly tried to hit the ball as far as possible, one blow at Mitcham Common in 1880 being carefully measured by England slow bowler James Southerton at 147 yards. The adulation Bonnor received meant that he was not lacking in confidence. When asked to name the three best batsmen in the world, he replied: 'Well you cannot get away from W.G. and [Billy] Murdoch isn't far behind. I would rather you did not ask me to name the third!'

Unfortunately his figures do not support the boast. In 17 Tests between 1880 and 1888 he scored only one century and averaged just 17. His first-class average of 21 from 148 matches is equally modest. Particularly at the start of his career, he was often out cheaply through trying to live up to expectations. The crowd came to see him slog and he felt obliged to respond from the very first delivery before he had the opportunity to weigh up the bowling. Later he tried to refine his technique and bat more steadily but it did not come naturally to him. As he tried to live down the reputation he had worked so hard at building up, he was once congratulated on hitting a ball over the fence and out of the ground. 'Why, I only blocked it,' protested Bonnor.

His nemesis was the Yorkshire and England slow left-armer Ted Peate, whose presence in the opposing team often caused him sleepless nights. On the evening before one Test, Bonnor practised batting against Peate in his hotel room but took such a mighty swipe at an imaginary ball that he shattered a china jug and basin! Peate paid tribute to Bonnor, calling him 'one of the most dangerous men I ever crossed,' qualifying his praise with 'but he would persist in trying to play the fancy game.' Peate went on: 'At Bradford, in June 1882, he was kind enough to hit me three times out of the ground for sixes. I had my revenge in another match, when he came in about 10 minutes from drawing-time. He went on playing over after over as nice as possible, until it got to the very last ball of the last over of the day. I sent him down what he evidently thought was a regular "sloppy" one, and of course he must let fly, with the result that he was caught at cover-point. He went out looking as if he would like to kick himself.' In the Old Trafford Test of 1884, Peate succeeded in pushing the big hitter so far back into his crease that his boot disturbed the stumps, Bonnor thus becoming the first player to be given out hit-wicket in a Test match.

If he sometimes struggled with his batting, Bonnor was worth a place in the Australian side almost on the strength of his fielding. His prodigious throwing ability made him an invaluable outfielder, only foolhardy batsmen being prepared to take a chance with his arm. He was also a genial fellow who, invited to play for the Non-Smokers in the annual fixture against the Smokers, duly arrived at the wicket with a large cigar in his mouth.

After retiring from cricket in the mid 1890s, Bonnor suffered from a heart condition but carried on working as a produce buyer. He died at East Orange, New South Wales, on 27 June 1912. Among the stories attached to this larger-than-life character is that he once hit a cricket ball 300 miles. It happened in 1890 during the Orange cricket competition when he lofted a ball out of the ground and on to a passing coal train, the ball subsequently being recovered 300 miles down the line. Thus, although factually true, the story is fanciful because in reality not even George Bonnor could hit a ball 300 miles…at least, not without taking his coat off.

Harold Gimblett
A Tortured Soul

Harold Gimblett enjoyed a fairytale start to his career in English county cricket and suffered a miserable ending. Fame came too quickly for the Somerset farmer's son, who was selected for his country little more than a year after playing village cricket. Gripped by doubt and depression, he was eventually ostracised by his county and finished up taking his own life at the age of 63.

The contrast between that dark day in March 1978, when Gimblett was found dead at his home in Verwood, Dorset, having taken an overdose of tablets, and the summer's afternoon in May 1935 when he burst spectacularly on to the county scene could not be more marked. Born in the west Somerset village of Bicknoller in 1914, Gimblett had made a name for himself as an explosive hitter in village cricket, as a result of which he was offered a month's trial by Somerset in 1935. He had no cricket bag and only a badly discoloured bat, and after just two weeks' working with the professionals, secretary John Daniell informed him that he was not up to the required standard and would therefore not be given a contract. The dejected Gimblett was about to catch the bus home when news reached the secretary that one of the Somerset players due to face Essex at Frome the next day was injured. With nobody else available at such short notice, Daniell was forced to turn to the young man he had just rejected. 'Do you know where Frome is, Gimblett?' he asked.

The secretary arranged that if Gimblett were able to catch the early morning bus from his home in the Quantocks to Bridgewater, wicketkeeper Wally Luckes would then give him a lift to Frome. Gimblett was up well before six o'clock on the morning of Saturday 18 May but not early enough to catch the first bus to Bridgewater. Instead he missed it by a few minutes and knew that the next one was not for another two hours. Carrying a small multipurpose bag that had been pressed into service to house his bat, flannels and shirt and some sandwiches made for him by his mother, Gimblett, with no backup plan, started walking down the country road in the vague direction of Bridgewater. Luckily, he soon heard a lorry approaching from behind and managed to thumb it down. When Gimblett revealed that he was going to Frome to play cricket for Somerset, the lorry driver didn't believe him but agreed to give him a lift to Bridgewater where wicketkeeper Luckes was waiting.

Using a spare bat offered to him by Arthur Wellard, Gimblett went in at number eight shortly after lunch, with Somerset in dire straits at 107 for 6. Fearlessly he set about the Essex bowling, which included England fast bowler Morris Nichols, reaching his 50 in 28 minutes and his century in 63. When he was finally out caught and bowled, he had made 123 out of 175 in 79 minutes, his innings including three sixes and 17 fours. The whirlwind knock would win him the Lawrence Trophy for the fastest hundred of the season.

Fleet Street lapped up the fairytale story and sent photographers and reporters to the family farm, but the hero of the hour was distinctly uneasy. 'I savoured the moment,' he said years later, 'but loathed the publicity that followed.'

Naturally Somerset reconsidered their decision to release him, and in his next innings he made 53 against the star-studded Middlesex attack at Lord's despite being so crippled by injury that he needed the services of a runner. Although his form tailed off, he recaptured it in glorious fashion the following summer, scoring over 1,600 runs and earning an England call-up against India at Lord's. Instead of being delighted at the selection so early in his career, he felt terrified, convinced that he was not yet ready for such an accolade and worried about the responsibility of representing his country. 'I can remember listening to the 12 names announced on the radio,' he said later. 'The names were given in alphabetical order and I prayed that I wouldn't be included.' In his first Test innings he made just 11 but, with a little help from Jack Hobbs who, using his umbrella as a bat, taught him how to cope with the inswinger, Gimblett top scored with 67 not-out in the second innings (finishing with five successive boundaries) as England won by nine wickets. However, he failed in the next Test, after which, to his enormous relief, he was dropped. His only other Test appearance produced two scores in the low 20s against the West Indies in 1939.

Whatever doubts Gimblett harboured at Test level did not affect his county career as he passed 1,000 runs for Somerset every season between 1936 and 1953. He scored over 23,000 runs at an average of 36 and hit 50 centuries and 265 sixes, the only blip being in 1938 when he adopted a more cautious approach that failed to suit his game. Usually opening the batting, he attacked freely and ferociously, employing the hook shot to great effect. He once hit three sixes in an over during which his partner appealed against the light.

To his surprise and dismay, he was recalled to the England line-up against the West Indies in the summer of 1950 but a carbuncle on the back of his neck conveniently ruled him out. That winter he went to India with a Commonwealth team but lost two stone because, sickened by the continual smell of curry, he completely lost his appetite. On his return to England he struggled for form initially and, feeling increasingly morose, was advised by his doctor to take a break from cricket in July. The rest seemed to work wonders because he came back to score three centuries in August. He maintained his form over the next two summers but was becoming isolated from the rest of the team, withdrawing more and more into his own private world. By the end of 1953 he was taking pills to help him sleep and more pills to wake him up. 'The world was closing in on me,' he said later.

On medical advice, he was sent to a mental hospital for four months and given electroconvulsive therapy. 'There were several of us having it twice a week,' he recalled. 'I felt like death and I remember joking to the others: "Well, I open for Somerset so I may as well go in first."'

He was released in time for the start of the 1954 season but knew immediately that he would struggle to get through it. Batting in the first match at Nottinghamshire, he nearly walked off halfway through his innings. He was persuaded to continue and ground out an uncharacteristically slow 29 before being able to adjourn to the dressing room, where he sat on a bench and launched a bitter diatribe that led to him being reported to the secretary for setting a bad example to the younger players.

Matters came to a head in the next match, which was against Yorkshire at Taunton. Caught off the bowling of Fred Trueman for a duck, Gimblett trudged back to the pavilion, packed his bags and went home. It would be his last match for the county.

He returned to hospital as a voluntary patient but avoided all contact with Somerset County Cricket Club until, a few months later and feeling a little brighter, he decided to go and watch the Pakistan tourists play at Taunton. With the permission of the scorer, he sat quietly in the scorebox but when word got around that Gimblett was at the ground, he was summoned to the secretary's office. 'He ordered me out of the ground,' recalled Gimblett. 'I was speechless.' The incident, which sparked angry recriminations on both sides, marked the end of his long and distinguished association with Somerset. The fairytale had turned sour.

His cricket career over, Gimblett worked in a steelworks until he swapped the claustrophobia for the outdoor life as a cow herder in Wales. He assisted in cricket coaching at Millfield School for 20 years and helped deliver hot lunches to the elderly, but the resentment he felt at his past treatment never departed. A year before his death, his bitterness was exacerbated when he was refused entry to the Long Room at Lord's.

At his best, Harold Gimblett was a dashing batsman and useful change bowler, a man capable of destroying the finest attacks in county cricket. Even at his most melancholic he could still display a dry wit. His last captain at Somerset, Ben Brocklehurst, often made a point of seeking his advice, if only to make him feel wanted, and once asked him which roller should be used between innings. Gimblett replied with a tired smile: 'That damn pitch has been rolled with heavy and light rollers for a great many years – and it won't make any difference which one is used now!'

Gilbert Jessop
The Croucher

Like Harold Gimblett, Gilbert Jessop's introduction to county cricket was spectacular and brutal. On his first-class debut for Gloucestershire in 1894, the 20-year-old arrived at the wicket to save a hat-trick. Most young batsmen would have played a tentative defensive stroke, but not Jessop. He lashed the hat-trick ball for four, smashed another boundary later in the over and in the process set out his stall for a 20-year assault on the world's bowlers that made him one of the biggest draws in the game.

Physically at least, Jessop did not look like a typical big hitter. He was only 5ft 7in tall and weighed a modest 11 stone, his crouching stance with feet apart as he shaped to play making him appear smaller still. In fact, his stance suggested a dour stonewaller such as 'Slasher' Mackay rather than the most exciting batsman of his day. But his secret weapons were a heavy bat, a keen eye, an agile brain and fast feet. He could not hit the ball the distance of a Bonnor or a Thornton but no batsman was ever so consistently aggressive. *Wisden* wrote: 'Extraordinarily quick on his feet, he was ready to hit firm-footed if the ball were pitched well up and equally, when it was of shorter length, to dash down the pitch and drive...Lightness of foot allied to wonderful sight made it possible for him to run out to the fastest bowlers of his time – Richardson and Mold – and at the peak of his form pull or straight-drive them with almost unerring certainty. No one ever approached him in this particular feat; indeed, nobody else could have attempted it with reasonable hope of success.'

Few batsmen were capable of punishing the bowling with such a variety of strokes. Not only would he advance down the wicket to the fast bowlers with the intention of making them drop the ball short but when they did so, he would cut or pull the ball with unsurpassed ferocity. His footwork was so nimble that he had the ability to cut balls off leg-stump or pull from outside off-stump. On his day – and there were many of them – he was virtually impossible to bowl at, prompting Sir Jack Hobbs to remark: 'He made me glad that I was not a bowler.'

Named after W.G. Grace, Gilbert Laird Jessop was born in Cheltenham on 19 May 1874. In the early years of his career he was a formidable fast bowler as well as a pugnacious batsman and a brilliant fielder in the covers, where his speed over the ground saved countless runs. In one season alone he ran out 30 batsmen. A year after his fearless debut for Gloucestershire, he hit 63 out of 65 in less than half an hour against Yorkshire. By 1897 he was representing Cambridge University, scoring 101 out of 118 in 40 minutes against Yorkshire at Harrogate, an innings in which he hit the ball out of the ground six times and a dozen times over the ropes, the latter only counting for four in those days. He made 1,219 runs that summer and collected 116 wickets at less than 18 apiece. On a tour of America with Plum Warner's side, poet Ralph Paine described Jessop as 'the human catapult who wrecks the roofs of distant towns when set in his assault.' The runs continued to flow, although when he was selected for his first Test – against Australia at Lord's in 1899 – it was primarily for his bowling. However, he strained his back after being overbowled in that match and was never quite as effective again, but the injury didn't stop him opening the bowling for England in Sydney on the 1901–02 tour and taking the first four Australian wickets.

Meanwhile his batting went from strength to strength. On 12 occasions he reached his 100 in under an hour and in total he hit 53 centuries, including five scores of more than 200, testament to his incredible stamina and concentration. Among his most destructive innings were a knock of 157 out of 201 in an hour against the West Indies at Bristol in 1901 and two years later a blistering 286 out of 335 in 175 minutes for Gloucestershire against Sussex. He could be almost as dangerous at Test level. Against Australia at the Oval in 1902, England, chasing 263 to win on a bowlers' wicket, had lurched to 48 for 5 when Jessop came to the crease. He proceeded to hit 104 out of 139 in an hour and a quarter, twice sending the ball on to the roof of the pavilion, and paving the way for England to scrape home by one wicket. Then in 1907 he scored 93 in 75 minutes against a battery of South African googly bowlers whom he had never encountered before. But for the fact that his Test appearances overseas were restricted because sea journeys made him extremely ill, he would undoubtedly have played more than 18 times for his country. On his sole trip to Australia in 1901–02 he actually met his future wife on the voyage home. Perhaps the experience dissuaded him from further travel.

His last Test appearance was against South Africa in 1912 but he played for Gloucestershire for a further two years before serving as a captain in the Manchester Regiment during the First World War. However, he was invalided out with heart problems in 1918 and that put an end to his cricketing career. He retired having scored 26,698 first-class runs at an average of 32.63.

Jessop's sporting prowess extended beyond cricket. He played rugby for Gloucester, football for the Casuals, could run the 100 yards in just over 10 seconds and was a fine hockey player, billiards player and golfer.

When he died in Dorset on 11 May 1955, aged 80, tributes poured in to the man affectionately known as 'The Croucher'. Many correspondents recounted tales of his legendary hitting, among them Neville Cardus who remembered when, as a small boy, he watched Lancashire play Gloucestershire at Old Trafford. Cardus missed the last few minutes before lunch so that he could buy some lemonade for the interval. His head barely reaching above the counter, he had just given his order when there was an almighty crash that sent glasses and crockery flying everywhere. Young Cardus feared the end of the world had arrived but the barman had seen it all before and was able to reassure him. 'Don't worry, son,' he said. 'It's only Mr Jessop just beginning his innings.'

Kevin Pietersen
Striking A Pose

There was always a danger that Kevin Pietersen would be known more for his appearance than his batting. For a while the blue hair, earrings and tattoos threatened to overshadow his considerable talent – until his outstanding performances in the 2005 Ashes series ensured that he was noticed for all the right reasons. Pietersen himself could never understand what all the fuss was about anyway. 'My hair doesn't make me play cricket any differently,' he says. 'Just because I've got a stupid haircut or diamond earrings, it's not going to make me cover drive a ball any differently.'

It was England fast bowler Darren Gough who talked Pietersen into doing something unusual with his hair. The result was a peroxide streak down the middle that made him look like a dead skunk. Apparently Gough also suggested the earrings and the three lions England tattoo on Pietersen's arm. Some might say Gough has a lot to answer for. In fairness, Pietersen has never been backward in drawing attention to himself, both on and off the field. Seen by some as a strutting peacock (and not just because of his occasionally blue hair), nobody could ever accuse him of lacking confidence yet he has found an unlikely ally in Geoffrey Boycott, whose own idea of a radical hairstyle would have been to move his parting a quarter of an inch to the left. Boycott has said of Pietersen: 'He is a belligerent individual. He is cocky and confident. There is a touch of arrogance about him. I love it, so long as he produces runs.'

Pietersen has certainly done that, but more importantly he introduced much-needed aggression into England's batting, equalling Viv Richards's record as the fastest batsman to reach 1,000 runs in one-day internationals. Before the South African-born strokemaker arrived on the international scene in 2004, too many English batsmen appeared overawed by the likes of Shane Warne, Glenn McGrath and Muttiah Muralitharan. The summit of their ambition seemed to be survival. From the outset, however, Pietersen made it clear that he was not going to be intimidated by any bowler, regardless of their reputation. How many people would dare to reverse-sweep

Muralithan for six, as Pietersen did at Edgbaston in 2006? He has taken the attack to the world's finest with some breathtaking demonstrations of powerful hitting, and an average of over 50 in both Tests and one-day internationals indicates that he has been successful more often than not.

Nothing seems to faze him. Having rejected his native South Africa, he was anticipating a hostile reception when England toured that country in 2005 and was not disappointed. He responded with an extravagant badge-kissing celebration on reaching his maiden international century in the one-day match at Bloemfontein, which further antagonised the spectators, who turned their backs on him as he returned to the pavilion. But far from retreating into his shell he resumed the offensive with two further tons, eventually winning over the crowd, who greeted his third century with a standing ovation. Later that year, six dropped catches in the Ashes series might have dented the confidence of a lesser man. Those who considered him too brash, too arrogant, were queuing up to take potshots at him but again Pietersen showed his mettle when it mattered. With the outcome of the series in the balance, he struck a majestic 158 at the Oval to secure the draw England required to regain the Ashes at long last.

Pietersen was born in Pietermaritzburg, South Africa, in 1980. He made his first-class debut for Natal at the age of 17 but was regarded predominantly as an off-spin bowler and a hard-hitting lower-order batsman. In 1999 he impressed Nasser Hussain's England tourists by taking four top-order wickets and, batting at number nine, hitting an unbeaten 61 off 57 balls. Despite this praise he was dropped from Natal's first team, largely he felt because of the country's quota system, whereby, in an attempt to redress the injustices of apartheid, provincial sides were required to include at least four non-white players. Pietersen believed that players should be judged on merit and has since been outspoken in his criticism of the scheme. Being eligible to play for England by virtue of his English mother, Pietersen decided to try his luck in Britain and spent five months as the overseas player for Staffordshire club Cannock, helping them to win the Birmingham and District Premier League in 2000. His first spell away from home saw him living in a single room above a squash club, working in the club bar and listening to 'those horrible Black Country accents'.

Hussain had advised him to seek employment with an English county and his fairy godmother duly arrived in the form of Nottinghamshire's South African coach Clive Rice, who had seen Pietersen play as a schoolboy back in 1997. Rice offered Pietersen a contract with Notts and in his first season he made 1,275 runs at an average of 57.95, the highlight being an unbeaten 218 in a sixth-wicket stand of 352 against Derbyshire.

Wisden wrote: 'If he can maintain his first season's form, the name of Pietersen should be pencilled in for future Test squads.'

The form was continued in 2002, with Pietersen scoring four consecutive centuries (254 not-out, 122, 147 and 116) in the space of a single week in August. He followed up with 1,546 first-class runs in 2003 plus 764 in limited-overs cricket, and on that winter's National Academy tour of India he hit three centuries in his six first-class innings to finish with an average of more than 100.

But storm clouds were gathering on the horizon. Pietersen's confident approach was not to everyone's taste in the Nottinghamshire dressing room. There was a feeling that he saw himself as a square cut above the rest of the players, a view that was reinforced when, following the county's relegation in 2003, he asked to be released from his contract. The unrest provoked an unseemly spat, captain Jason Gallian allegedly throwing Pietersen's kit bag off the balcony at Trent Bridge. Pietersen was forced to honour the final year of his contract but found it a depressing experience and further fuelled the ill-feeling by describing the county's director of cricket, Mike Newell, as 'a very insignificant figure in my life.' In October 2004 Pietersen was finally free to join Hampshire.

By then Pietersen had also served his four-year qualifying period at county level and was immediately called into the England side for that winter's one-day internationals in Zimbabwe. Naturally, international cricket held no terrors for him and he averaged 104 in his three innings. England had found a new star, and moreover one with sufficiently broad shoulders and sufficiently thick skin to cope with the attendant publicity, even when it focused on a private life that often appeared to be as colourful as his hair.

His first Test appearance came in the unforgettable Ashes series of 2005 and although England began with a crushing defeat at Lord's, KP, as he was now universally known, top-scored in both innings, only the fourth English player to do so on his debut. He followed up with a crucial 71 in the first innings at Edgbaston but then posted a run of relatively disappointing scores until hitting his maiden Test century at the Oval, riding his luck after being dropped twice before he had reached double figures. His belligerent 158 included seven sixes, a record for an England player in an Ashes innings.

Although Pietersen is capable of playing a patient innings, he is at his best when on the attack, using his 6ft 4in frame to bludgeon the bowling into submission. The one-day game could have been invented for him, and it is no surprise that he has developed into one of its leading exponents.

Not that he is any slouch in Test cricket and his 142 in the Second Test against Sri Lanka in 2006 took him past the milestone of 1,000 Test runs in only his 12th match. Indeed, his total of just under 2,500 runs from his first 25 Tests has only ever been beaten by one man – Donald Bradman. If you have to come second, even Pietersen would probably acknowledge that Bradman is not a bad person to lose out to.

He was again England's most effective batsman in the disastrous 2006–07 Ashes series in Australia and his performances at the 2007 World Cup, including 104 off 122 balls against Australia and 100 in 91 balls against the West Indies, led to him being named the International Cricket Council's number-one ranked batsman in the world for one-day internationals. He finished the tournament with 444 runs at an average of 55.5 and was described by one writer as shining in the England team 'like a 100-watt bulb in a room full of candles'.

The early summer of 2007 saw a slump in form, which he blamed on fatigue, but again he responded in the most positive manner, with 134 in the First Test against India at Lord's (hailed as his best century to date) followed by another century in the Oval Test. Anyway, as Pietersen himself remarked of his temporary loss of form, without a trace of modesty: 'Even legends have quiet times.'

Charles Thornton
Bun Lover

While fielding at long leg for Eton in a schoolboy match, Charles Thornton summoned a vendor of cakes and pastries and proceeded to eat a jam-filled bun on the field of play. He was evidently so hungry that not even the threat of impending action could persuade him to relinquish the repast, for he held on to a high catch while devouring the last few mouthfuls. The incident earned him the nickname of 'Buns' for the remainder of his career, although it was as a prolific big-hitter rather than as a prolific consumer of confectionery that he ultimately earned his reputation.

Thornton was a contemporary of George Bonnor and was able to hit the ball every bit as far as the Australian. He recorded six measured hits of over 150 yards and in 1876, while practising for a match between Brighton and Horsham at Hove, he drove a ball over the entrance gate and into the street, where it landed among a group of startled cabbies. The blow was variously measured at anything between 160 and 168 yards but was nevertheless confidently listed in three separate publications of the period as 'the longest authenticated hit ever made'.

Unlike Bonnor, who operated from a standing start and relied on his muscular physique, Thornton favoured the mobile approach that would later be the trademark of Gilbert Jessop. To assist in his movement at the crease, Thornton never wore any leg padding, apart from small shin-pads inside his stockings, and rarely wore batting gloves, believing that they prevented a full swing of the bat. Although six-foot tall, Thornton did not possess the build of Bonnor but was very strong in the hips, and this, coupled with the momentum achieved by his nifty footwork, enabled him to propel the ball vast distances with a wonderfully free flourish of the bat.

The son of a vicar, Charles Inglis Thornton was born at Llanwarne, Herefordshire, on 20 March 1850. He spent three years in the Eton first XI (one as captain) and also won school contests for throwing the cricket ball and putting the shot. He first gave notice of his forceful batting at Lord's in 1868 when, playing for Eton against Harrow, he drove a ball over the old pavilion, a shot considered by no less an authority than former England stalwart John Lillywhite to be the best straight drive he had ever seen. From Eton he went to Trinity College, Cambridge, where he played for the university team, captaining it in 1872 when it beat Oxford by an innings. In the meantime he also played for Kent and was reported as hitting a ball 152 yards at Canterbury. On the same ground he once launched every ball of a four-ball over well beyond the boundary but the rules of the day meant that he was rewarded with only four runs for each stroke.

Although he made five centuries and compiled nearly 7,000 runs in a first-class career that stretched to 1897, Thornton's principal consideration when stepping out to bat seemed to be to hit the ball as far as possible. Playing at the Oval in the early 1870s, he struck a delivery from Surrey's James Southerton so far that wicketkeeper Edward Pooley was heard to exclaim: 'So 'elp me God, Jimmy, I believe it's gone on to Brixton Church!'

He played for Middlesex from the 1870s and thereafter for a number of scratch sides but reserved his finest blows for Scarborough, where he is reputed to have hit one ball from Tom Emmett into the sea. This may have been an exaggeration and a more credible story is that he drove a ball over a four-storey house in an adjoining street. Playing there for the Gentlemen against I Zingari in 1886, he hit a memorable 107 in only 70 minutes, sending eight balls clean out of the ground. On another occasion – against Merchant Taylors – he lost seven balls. His wicket was greatly prized. When Scarborough visited neighbours Malton in 1922, a fielder was so intent on trying to catch Thornton on the boundary that he forgot to look where he was going and finished up in the pond that bordered the ground! Thornton was largely responsible for the creation of the Scarborough Festival, although not everything about the Yorkshire resort was to his liking. Striding out to the middle to start his innings, he heard a brass band playing in the distance. This distracted him to such an extent that he issued instructions for the musicians to stop playing. The command was obeyed but Thornton was out for a duck anyway. Hours later, he was still blaming his dismissal on the band.

He once visited the cricket ground at Oakham School and, with nobody recognising him, was invited to play as a substitute. He went on to hit 188 in two hours, sending the ball out of the ground no fewer than 13 times. His mastery of batting was such that he hit upon the idea of playing an innings 'ball by ball, in the manner of certain well-known batsmen'. However, the ingenious scheme foundered all too swiftly, Thornton being out first ball after, according to observers, 'leaving the ball alone in the customary manner of a certain defensive player'.

Away from cricket Thornton earned his living in the timber trade for 35 years and was also an enthusiastic motorist and traveller, journeying through Japan and Russia and penning a book titled *East and West* about a trip around the world. He was nearly trapped in Berlin when the First World War broke out. He died in London on 10 December 1929 but his exploits were immortalised by a verse, *A Song for the Slogger,* which had first appeared in *Punch* years earlier:

'Here's health to you "Buns!" may you score lots of runs,
And oft stir the crowd with your spirit unfailing.
How often I'd watch when they "bowled for a catch",
And you gave 'em one, truly, but in the next parish!'

The rhyme may have left something to be desired but the sentiments were worthy.

Albert Trott
A Sad Decline

The haphazard life of Middlesex all-rounder Albert Trott is best summed up by his benefit match against Somerset at Lord's over Whitsun in1907. In dire straits financially – partly due to his love of ale, which he used to share with spectators while fielding on the boundary – Trott was hoping for a bumper payout from the holiday crowd. However, he quite forgot himself and, with thousands of spectators still waiting to pay cash tribute to one of the county's most popular players, he took a double hat-trick in the same innings, as a result of which the match finished a day early and he was deprived of urgently needed gate receipts. Afterwards he said ruefully: 'I'm bowling myself into the workhouse.'

Seven years later, aged just 41 and beset by illness as well as debt, Trott wrote his will on the back of a laundry ticket, leaving all his worldly possessions – his clothes and £4 in money – to his landlady. Then he shot himself.

It was a tragic end for one of cricket's most boisterous characters – a man who, in his newspaper column, angered the MCC by criticising a fixture in which 'the beer gave out after lunch', and who once threw a Middlesex team-mate over his knee in the dressing room and spanked him with a hairbrush as punishment for sloppy fielding that had cost the match. 'Albatrott', as he was known to friend and foe, was very much the Freddie Flintoff of his day.

The son of an accountant, Trott was born in Melbourne, Australia, on 6 February 1873. As a teenager he learned to spin the ball by placing a large wooden crate in front of the stumps and spinning the ball around it. As his career developed he tended to rely less on spin and more on change of pace, slipping a quick yorker into the mix at will. One of his swifter deliveries is said to have killed a swallow. Before Trott took the field for the Players against the Gentlemen at the Oval in 1903, wicketkeeper Herbert Strudwick, who was unfamiliar with his bowling, asked him how he signalled his faster ball. 'That's all right,' replied Trott cheerfully, 'you'll soon find it.' Strudwick habitually stood up to slow bowling but then in his third over Trott whipped in a demon yorker that landed painfully on Strudwick's left foot. As the wicketkeeper hobbled around in agony, Trott laughed: 'Did you find it?'

Trott burst on to the scene in the winter of 1894–95 with a succession of outstanding performances with both bat and ball against Andrew Stoddart's England tourists. In eleven-a-side matches against the Englishmen he scored 331 runs in nine innings and took 19 wickets. His finest hour came in the Adelaide Test in which he made 38 and 72 (both not-out) and took 8 for 43 in the second innings. In the next Test at Sydney he scored an unbeaten 86 but surprisingly was not asked to bowl by captain George Giffen. Although less successful in the final Test at Melbourne, his batting average for the series was 102.5 and it was widely expected that he would be selected for the 1896 tour of England – particularly as his older brother Harry was captaining the side. However for reasons that were never properly explained, young Albert was sensationally omitted from the touring party.

Dismayed by the rejection, Trott sailed to England independently, paying for his own passage, and, encouraged by Australian umpire Jim Phillips, decided to qualify for Middlesex. He achieved his goal in 1898, taking 102 wickets in the season, although not everyone approved of the switch. One opponent claimed that Trott had 'no more right to play for Middlesex than Stalin has to lead the Guards Brigade.' His controversial change of allegiance was completed when he played for England on the 1898–99 tour of South Africa, taking 17 wickets at less than 12 runs apiece in the two Test matches. On that tour Trott went out of his way to collect as many native weapons as he could lay his hands on and managed to acquire a splendid assortment of battleaxes and blunderbusses. These travelled everywhere with him by rail but when the England train was involved in a collision, the force of the impact sent Trott's weapons flying about the carriage and he finished up with a dislocated thumb.

The next two summers saw Trott at the peak of his powers. In 1899 he scored 1,175 runs and took 239 wickets and the following year he hit 1,337 runs and snapped up 211 wickets. He was also a brilliant fielder. His massive hands held 452 catches in the course of his first-class career and he was possibly the first man to slide into the ball in the outfield, gather it up and throw in one movement. Wonderfully inventive, he ran out a Somerset batsman by throwing the ball backwards through his legs to break the wicket.

Trott loved a challenge, and the one he had set himself was to become the first player to hit a ball over the pavilion at Lord's. He prepared for the attempt for some months with the help of an extraordinarily heavy bat, weighing more than three pounds. His moment came on 31 July 1899, fittingly in the match between MCC and the visiting Australians. Trott set about wreaking revenge on his native country – and on bowler Monty Noble in particular – with a display of mighty hitting. One blow landed just short of the pavilion rails, the next pitched on the seats. After these two sighters, he launched a huge blow that sent the ball soaring over the Lord's pavilion and into the garden of the ground's dressing-room attendant Philip Need. From then on, Trott's reputation as a big hitter went before him. In the same season he scored 164 for Middlesex against Yorkshire, offering just one chance in the innings – a lusty swipe to long-on – but the fielder, losing the ball in flight, was so horrified to see it suddenly bearing down on him at pace that he opted to leave it. Yet ultimately Trott's record-breaking hit was to prove a mixed blessing, for he became increasingly obsessed with clearing pavilions wherever he played and the relentless pursuit ended up ruining him as a batsman.

The other factor in his swift decline was alcohol. He started drinking more – particularly when it was offered by admiring Lord's spectators – but in doing so he put on weight and began to lose his athleticism. He could no longer bowl the faster ball that had been his most feared weapon. It saddened his team-mates to see such a popular figure struggle, Middlesex wicketkeeper Gregor MacGregor once saying to him: 'What a pity you haven't got a head instead of a turnip. You'd be the best bowler in the world!'

Trott's bowling was rarely as effective after 1903, the ironic exception being his own benefit match. In 1910 he quit playing (having scored over 10,000 runs and captured more than 1,500 wickets) and took up umpiring. Four years later he was dead, discovered in the seedy London lodgings where he had lived alone, surrounded by empty beer bottles.

Albert Trott's legions of fans preferred not to dwell on his unhappy later years but to recall the sheer vitality of the man at his peak. He was a renowned practical joker, as one opposing batsman, who dared to suggest that Trott's bowling was overrated, discovered to his cost. As the batsman in question took guard, he was handed a folded piece of paper by Trott with instructions not to read it until his dismissal. Trott's first ball hit the batsman in the stomach, his second eluded a mighty swing, and his third knocked back the middle stump. On his way back to the pavilion the crestfallen batsman opened the note. It said: 'Trott to receive £5 if he hits you first ball, gives you one you cannot hit, and clean bowls you in the first over. Is he a good bowler?'

Arthur Wellard
The Terror Of Taunton

Somerset all-rounder Arthur Wellard did not believe in doing things by half. Of the 125 championship wickets he took in his first season for the county, no fewer than 69 were clean bowled – a ratio that he often maintained through his career. But it was as a ferocious batsman that he entered local legend, hammering more than 500 sixes in first-class cricket, a figure that accounted for a quarter of his overall total of runs. Nobody was safe from a Wellard onslaught – least of all the fish in the River Tone flowing past the county ground at Taunton.

He was even more dangerous at Wells, where he profited from the shorter boundaries by twice hitting five sixes in an over. In 1936 he struck Derbyshire slow bowler 'Tosser' Armstrong for five consecutive sixes there, his 86 in 62 minutes (following on his nine-wicket match haul) giving Somerset victory by one wicket. Two years later he hit five sixes off Kent's Frank Woolley but, going for a record-breaking sixth off the final ball of the over, was dropped by Bryan Valentine just in front of the sightscreen and had to settle for running a single. Wellard sealed Somerset's victory by collecting 13 wickets in the match. As if his batting and bowling were not sufficient to make him a formidable adversary, in the field he would station himself at silly mid-off and take his false teeth out on hot days. To say the least, the sight had an unsettling effect on the batsman and was considered by some opponents to be bordering on gamesmanship.

Wellard was born in Southfleet, Kent, on 8 April 1902 and first played for Bexley, heading the club's batting and bowling averages for three years. He applied to Kent for a trial but was told bluntly that he would be better advised trying for a career in the police force. Fortunately he came to the attention of Somerset, who were more appreciative of his abilities, and he made his debut for them in 1927. His impact was instantaneous. A tall, powerfully-built man with a distinctive leap in his delivery stride, he was a lively opening bowler who could not only produce away swing but also a vicious breakback that shattered many a set of stumps. With a bat in his hand, initial appearances could be deceptive, for he was wont to play the first few balls with textbook defensive shots before, unannounced, taking aim at the nearest allotments. In 1933 he hit 51 sixes; in 1935 he struck a record 72, following it up with 57 in both 1936 and 1938.

His value to the team was immeasurable. Against Hampshire at Portsmouth in 1933, Wellard went in to bat with Somerset faltering at 38 for 6, but he made 77 out of 94, took 7 for 43, and then hit 60 in the second innings. His form earned him two Test appearances – against New Zealand at Old Trafford in 1937 and against Australia at Lord's in 1938. In the latter he batted with uncharacteristic restraint to help Denis Compton in a vital eighth-wicket stand of 74 on the last day, although he did briefly revert to type to launch one six into the grandstand. He was selected for the 1939 tour of India but the outbreak of war forced its cancellation and prevented him adding to his caps. He managed to keep his hand in during the war and hit a whirlwind 50 in just eight minutes in a match at Hayes.

Even though he was now well into his 40s, he resumed his career with Somerset after the war but the ravages of age obliged him to turn increasingly to bowling off-breaks. However, he was not above catching the batsman unawares by slipping in a much faster ball with echoes of his younger days. He played his last game for the county in 1950, having scored 12,485 first-class runs at an average of 19.72 and taken 1,614 wickets at 24.35 apiece. He later played in the Birmingham League and died at Eastbourne on New Year's Eve 1980.

Arthur Wellard's exploits on the field made him an obvious favourite with Somerset fans but he was also a popular figure in the dressing room. The gaudy clothes he wore when he first arrived from Kent stood out among the more rustic attire of some of his team-mates and he was also an enthusiastic drinker and gambler. He attended the races whenever possible, while any stoppage for rain brought out his pack of cards for a game of poker or brag. By the time the sun had come out again, he was nearly always better off financially. 'He could remember the position of every card in the pack,' sighed team-mate Bill Andrews. 'He was out of our class.'

FAST AND FURIOUS

Billy Bestwick
An Unquenchable Thirst

For a bowler to take all 10 wickets in an innings is always a remarkable feat, but for Derbyshire's Billy Bestwick it bordered on the miraculous. Not only was he 46 when he tore through the Glamorgan batting at Cardiff in June 1921, but it was nothing short of amazing that he was playing at all.

Nobody disputed Bestwick's ability; the broad-shouldered miner had been a formidable fast bowler for a number of years, combining genuine pace with nagging accuracy. But winters working at the coal face had also given him a raging thirst, which, as one writer put it, could be measured in gallons rather than pints. Bestwick had been drinking heavily for longer than anyone – and certainly he – could remember, matters having reached the point where the county appointed a minder to keep an eye on him during away trips. One of his team-mates (usually Arthur Morton) was instructed to stay with Bestwick at all times and make sure that he did not hit the ale. But Bestwick was a wily old fox and used to give his minder the slip by entering a shop via the front door and sneaking out the back. A couple of late-night drinking sessions left him virtually incapable of playing any meaningful part in the 1921 fixture with Gloucestershire at Bristol, a report for the game reading: 'Bestwick occasionally suffered from a "thirst" and as a result was unable to bowl or field much in Gloucestershire's second innings.' It did not bode well for the next match in Cardiff.

The Sunday rest day proved disastrous and Bestwick was considered unlikely to be fit to bowl in Glamorgan's second innings. However, captain George Buckston decided to teach him a lesson and, in an inspired move, put him on to open the bowling. The bleary-eyed Bestwick took a wicket with his fifth ball and thereafter maintained admirable line and length, ripping out the entire Glamorgan side before lunch, finishing with figures of 10 for 40 from 19 overs. Seven were clean bowled and he wrapped up the innings with three wickets in four balls. Rarely has a finer performance been given under the influence, and no doubt Bestwick celebrated in his own inimitable way.

He was born at Heanor, Derbyshire, on 24 February 1875 and first played for the county at the age of 23. Despite his powerful build he was a hopeless batsman with a career average of less than five, his highest score being 39 against Leicestershire in 1900. Fortunately his deficiencies with the willow were ably compensated by his bowling, which saw him to pass the 100-wicket mark in 1905, 1906 and 1908. He only needed a short run, using his body strength to generate pace and lift, which meant that he was able to bowl for long spells. His fondness for a drink was already well known but his self-discipline deteriorated after his wife died in 1906, leaving him with a young son to raise. In January 1907 he was involved in a drunken brawl at Heanor with an unsavoury character called William Brown, who pulled a knife on Bestwick and cut his face. When Brown was stabbed to death later that night, Bestwick was arrested and charged with manslaughter. However the inquest ruled that he had acted in self-defence after Brown had again lunged at him with the knife, and consequently the charge was dropped.

The incident did nothing to curb Bestwick's drinking and he was often unable to open the bowling after a heavy night on the ale. In 1909 Derbyshire finally lost patience with him, suspending him in the summer and releasing him at the end of the season. At 34 and with an undesirable reputation, he seemed finished and drifted into professional league cricket in South Wales, also making a few appearances for Glamorgan who were not a first-class county in those days. But when county cricket resumed in 1919 after the First World War, Bestwick surprisingly returned to Derbyshire, having obviously been forgiven for his past misdemeanours. Although in his mid-40s, his work as a miner had kept him fit and he was to enjoy something of an Indian summer.

He played only one match in 1920, when Derbyshire lost 17 of their 18 matches (the other being abandoned), but in 1921 he took 147 wickets at an average of 16.72, including five in an innings on 17 occasions and that alcohol-induced, 10-wicket haul at Cardiff.

His drinking continued to cause problems and the following year, after another night out, he was left at the team's hotel before the game at Worcester. Angry and hungover, he made his way to the ground, paid to get in, and sat in the stand, from where he loudly barracked his own side. Remarkably, he was again forgiven and later that summer he was joined in the Derbyshire team for two games by his son Robert. In the match against Warwickshire the Bestwicks came up against another father and son duo, Willie and Bernard Quaife.

Billy Bestwick outlasted young Robert in the first-class game, playing on until he was 50. He finally retired in 1925, having taken 1,457 first-class wickets, and, in another unpredictable twist, became an umpire! Fears that he might see four batsmen running at a time proved unfounded as he cut back on his drinking (no longer being able to sweat it out with a long spell of bowling) and was rewarded by being asked to officiate in three Tests between 1929 and 1930. He died in Nottingham on 2 May 1938. It is not known whether his liver was donated to science.

Roy Gilchrist
Jamaican Firebrand

West Indian fast bowlers are not necessarily known for their easy-going nature on the cricket field. Charlie Griffith, Andy Roberts, Curtly Ambrose – to name but three – were intimidating figures, but they were positive pussycats compared to Roy Gilchrist. To put it mildly Gilchrist led a troubled life, both in and out of sport. He was thrown out of Test cricket for deliberately bowling beamers, struck a batsman on the head with a stump during a charity match, and was sentenced to three months' probation for assaulting his wife following a violent row. Depending on your point of view, Gilchrist's wild behaviour was either, as author Michael Manley suggested in *A History of West Indies Cricket*, the unfortunate product of his impoverished upbringing, or, as blunt-speaking Australian umpire Cec Pepper believed, down to the simple fact that he was a 'bloody nutter'.

Gilchrist was born in Jamaica in 1934 and endured a tough childhood on a sugar plantation. A small man, with short legs and long arms, he did not possess the standard fast bowler's build but he was capable of generating tremendous pace, assisted in no small part by a personality that was surly on his good days, volatile on his bad. He could deliver an awesome bouncer but, more worryingly, considered the beamer to be a legitimate weapon. 'I have searched the rule books,' he once said, 'and there is not a word in any of them that says a fellow cannot bowl a fast full-toss at a batsman. A batsman has got a bat and they should get the treatment they deserve. Unless he hasn't got the technique or the courage...'

Gilchrist made his debut for Jamaica in 1956 and performed well enough to be selected for the West Indies' tour of England the following year. Despite incurring an injury partway through the tour, he managed to take 10 wickets in four Tests and certainly made his presence felt on the English players, not least with Fred Trueman, with whom he exchanged a series of bouncers, at the end of which Trueman threatened to 'pin 'im to t' bloody sightscreen'.

Retained for the 1957–58 series against Pakistan in the Caribbean, Gilchrist snapped up 21 wickets and almost certainly contributed to the downfall of others as the Pakistani batsmen were visibly unsettled by his raw pace, several showing no inclination to face him. A year later, he toured India, forming a terrifying new-ball partnership with Wes Hall. Gilchrist was at his most venomous on the subcontinent and soon the Indian batsmen were reeling from his blows. They escaped with a draw in the First Test, despite a barrage of bouncers – and the occasional beamer – from Gilchrist, who wrote gleefully: 'Real India rubber men those batsmen – the way they bounced about.' However, his captain, Gerry Alexander, was distinctly unimpressed and warned him to cut out the beamers.

Alexander found the rebellious Gilchrist impossible to handle, and relations between the two men quickly became strained. After Gilchrist swore during a net session, Alexander demanded an apology and when none was forthcoming, he told the fast bowler that he was going to be thrown off the tour. However, a delegation of younger players pleaded Gilchrist's case and he was allowed to stay – on condition that he behaved himself in future. He missed the Second Test with a pulled muscle but returned to wreak havoc against Combined Universities before picking up nine wickets in the Third

Test to seal a comfortable West Indies victory. He collected another five wickets in the Fourth Test, but some of the media were unhappy about the pace battery and condemned what they called 'terror tactics'. Gilchrist was accused of deliberately overstepping his bowling mark by as much as four yards in order to intimidate the batsmen further.

After a draw in the final Test, the West Indies' last match on the Indian leg of the tour was against North Zone at Amritsar. North Zone were captained by Swaranjit Singh, whom Alexander knew from their days together at Cambridge University. On the eve of the match Gilchrist heard that Singh had been making disparaging remarks about his bowling and was boasting about how he would deal with him. It was a red rag to a bull: Gilchrist decided he was going to make Singh pay by dislodging his turban, either with a bouncer or a beamer.

In the first innings Gilchrist bowled Singh first ball, but in the second the batsman appeared more settled and had reached double figures when, in the over before lunch, Gilchrist sent down a brutal bouncer. The next ball was pitched up and driven for four, whereupon Singh taunted the bowler: 'You like that one? Beautiful wasn't it?' An enraged Gilchrist responded by unleashing a vicious beamer – 'the fastest ball I had ever let rip in my life'. Still dazed, Singh edged the next ball to short leg, where Alexander dropped it. This was the last straw for Gilchrist, who delivered another nasty beamer that 'must almost have singed his beard'. Alexander issued a final warning but Gilchrist paid no attention and sent down yet another beamer. At lunch the captain told him that he would play no further part in the match and a hastily convened meeting of the selectors unanimously agreed to send Gilchrist home while the rest of the party went on to Pakistan. Amid the furore there were unsubstantiated rumours that Gilchrist had pulled a knife on Alexander.

Gilchrist never played Test cricket again. Alexander's successor, Frank Worrell, asked for him to be included in the party to tour Australia in 1960 but the selectors rejected the idea out of hand. Gilchrist played just seven more first-class matches – six of them, ironically, in India where he had been hired to harden Indian batsmen to pace bowling.

He went on to play in the Lancashire League for a variety of clubs, taking 100 wickets every year until 1979 and performing the hat-trick on no fewer than 37 occasions. However, his violent temper was always liable to bubble over, as was the case when he attacked a batsman with a stump. Sentencing him in 1967 for the assault on his wife, the judge remarked: 'I hate to think English sport has sunk so far that brutes will be tolerated because they are good at games.'

After fathering seven children, Gilchrist returned to Jamaica in 1985 and was stricken with Parkinson's disease. He died on the island in 2001, aged 67.

No less an authority than Gary Sobers said Gilchrist was the fastest bowler he had ever faced. The sad thing is that if he had not been so intent on causing physical injury to opposition batsmen and could somehow have controlled his temper, Roy Gilchrist might well have become one of the world's great fast bowlers instead of being thrown out of the international arena after just 13 turbulent Tests.

Merv Hughes
The Walrus

Writing in the *Daily Telegraph*, journalist Martin Johnson offered a perceptive and withering assessment of Australian pace bowler Merv Hughes: 'Hughes's appearance alone was comical enough, with a stomach that was the rough equivalent of a female kangaroo with quadruplets stuffed into its pouch, and a coiffeur apparently entrusted to an inebriated sheep-shearer somewhere in the Outback. His mincing approach resembled someone in high heels and a panty-girdle running after a bus, and from beneath the furry koala attached to the underside of his nose would pour forth words of such eloquence and sensitivity – "I'll bowl you an effing piano, yer pommie pooftah, let's see if you can play that!"'

For all his 53 Tests and the 212 wickets he took in those matches, Hughes is chiefly remembered for two things: his walrus moustache and his sledging. Often the two were inseparable in the minds of opposing batsmen. After England's fresh-faced newcomer Mike Atherton had been subjected to the Hughes treatment in the 1989

Ashes series, he wrote of his tormentor: 'He snarled at me constantly through his ludicrous moustache. He was all bristle and bullshit and I couldn't make out what he was saying, except that every sledge ended with "arsewipe".'

It is rumoured that Hughes insured his moustache for £200,000 – against what, who knows? How many batsmen take to the field carrying a razor? The nearest anyone came to deflowering him was when the little Indian, Venkatapathy Raju, gave it a playful tug. On a pro-rata basis his other trademark physical feature, his stomach, should therefore have been insured for several million.

As he came charging in off that faintly effeminate run-up, the moustache and potbelly made him resemble an angry water buffalo, an image enhanced by the vitriol he proceeded to snort. To this day, Hughes remains unrepentant about his verbal insults, unsurprisingly since he claims he got a quarter of his victims through sledging. 'The way I see it is that no one who plays Test cricket is less than highly competent at his art. Therefore it was my job to make sure I exposed any weakness in temperament, and if I wasn't giving the batsman heaps, then in my book I wasn't doing my job. Mike Atherton described my behaviour on the field as suggesting that I had no respect for English batsmen, but he couldn't have been more wrong. I only ever sledged batsmen that I respected. Take Graeme Hick. He was a real danger and the fast bowlers did target him. Because Graeme had such fantastic ability, we would test him in other ways.'

Those 'other ways' included such comments as 'Does your husband play cricket as well?' and 'Mate, if you turn the bat over you'll find the instructions on the other side.' Hick-baiting became a national pastime for the Australians – and for Hughes in particular – and unfortunately the recipient was too shy and retiring to respond in kind. Sensing that it was an unequal battle, umpire Dickie Bird once berated Hughes after one volley of abuse: 'Mervyn, Mervyn, those are terrible things to say. What has that nice Mr Hick ever done to you?' To which Hughes replied with rare imagination: 'He offended me in a former life.'

If Hick lived up to his billing as ideal victim material, Atherton proved a tougher nut to crack. 'When I first saw him,' says Hughes, 'I thought, "What a skinny little twerp," and his body language looked totally defeatist. But he turned out to be one of the toughest characters I've ever bowled to. He gave as good as he got. His sledging was always more subtle and intelligent than my basic stuff. It would often take me three overs to understand what he meant.'

Robin Smith was another English batsman who was more than capable of standing up to Hughes. After beating Smith's outside edge, Hughes growled: 'Smith, you can't effing bat to save your life.' Smith promptly smashed his next ball for four, wandered down the pitch and said: 'Make a good pair, don't we? I can't effing bat, and you can't effing bowl!' Hughes was less than amused.

He reaped greater reward when taking on Pakistan's Javed Miandad at Adelaide in 1991. Reacting to taunts about speaking in Urdu instead of English, Miandad allegedly called Hughes a 'fat bus conductor'. Hughes then got him out with a vicious delivery and shouted out 'Tickets, please' as Miandad headed back disconsolately to the pavilion, the latest victim of the master sledger.

Mervyn Gregory Hughes was born in Euroa, Victoria, in 1961. He started his career playing district cricket with Footscray in 1978–79 and proved so successful that three seasons later he graduated to the Victoria side. He made his Test debut in 1985 against India at Adelaide but figures of 1 for 123 meant that he was rested until the following year's Ashes series. He recorded his best Test figures – 8 for 87 – at Perth in the 1988–89 series against the West Indies, including a bizarre hat-trick. He had Curtly Ambrose caught behind with the last ball of one over, ended the West Indies' first innings by dismissing Patrick Patterson with the first ball of his next over and then, more than a day later, trapped Gordon Greenidge lbw with the first ball of the West Indies' second innings.

Nicknamed 'Fruitfly' after that other great Australian pest, the 6ft 4in Hughes became a crowd favourite the world over. Fans loved his curious run-up, which at times stretched to 45 paces, his wholehearted enthusiasm, his evident love of the good life, and his banter, even if it was directed at their team. Above all, they loved his drooping moustache and demonstrated their affection by wearing false imitations. They even stood behind him and mimicked his extravagant limbering up exercises as he prepared for the call to join the attack. On his second visit to England, in 1993, the crowd chanted 'Sumo' whenever he ran into bowl.

Hughes might never be listed among the all-time great Australian fast bowlers – he was no Lillee or Lindwall – but he was a willing workhorse and once he stopped trying to bowl too fast or live up to his image by mixing in too many bouncers, he developed into a first-rate Test cricketer. His worth to his country was amply illustrated on the 1993 Ashes tour when, after pace partner Craig McDermott had been ruled out with a twisted bowel, Hughes bowled 300 overs in the six-Test series, capturing 31 wickets. His never-say-die attitude was also evident in the field, notably during the Lord's Test of that series when he chased what appeared to be a lost cause to the boundary and succeeded in running out Atherton for 99. His batting also improved considerably. He failed to score in his first three Tests but by 1989 at Headingley was capable of hitting 71 off the English attack (albeit by largely agricultural methods) and he went on to score over 1,000 runs in Test cricket at a respectable average of 16.64.

He played his final Test in 1994 against South Africa at Cape Town, his career ending prematurely due to his love of beer and pizza, the combination of which caused his stomach to expand and his knees to suffer accordingly. In 2005 eyebrows were raised when he was chosen to replace Allan Border as a selector for the Australian team. Foul-mouthed Merv Hughes, the erstwhile scourge of sensitive batsmen, had gone all respectable.

John Jackson
The Foghorn

It was a sound that became frighteningly familiar on cricket grounds the length and breadth of England in the 1850s and early 1860s: that of John Jackson blowing his nose like thunder to acclaim the fall of another wicket to his fast bowling. The ritual, which earned him the nickname of 'Foghorn', was said by some to be a trumpet of prophecy – a prophecy that further wickets would soon fall to the demon paceman. The fact that he picked up 655 wickets in his first-class career suggests that his nostrils were working overtime.

Jackson was one of the most feared bowlers of his day. He was a big, powerful man, standing over 6ft tall and weighing 15 stone, and his rhythmic, round-arm delivery generated sufficient pace to render batsmen what one chronicler described as 'a trifle apprehensive'. 'His action was so easy,' wrote another, 'that he looked as if he were a piece of machinery in motion.' Few relished facing him in full cry. Struck on the foot by a particularly quick ball, a batsman by the name of Ludd hobbled around in agony while Jackson appealed for lbw. When the umpire ruled 'not-out', Ludd replied: 'Mebbe not, but I'm a-goin'.' With that, he retired to the safety of the pavilion.

Jackson appeared to have no qualms about increasing Florence Nightingale's workload. Rueing the fact that he had never taken all 10 wickets in an innings, he suddenly remembered a game for the North versus the South. 'Ah bowled out nine of them and lamed Johnny Wisden so's he couldn't bat, which was just as good, wasn't it?'

His capacity for inflicting grievous bodily harm on opposing batsmen was immortalised by a *Punch* cartoon that showed a gentleman returning from the wicket, swathed in bandages from head to toe. Asked what had happened, he said he'd faced an over from Jackson – 'first ball 'it me on the 'and; the second 'ad me on the knee; the third was in my eye; and the fourth bowled me out.'

Little wonder that batsmen did not stay around long when Jackson was bowling – in fact when he was at his best between 1857 and 1863, only one player scored a century against him.

He was born in Bungay, Suffolk, on 21 May 1833 of gypsy stock, but his family moved to the Nottinghamshire village of Wellow when he was a week old. As a boy, he used to run barefoot after the hounds and practised his marksmanship by throwing stones at anything and everything. To make money he would walk seven miles from his home to the cricket ground in Southwell to bowl or field for the club members for sixpence an hour, and then walk home again. Financially astute even at a young age, he always insisted on being paid in cash. This demand continued when he became a professional cricketer, and he used to keep the coins in the pocket of his trousers while playing. Once in the middle of an innings he had so many sovereigns in his trouser pocket that it gave way and the coins rolled all over the wicket. His team-mates immediately rushed to collect them but Jackson brusquely waved all assistance away. He was not a man to upset.

He first played for Nottinghamshire in 1855 and remained with the county until 1866, apart from a season with Kent in 1858. In 1859 he took part in the first overseas cricket tour when he was a member of the England team that visited North America and four years later he toured Australia. His strike rate in senior cricket was phenomenal. In 1857 he took 111 wickets at 8.07; in 1858, 132 wickets at 9.30; and in 1860, 120 wickets at 8.77. His best figures were 9 for 27 and he took five wickets in an innings on 59 occasions. His career bowling average was an oustanding 11.52.

Given his record and general demeanour, it comes as no surprise to learn that he took it personally if anybody hit him to the boundary. When 'Buns' Thornton had the temerity to drive him out of the ground twice off successive balls, Jackson snarled: 'Oh, to hell with that kind o'batting!' Thornton escaped lightly; generally any insubordination on behalf of the batsman caused Jackson to bowl and act even more aggressively than usual. He was continually involved in scrapes – on and off the field. Following an accident in the nets at Cambridge, brandy was brought from the pavilion to be rubbed on Jackson's injured nose, but as he later related gleefully: 'I drank the brandy and went to the pavilion for hot water!'

His strength also made him a dangerous batsman and against Kent in 1863 he took 13 for 43 and hit 100 in his only innings. That was his sole century but he scored nearly 2,000 runs in the course of his first-class career. *Scores and Biographies* said of him: 'As a batsman, he was far above the average, being a fine, free and powerful hitter, especially forward and to leg.' In the field, he started out at short-slip before moving to the outfield, although he occasionally operated as an emergency wicketkeeper.

By the age of 33 he had burnt himself out and 1866 was his last season for Notts. Five years later he moved to Liverpool, where he worked in a warehouse while continuing to play club cricket for Burnley and Richmond (Yorkshire). He also umpired first-class matches until the mid-1880s. A benefit match in his honour at Trent Bridge in 1874 raised the sum of £300 but this did not prevent him sinking into debt. He died in poverty in Liverpool on 4 November 1901, a pale shadow of the man whose nasal bellow had once put the fear of God into English batsmen.

Dennis Lillee
The Ultimate Competitor

'For me, Lillee was very special,' wrote umpire Dickie Bird in his autobiography. 'He had a beautiful approach to the wicket; stood up in his delivery stride, left knee stiff as a poker; his follow-through was perfection; and his whole action poetry in motion. He had so much control and variation. It was wonderful for me to stand there and watch him.'

Not so pleasurable, however, for opposing batsmen, forced to take evasive action from one of the numerous venomous bouncers Lillee bowled during his 13-year reign as the spearhead of Australia's attack, nor always for his captains. Stubborn and forthright, Lillee was never an easy man to captain, a point acknowledged by one of his Australian national team skippers, Kim Hughes, who said knowingly: 'Dennis could be awkward. And he enjoyed being awkward, especially with me.' The sentiments were echoed by another of Lillee's captains, Greg Chappell, who nevertheless realised that the odd fallout was a small price to pay for having a bowler of Lillee's talent in the side. 'Dennis was such a strong-willed bugger,' said Chappell, 'and such a good bowler you had to accept that occasionally he would get pig-headed. The adrenalin would pump so fast he would go over the top.'

He certainly lost his temper against the West Indies at Brisbane in 1979 when his frustration at having to bowl on an unresponsive pitch suddenly boiled over. Lillee announced that he was going to bowl an off-break, prompting wicketkeeper Rod Marsh to stand up to the stumps, but instead he delivered a ferocious bouncer, which a startled Marsh was forced to fend away with his gloves. A furious Chappell read Lillee the riot act, pointing out that his reckless actions could have killed his team-mate.

Later that year Lillee brought Greg Chappell further strife when stepping out to bat in the Perth Test against England with an aluminium bat. Concerned that the ball was not coming off the bat properly, Chappell instructed 12th man Rodney Hogg to give Lillee a conventional wooden bat. At the same time England captain Mike

Brearley complained to the umpires that the metallic bat was damaging the ball. Lillee flatly refused to change bats until Chappell handed him a wooden bat and told him to shut up and get on with the game, causing an angry Lillee to throw the aluminium bat some 40 yards away in disgust. After that, metal bats were banned.

The Brisbane match was not the first time Lillee had vented his frustrations by bowling off-spin. At the Oval in 1975 he was annoyed because umpire Dickie Bird refused to change a ball that had gone out of shape. 'What can I do with that?' he moaned, tossing the ball to captain Ian Chappell. 'I'm a fast bowler, not a miracle worker.' He made his point by sending down a perfect off-break, whereupon Bird defused the tension by claiming that Lillee was the best off-spinner he had seen all season. Next over, Bird agreed to change the ball.

Bird enjoyed a friendly relationship with Lillee, happily recounting how Lillee slipped a rubber snake into his umpire's coat and on another occasion borrowed Bird's white cap to conduct the moving of the Oval sightscreens, but it is doubtful whether the affection is shared by Pakistan batsman Javed Miandad, who was involved in a nasty scrap with Lillee at Perth on his country's 1981–82 tour. As Miandad ran through for a single, Lillee appeared to kick the batsman's pads, at which the volatile Pakistani tried to attack Lillee with his bat, forcing the intervention of umpire Tony Crafter. Henry Blofeld wrote in the *Cricketer*: 'Over the years Lillee has been involved in probably more unpleasant incidents than any other Test cricketer. He has seemed almost to make a habit of trying to bait and upset his opponents in the most petulant manner.' It has to be said that Blofeld was not overly fond of Lillee at the best of times. He once wrote of him: 'He was starkly sinister and, when he thought he had trapped the batsman lbw or had him caught at the wicket, downright terrifying. As he yelled his appeal he would turn round to face the umpires squatting on his haunches with both hands raised and his pointing index fingers already anticipating the decision.' A Lillee appeal to an umpire was almost a command.

In 1984, less than four weeks after making his final appearance for Australia, Lillee was involved in another controversy while captaining Western Australia in a Sheffield Shield match against Queensland, this time over a drinks break. Although the umpires had decreed that drinks should not be taken, because the morning session had been curtailed by rain, Lillee appeared to overrule them by ordering drinks to be brought on to the field. The umpires reported him for acting in a 'provocative and disapproving manner', and he was suspended from all cricket for a month despite insisting that he had simply misinterpreted the rules.

Even so the confrontations that have sometimes dogged Lillee cannot overshadow his enormous contribution to the Australian team. In 70 Tests he took what was then a world record 355 wickets despite the fact that his career was nearly ended in its infancy by a series of stress fractures in his back. He was born in Subiaco, Western Australia, in 1949, making his debut for his home state at the age of 20. Within two years he had been selected for the national side and repaid the confidence in his ability by taking 5 for 83 in his first Test, against England at Adelaide. He followed that up with a successful tour of England in 1972, collecting 31 wickets in the Test series at an average of just 17.67. He was a fearsome adversary with his shoulder-length hair and raw aggression, and left the batsman in little doubt as to his intentions. He explained: 'I try to hit a batsman in the rib cage when I bowl a purposeful bouncer, and I want it to hurt so much that the batsman doesn't want to face me any more.'

Then in 1973 he was diagnosed with four spinal stress fractures, but battled back to fitness with the help of a strict physiotherapy regime and a reshaped bowling action. The new-look Lillee teamed up with Jeff Thomson to destroy England 4–1 in the 1974–75 Ashes series, Lillee's bowling being timed at 96mph. Worryingly for England, Thomson was even faster. That summer Lillee demonstrated rare prowess with the bat, hitting an unbeaten 73 against England at Lord's – his highest Test score. His involvement with Kerry Packer's World Series ruled him out of Test cricket from 1977 but by the start of the next decade he was back breaking records and batsman's hearts in equal measure. The most famous scorecard entry, 'c Marsh b Lillee', appeared no fewer than 95 times in Tests as Lillee formed a deadly double act with wicketkeeper Rod Marsh, the man he had once nearly killed. After retiring from international cricket, Lillee continued playing for Tasmania until 1988 before becoming one of the world's leading fast-bowling coaches.

If anyone can teach young players the art of fast bowling, it is Dennis Lillee. And despite his highly competitive nature and the odd fit of pique, the England players, at least, held him in great respect. David Gower said: 'Dennis, like most Australian cricketers, was never short of the odd word, but what I particularly liked about the guys of that era – the Chappells, Marsh, Thomson etc. – was that what happened on the field mattered not a jot off it. You could be smacked in the ribs at five minutes to six, and at five past the first two people into the dressing room to apply a cold beer to the bruise (plus a few more internally) would be Lillee and Marsh.'

Fred Spofforth
The Demon

Fred Spofforth was the Dennis Lillee of his day; fast, hostile, ultra-competitive, the terror of English batsmen. Even Spofforth's moustache and long nose were replicated in Lillee nearly a century later, as if part of an Australian fast bowler's genes. So distinctive was Spofforth's aquiline hooter that when he ran into bowl with a lively Catherine wheel action, he was described as being 'all arms, legs and nose.' Above all, it enabled him to smell fear in English batsmen.

Australia's first genuine fast bowler, Spofforth's name will forever be associated with the Ashes, for it was his ferocious bowling performance at the Oval in 1882 that brought about England's shock defeat – their first against Australia on home soil – and resulted in the famous mock obituary 'in affectionate remembrance of English cricket' that appeared shortly afterwards in the *Sporting Times*. There was precious little goodwill between the two sides from the moment W.G. Grace had disgracefully run out Australia's Sammy Jones when the latter left his crease to do a spot of gardening on the pitch. At the end of the innings an incensed Spofforth stormed into the England dressing room, called Grace a cheat and warned: 'This will lose you the match!'

With England needing just 85 to win, Spofforth's words were probably dismissed as bravado but even when England reached 51 for 2 – and victory was within touching distance – he was still insisting to his team-mates: 'This thing can be done.' And so it proved. Spofforth's last 11 overs included 10 maidens and were bowled for two runs and four wickets as England crumbled, the finish being so tense that one spectator was reported to have died of heart failure while another – Epsom stockbroker Arthur Courcy – was said to have chewed through the handle of his brother-in-law's umbrella. England were finally bowled out for 77, giving Australia victory by seven runs. Spofforth took 7 for 44 in that innings, giving him match figures of 14 for 90 – an Australian Test record that stood for 90 years until Bob Massie took 16 for 137 against England at Lord's in 1972.

After that historic Oval Test, Spofforth was dubbed the 'demon bowler' by the English media, a fearsome reputation that he earned partly by being the first bowler to use eye-to-eye contact to intimidate batsmen. Although he was lean, at 6ft 3in tall he cut an imposing figure and he was also immensely strong, capable of bowling longer spells than most fast bowlers. He had the ability to move the ball sharply into the batsman and, particularly in later years, varied his pace intelligently off what was a relatively short run-up. As shrewd a judge as Lord Hawke considered him to be the most difficult bowler he had ever played against.

Frederick Robert Spofforth was born at Balmain, Sydney, on 9 September 1853 and followed his father into banking, working as a clerk for the Bank of New South Wales. As a young cricketer he began bowling fast underarm but switched to overarm after watching England's George Tarrant in action on a tour to Australia. In 1874 Spofforth was a member of the New South Wales XVIII that played W.G. Grace's England team and three years later he was selected to play in the First Test against James Lillywhite's England tourists. However, he refused to play because Jack Blackham had been chosen as wicketkeeper in preference to Spofforth's New South Wales colleague Billy Murdoch. It was only when Murdoch was picked for the following match that Spofforth made his Test debut. Against England at Melbourne in 1879 he became the first man to take a hat-trick in Test cricket, finishing with match figures of 13 for 110. In total he played 18 Tests between 1877 and 1877 and took 94 wickets at 18.41 apiece. On three of his five tours of England he took over 100 wickets and in 1884 managed a remarkable 216. He was said to be almost unplayable on bad wickets. Although he once rode 400 miles to play in a country match and clean bowled all 20 wickets, it was usually the big occasion that inspired him to his greatest feats. He was also a decent batsman (going in last in an 1885 Test, he top scored with 50) and an outstanding fielder, both close to the wicket and in the outfield. Asked the secret of his close catching, he explained, tongue firmly in cheek: 'When I was quite young I made a boy, when out for a walk, throw stones into a hedge, and as the sparrows flew out, I caught 'em!'

He quit Test cricket prematurely to concentrate on his business career and in 1888, having married the daughter of a wealthy English tea merchant, settled in England as the Midlands representative of the Star Tea Company, later rising to managing director. He kept his arm in by playing a few games for Derbyshire and spent nearly a decade with the Hampstead club. In 1896, at the age of 42, he was still good enough to take 8 for 74 for the MCC against Yorkshire.

The once dreaded Demon became a genial raconteur of tall stories – not that his exploits with the ball needed any embellishment – and by the time of his death in Surrey on 4 June 1926, the scourge of the English had blended effortlessly into Home Counties society.

Fred Trueman
Fiery Fred

One day Yorkshire were playing the Combined Universities and following the fall of a University wicket a slim figure, elegantly attired in spotless Savile Row flannels and new boots, came out to bat. He wore his cap at a jaunty angle and had a silk scarf around his neck. On his way to the crease he demonstrated perfectly timed strokes that despatched the imaginary bowlers to all parts of the ground. The Yorkshire players watched his approach in silence. Surveying the scene imperiously, he then took guard and spent an entire minute making his block hole. Finally, after another study of the field placings, he was ready to receive his first ball. Fred Trueman bowled it and knocked two of the stumps clean out of the ground. As the batsman turned and walked languidly back to the pavilion, Trueman called out: 'Bad luck, sir. You were just getting settled in.'

The anecdote is typical Trueman – a man who epitomised Yorkshire bluntness and could be as devastating with his tongue as with a cricket ball. From stout northern mining stock, he particularly enjoyed deflating Oxbridge students and their privileged upbringings. In another match against a university side he bowled one of the undergraduates with a beauty. As the young man passed Trueman on the way back to the pavilion, he said politely: 'Well bowled, Mr Trueman, that was a beautiful ball.'

'Aye,' replied Trueman, 'and it was bloody wasted on thee!'

If Trueman was forthright as a player, he was even more opinionated in retirement. He claimed that Ian Botham couldn't bowl a hoop downhill, that the only head bigger than Tony Greig's was Birkenhead, and suggested that the only reason Geoffrey Boycott had bought a house by the sea was so that he could go for a walk on the water. The fumbling fielding of Essex captain Keith Fletcher at Test level also attracted Trueman's mocking wit. When the Headingley wicket was sabotaged by protesters in 1975, Trueman, whose views were generally a little to the right of Genghis Khan, growled: 'I'd throw them off the top of the pavilion. Mind, I'm a fair man, I'd give them a fifty-fifty chance. I'd have Keith Fletcher underneath trying to catch them.'

Trueman's unwavering self-confidence gave him the licence to speak his mind. He was only half-joking when he said he wanted his autobiography to be titled *The Greatest Bloody Fast Bowler That Ever Drew Breath*. He never played down his achievements and it was said that, if invited, he could recite his 307 Test victims in decent chronological order. Many batsmen were frightened out purely by Trueman's reputation, a cartoon of the day depicting a West Indian mother urging her children to go to sleep 'or that Fred Trueman will come to get you.' Trueman enjoyed that.

He liked to crank up the intimidation by barging uninvited into the opposing dressing room before an innings. Puffing on his pipe, he would stand there surveying the room for nervous faces and past victims. Then with a shake of his head he would say something like, 'Dear, oh dear, I can see six or seven wickets in this room for FST [Frederick Sewards Trueman] today.' While the rest of the Yorkshire team walked out on to the field with the umpires, Trueman would stand at the bottom of the pavilion steps, waiting for the opposition's two opening batsmen to come out. As they walked through the gate,

Trueman would say: 'Don't bother shutting it. You'll be back soon.' His first-class record of 2,304 wickets at a cost of 18.29 apiece shows that he was usually right.

The sight of Trueman, black hair flopping, white shirt billowing in the breeze as he steamed in to bowl off that long run-up, was one of the finest images in sport. There was none of the languid grace of a Sobers; with Trueman it was all power and energy, culminating in a moment of delivery that Michael Parkinson described as 'the classic example of how the body should be poised to deliver a cricket ball with maximum velocity and accuracy.' For all his searing pace, few fast bowlers could compete with him in terms of line and length, and his ability to swing the ball away from the bat made many a slip fielder's reputation. John Arlott wrote of him: 'It is a mistake to think of Fred Trueman as simply a bowler of speed. He had outswing, inswing, a yorker that only Lindwall could match.' He revelled in his nickname of 'Fiery Fred' and although he could unleash venomous bouncers, there was never any hint of real malice. Not that he was quick to convey sympathy to a stricken batsman. When a short ball from Trueman hit a young Peter Parfitt in the face, the Middlesex batsman was forced to retire hurt. Bravely he resumed his innings later, whereupon Trueman appeared to display uncharacteristic concern. Subsequently he revealed that he had said to Parfitt: 'When I hit 'em they don't usually come back.' The one occasion when he did show genuine remorse was after felling his good friend Trevor Bailey with a bouncer. 'I'm sorry, Trevor lad,' said Trueman. 'There's many more I'd rather hurt than you.'

Trueman was the most popular cricketer of his day. Prime Minister Harold Wilson called him the 'greatest living Yorkshireman', high praise from one who had pretensions to the crown himself. But Trueman's appeal stretched well beyond his native county, and even non-cricket fans warmed to his straight talking and sharp sense of humour. Those rich, earthy tones were quintessentially English, and whilst he was undeniably the best bowler in a successful international team, he remained a man of the people, someone who appeared to be in his element down at his local pub setting the world to right over a pint and a few puffs on his pipe. To an entire generation the name 'Fred' could mean only one person – Fred Trueman.

From the moment he entered the world on 6 February 1931, in a terraced house in the South Yorkshire mining village of Stainton, he was a larger-than-life character. He weighed 14lb 1oz at birth, which, whilst not automatically suggesting a career as a fast bowler, at least ruled out ballet dancer as a likely occupation. His father Dick was a former stud groom, forced down the pits by hard times, and a keen weekend cricketer. Young Fred inherited his love of the game, although it nearly cost him dear when, at the age of 12, he was hit in the groin while batting at secondary school without a box. He missed two seasons and there were even fears that he might lose a leg too. Once recovered, he started playing club cricket, combining it from the age of 15 with work as an apprentice bricklayer – a job he kept until telling the foreman to 'bugger off'.

Meanwhile, his father had taken Fred for a trial with Sheffield United cricket team, arriving at the nets in Bramall Lane just as the coaches, Cyril Turner and Charlie Lee, were packing up for the day. Turner said to Lee: 'This bloke's brought his lad all the way from Maltby. Says he's a bit quick, so we'd better have a look at him.' Lee dutifully set up the nets and stumps again, padded up and went out to face the 17-year-old Trueman. The first ball flew over the top of the net, over the back wall and just missed a passing tram. The next three balls were equally wild, but when the youngster did find his line, a stunned Lee turned to see 'two stumps sticking out of the net like herrings on a Grimsby trawler'. Elevation to the Yorkshire team followed but Fred never forgot the debt he owed his father. When Dick Trueman died, Fred placed his first Yorkshire cap inside the coffin.

It was by no means all plain sailing with Yorkshire. Although his pace and action were much admired, Trueman was considered expensive, and his insubordination did not always go down well with the county committee. Consequently, even after taking 8 for 68 against Nottinghamshire in 1951, he was overlooked for the next match and instead found himself acting as 12th man for the second XI at Grimsby. Strangely, England appeared to show greater interest in his raw talent, and in 1952 Trueman obtained leave from doing his National Service with the RAF to make his Test debut against India. He burst upon the international scene in the most explosive manner imaginable, taking three instant wickets to reduce India to 0 for 4. Then in the Third Test he took 8 for 31, working up such a frenetic pace that several of the Indian batsmen timidly backed away to square leg. Twenty-two years later he met up again with Lt-Col. Hemu Adhikari, vice-captain of that Indian side, and remarked with typical candour: 'Hello, Colonel, glad to see you've got your colour back!'

Despite his success against India, Trueman was not yet reckoned to be anything like the finished article and he struggled badly on the 1953–54 tour of the West Indies, where he frequently voiced his displeasure at the local umpires. His indiscipline was threatening to jeopardise his career, to the extent that he was passed over in favour of Frank Tyson for the next Ashes tour, a grievance that he nursed for the rest of his days. Before the Headingley Test of 1956, chairman of selectors Gubby Allen put a handkerchief down in the nets and ordered Trueman, in front of a gathering Yorkshire crowd, to hit it. Trueman felt humiliated by the experience.

His fortunes changed when he bowled in harness with Lancashire's Brian Statham. They formed a formidable partnership, Statham's control perfectly complemented by Trueman's snarl and bite, both men capable of bowling for long spells. After tearing through another weak Indian batting line-up in 1959, Trueman even enjoyed a happy tour of the West Indies, this time showing the crowd his humour rather than his temper. In 1960 he took 46 Test wickets and, utilising his strength as a lower order batsman, hit 132 for Yorkshire in the County Championship, one of three first-class centuries in his career. He once smashed 26 off an over by Hampshire's usually economical Derek Shackleton. On his home ground in 1961, bowling off a shortened run, he helped England to their first victory over Australia for five years, and three years later, at the Oval against the same enemy, he became the first bowler to take 300 Test wickets. Acclaim was universal.

He played his final Test in 1965 but continued playing for Yorkshire for another four seasons and captained the county to victory over the 1968 Australian tourists. Thereafter, despite a brief comeback to play Sunday League cricket for Derbyshire, he concentrated his energies on after-dinner engagements and a long run as a plain-speaking member of radio's *Test Match Special* team, a platform which he used increasingly to bemoan the state of the modern game.

The man who was arguably England's finest-ever fast bowler died on 1 July 2006. A suitable epitaph might have been a comment he made on BBC radio in the 1990s, referring to an old black-and-white-film of him in action: 'I'd have looked even faster in colour.'

Sammy Woods
Champagne And Lobsters

As captain of Somerset between 1894 and 1906, Sammy Woods firmly believed in entertaining the crowds. 'Draws?' he once remarked. 'They're only for bathing in.'

Woods certainly gave value for money in that respect, first as a lively fast bowler, then as a hard-hitting batsman, but chiefly as a highly idiosyncratic leader of men. His daily diet would have had today's nutritionists scratching their heads in bewilderment. He liked a breakfast of champagne and lobsters, and before going out to bat always drank a double whisky and smoked a cheroot. His method of team selection was equally unconventional. When challenged as to why he had picked one particularly hopeless player, Woods replied: 'Oh, he is not much of a bat, he doesn't bowl and he can't field – but, by George, what a great golfer he is!' On another occasion he was about to lead Somerset on a journey north when he realised that he was three players short. After hastily enlisting the services of two of his godsons, he struck up a conversation with a fellow passenger on the train – a man who said he had made big scores in club cricket. Without a moment's hesitation, Woods asked him to complete the eleven. However the decision to include a total stranger backfired somewhat, as Woods himself admitted: 'He made nought and nought, and it turned out he hadn't played since he was ten but wanted to get a close view of the game for nothing.' But, by way of justification, Woods added: 'He was a very good whist-player.'

It was perhaps understandable that Woods appreciated sporting versatility, because not only did he play cricket for two countries (Australia and England), but he also won 13 rugby caps for England. And he was no mean boxer, ever willing to step into the ring as a challenger at West Country fairs.

Samuel Moses James Woods was born in Sydney on 13 April 1867 and as a boy boxed with the local Aboriginal champion. At the city's Royston College he showed he was no mean cricketer either, once taking seven wickets in seven balls! In 1883 he came to

England to complete his education and be trained as a 'proper gentleman'. His sporting excellence shone through at Cambridge University where, in 1888, he bowled so well that he was invited to join the Australian team that was touring England even though he had never played a first-class match in his native country. His three Tests against England were relatively undistinguished but he continued to excel for the University, becoming one of the finest fast bowlers in the country with an armoury that contained a cleverly disguised slower ball and a lethal yorker. He celebrated his first match as Cambridge captain by taking all ten wickets against C.I. Thornton's XI.

It was fortunate that he was an outstanding sportsman, for he was no academic. The story goes that he failed to answer a single question in his final exam at Cambridge University. Instead he wrote only 'Dam' and then left the hall. It is said that his dons, all of whom were cricket enthusiasts, would have passed him if only he had spelt the word correctly!

Moving west, Woods helped Somerset establish themselves in the County Championship and in 1892 he captured 153 wickets in all matches. From then on, however, injury began to take its toll on his bowling and he was forced to reinvent himself as an attacking batsman, hitting 215 in 150 minutes against Sussex in 1895. The following winter he was chosen for England's tour of South Africa, playing in three more Tests but proving ineffective on the matting wickets. He continued to prosper as Somerset captain and became a popular figure, often walking to the County Ground in Taunton from his home in Bridgewater and pausing to chat to locals along the way. Arthritis forced him to retire in 1910 at the end of a first-class career in which he had taken more than 1,000 wickets and scored over 15,000 runs. He suffered another body blow during the First World War when he damaged his back after a camel bolted from beneath him.

He continued to serve Somerset as secretary and in that capacity was placed in an invidious position when asked to umpire a match between his adopted county and his country of birth. He reassured both captains with the words: 'I will cheat fair.' He also helped out on the medical side and could often be seen attempting to wrench a dislocated shoulder back into place – usually with more enthusiasm than expertise. A regular spectator at home matches, he could be heard loudly haranguing anyone who happened to stray in front of the sightscreen, and right up until his death – on 30 April 1931 – he lived in local pubs and drank a bottle of whisky a day: his own man to the very end.

LIVES LESS ORDINARY

George Brown
High And Mighty

Following a minor altercation during Hampshire's game with Kent at Portsmouth in 1913, Kent fast bowler Arthur Fielder aimed a nasty bouncer at George Brown. Seeing it coming, the Hampshire batsman dropped his bat to the ground, stood up straight, took the full force of the ball on his chest and yelled, "He's not fast", before scoring on to score 71.

Brown was not a man to be cowed. He used to pride himself on batting without gloves against fast bowling and was, in the words of John Arlott, 'utterly fearless, over six feet tall, possessed of immense physical strength and with a deep tan, high cheek bones and imperious nose which gave him the appearance of a Red Indian chief.' He had a quick temper, could tear a pack of cards with his huge hands, and never forgot a slight. Once he deliberately blocked over after over of flighted leg-spin from Surrey captain Percy Fender whereas normally he would have attempted to hit him out of the ground. When Fender, frustrated at not being able to tempt the batsman into any sort of attacking stroke, finally asked what the problem was, Brown replied firmly that he was having the net that had been denied him the previous winter in South Africa. On that occasion Brown, a professional, had dutifully bowled to Fender, an amateur, in the heat for ages but when the time came for Fender to return the compliment, he simply walked off. Brown had been waiting for revenge ever since.

He also fell out with his unpredictable county captain, Lionel Tennyson, whose whims included reversing the entire batting order when the mood took him. In the match against Warwickshire at Southampton in 1926, Tennyson was so angry at his side's first innings batting display that he swapped everything around so that Brown, instead of opening the second innings, went in at number 10.

Brown showed his contempt for the decision by going out to the middle with a bat that was a veritable antique. It launched one six over the sightscreen but a few moments later a powerful pull shot split it in two. Instead of calling for a replacement, Brown ripped the blade apart, handed one half to the umpire and continued to bat with the other half!

George Brown was born at Cowley, Oxford, on 6 October 1887, and was a determined character even as a young man. In the spring of 1906 the 18-year-old walked the 60 miles from his home to Southampton for a trial, hauling a tin trunk containing all his worldly belongings, including a bat and a pair of plimsolls. Hampshire were suitably impressed and two years later he made his first-class debut. Not only was he a fine, aggressive left-handed batsman, capable of driving and hooking with immense power, but especially in the pre-war period, he was a genuinely fast right-arm bowler. In 1912 he took four major wickets against the touring Australians, enabling Hampshire to gain a famous victory – the last by a county side against Australia until Surrey repeated the feat 44 years later. Although he bowled less frequently towards the end of his career, he was still taking useful wickets in his 40s and finished up with a career total of 626 first-class victims at an average of 29.81.

As a fielder he was said to one of the longest throws in the game but he himself preferred fielding closer to the wicket, and, curiously, when he made his Test debut against Australia at Headingley in 1921 it was as a wicketkeeper, even though he was never his county's regular behind the stumps. But he was always more than willing to help out in an emergency. He kept wicket in all seven of his Test appearances and did so with considerable aplomb despite his relative lack of experience and the fact that he did so in his motorcycle gauntlets! He was also one of England's few successes with the bat in that 1921 series, averaging 50. When he retired from first-class cricket in 1933, he had hit 25,649 runs (including 37 centuries) at an average of 26.71, a figure that would have been considerably higher had he not struggled to motivate himself against lesser opposition.

On his death at Winchester on 3 December 1964, George Brown's ashes were scattered over the county ground at Southampton and Hampshire supporters mourned one of cricket's few bowler/wicketkeeper/batsmen.

Bob Crisp
The Adventurer

It is no exaggeration to say that Bob Crisp led a life of extreme highs and lows. He climbed Mount Kilimanjaro twice in two weeks and during the Second World War was wounded five times as a tank commander in the Western Desert. On the cricket field he holds the distinction of being the only bowler to have taken four wickets in four balls on two separate occasions, yet he also suffered the ignominy of bagging pairs in two successive Tests. He was not a man who believed in half measures.

He was born in Calcutta on 28 May 1911, but educated in Rhodesia. As a young man he was essentially an adventurer who fitted in cricket as a sideline, but his figures of 9 for 64 for Western Province against Natal in 1933–34, which included his second feat of four wickets in four balls, propelled him on to the international stage. Thus, in 1935 he and Dennis Tomlinson became the first Rhodesians to be picked to play for South Africa, Crisp receiving the news shortly after his return from climbing Kilimanjaro. On that tour of England his brisk right-arm bowling brought him 107 wickets, including 5 for 99 in the Old Trafford Test. South Africa won the series 1–0 by virtue of victory at Lord's, the other four Tests all being drawn. Crisp then played four Tests in South Africa against the visiting Australians in 1935–36, in the course of which he failed to trouble the scorer on four successive occasions. That series marked his last Test appearance, and although he briefly tried his luck with Worcestershire in 1938, his first-class career was effectively ended by the War. In 62 matches he took 276 wickets at an average of just under 20 and averaged 13 with the bat.

But that was by no means the end of the Bob Crisp story. As a wartime commander with the Royal Tank Regiment in Greece and North Africa, he had six tanks blasted from under him in a month but refused to admit defeat, his determination to carry on fighting earning him a Distinguished Service Order for gallantry. However, it appears that he was almost as great an irritant to the Allied military authorities as he was to the Germans, as a result of which General

Montgomery intervened personally and prevented him being awarded a Bar the following year, his second honour being downgraded to a Military Cross. Crisp was mentioned in despatches four times before being invalided out in Normandy, having nearly died from his wounds and the subsequent infection. When King George VI asked him whether his bowling would be affected, Crisp replied: 'No, sir. I was hit in the head.'

Crisp never did play again and turned instead to journalism, founding *Drum*, a magazine aimed especially at black South Africans. Returning to England, he worked for the *Daily Express* and the *East Anglian Daily Times*, and, forever in search of a new adventure, also tried his hand at mink farming. He wrote two accounts of his wartime experiences – *Brazen Chariots* and *The Gods Were Neutral* – before abruptly quitting England to live in a Greek hut for a year. Later, when informed that he had incurable cancer, he promptly spent a year walking round Crete, selling the story of his trek to the *Sunday Express*.

The seemingly indestructible Bob Crisp passed away in Colchester, Essex, on 3 March 1994, aged 82. He died with a copy of the *Sporting Life* on his lap, having just lost a £20 bet.

Monty Panesar
Cause For Celebration

When he first burst on to the England scene, Monty Panesar was viewed by some as little more than a comic figure. There were the wildly over-the-top celebrations and the high-fives that greeted a wicket, the hopelessly inept fielding and the batting that was only marginally better. To all intents and purposes he was Phil Tufnell in a *patka* (the small turban-like headgear that Panesar wears). But the man mocked as more Monty Python than professional cricketer has forced a change of opinion. True, his manic gambolling down the pitch at the fall of a wicket remains risible and he still isn't exactly Jonty Rhodes in the field but he has developed into a left-arm spin bowler of genuine quality while retaining that engaging enthusiasm. In short, he has become something of a national hero.

Fans have taken the first Sikh to represent England to their hearts. They turn up to matches in *patkas* and false beards and cheer his every move. Before the 2006–07 tour of Australia, there were fears that he might be singled out for abuse both by the crowds and the players, although Panesar himself remained refreshingly level-headed about the prospect. 'Aussie sledging?' he said. 'I'm just glad they've heard of me!' As it was, Australians fans, always appreciative of a real character, quickly warmed to Panesar.

It is his wicket-taking celebration – dubbed the 'Monty macarena' – that has attracted so much attention. In the *Mail on Sunday*, Peter Hayter described it as 'one of the wonders of the modern cricket world – eyes blazing, mouth wide open, arms akimbo, knees pumping, high-fives missing by miles.' Panesar makes no apology for the routine and says that it is born out of his roots in park cricket. 'My background is different from most England cricketers in that until I was about 18 I only ever played cricket in parks and council recreation grounds. So when I take a wicket in international cricket, to me it's like picking a lad from park football and watching him score the winning goal for England in the World Cup final. That's why I start running around and jumping up and down when I take a wicket. My enthusiasm is such a key part of how I am as a cricketer. I'm not trying to pressurise or intimidate the batsman or the umpire. That just isn't me. I think most umpires know what I am like now, I've been the same since I was very young. But I've never been warned by an umpire for excessive appealing. Sometimes I have been told to calm down a bit but that's all. You can't play international cricket without trying to be as competitive as possible, but with me what you see is what you get – I am always smiling and excited because I just enjoy playing so much.'

England's latest cricketing cult hero was born Mudhsuden Singh Panesar in Luton in 1982, but his aunt's pet name for him, Monty, was the one that stuck. At 10, he was taken by his father to Luton Indians Cricket Club, where he initially bowled seamers before changing to finger-spin, using his large hands to turn the ball prodigiously. He worked hard on improving his game and after being spotted by Bedfordshire at 17, he won a trial with Northamptonshire and a place in the England Under-19 team. So intent was Panesar on perfecting his craft at Northampton that his second XI coach, Nick Cook, used to have to send him away. Panesar recalls: 'He'd say, "Listen, no more bowling now, go home." But I see it as fun, I don't see it as practice.'

Panesar made his first-class debut in 2001 but his appearances over the next few years were limited because he was busy studying computer science at Loughborough University. As soon as he had graduated in 2005 he became a regular in the Northants side and finished that season with 46 Championship wickets in eight matches, earning him a late call-up for England's tour of India. He made his England debut in the First Test at Nagpur and picked up his first Test wicket by trapping his boyhood hero, Sachin Tendulkar, lbw. Unfortunately his skill with the ball risked being overshadowed by his incompetence in the field when, in the Third Test at Mumbai, he made a hash of a steepling catch at long-off after losing the ball in the sun. The ball eventually landed five yards away from him, his floundering attempt suggesting that his hands and eyes were not on speaking terms. He redeemed himself a few minutes later by holding on to a similar chance but in his next Test, at Lord's, he spilled another sitter, after which he decided to have his contact lenses altered slightly. The fans loved his fumbling fallibility – it was all part of his appeal – but predictably England coach Duncan Fletcher was less enthusiastic and suggested that it could cost Panesar his place in the side.

Fortunately, by the end of the summer of 2006 his bowling had made him almost indispensable to England, regardless of his fielding. His days as a seam bowler had encouraged him to push the ball through at pace but he also had the ability to deceive batsman in the flight. He took 5 for 78 against Sri Lanka at Trent Bridge and 5 for 72 against Pakistan at Old Trafford, then at Headingley – a pitch not renowned for helping spinners – he produced a perfect delivery to bowl Pakistan's Younis Khan. In the same match he claimed another prize scalp in Inzamam-ul-Haq, who overbalanced and dislodged the bails with his ample stomach, to help England to victory. He even displayed hitherto hidden expertise with the bat, hitting 26 off 28 balls against Sri Lanka at Trent Bridge, including a swept six off Muttiah Muralitharan.

After such a successful summer, he was seen as a potential match-winner in Australia, only to be overlooked for the first two Tests in favour of a semi-fit Ashley Giles. Fans chorused their disapproval and BBC Radio Five Live started a petition demanding Panesar's recall to the side. He was finally selected to play in the Third Test at Perth and responded with 5 for 92 in the first innings, becoming the first English spinner to take five wickets in an innings on that ground. He also made an unbeaten 16 with the bat. In the summer of 2007 he achieved another landmark when his match figures of 10 for 187 against the West Indies at Old Trafford made him the first English spinner to take 10 wickets in a match since Phil Tufnell.

Other comparisons with Tufnell are now a thing of the past. Whereas Tufnell was a rebel who sometimes found it hard to accept – or even stay awake during – advice, Monty Panesar is an eager listener, always willing to work at his game. Nobody could ever describe Tufnell as an enthusiast. Besides, if Panesar's batting continues to improve, he is in danger of acquiring a Test average in double figures. That was something Tufnell (average 5.10) could only dream of.

Bobby Peel
Drunk In Charge

A loyal servant to Yorkshire for 15 years, Bobby Peel was probably the finest slow left-arm bowler in England in the late 19th century. His mastery of line and length plus a devastating quicker ball had earned him 20 appearances for his country and more than 1,500 first-class wickets, which, even in those days of helpful pitches, was a splendid total. Quite apart from his bowling, he was an excellent fielder at cover point and a more than capable batsman, having twice hit double centuries for his county. Yet on an August day in 1897 his career was brought to a sudden end when he was found to be drunk on the field of play.

At 40, Peel was the senior professional in a Yorkshire side ruled by the iron hand of Lord Hawke, the county captain who had already overseen the departure of a number of the old guard. Peel's fondness for a drink or several was an open secret. He often turned up for matches in an inebriated state and was once described by *Wisden* as 'having to go away' during a game.

On 19 August Yorkshire were due to start their fixture against Middlesex at Bramall Lane, Sheffield, a match that marked Peel's return to action after he had been 'indisposed' on the last day of his previous appearance a month earlier. *Cricket* magazine diplomatically described the Middlesex game as 'his first appearance after a long illness'. Much was expected from their star spinner but it immediately became apparent that any such hopes were wildly optimistic when Peel staggered down to breakfast at the team hotel in a state of some dishevelment. Alarmed by his condition, team-mate George Hirst urged him to return to bed to sleep it off and in the meantime tracked down Lord Hawke, explaining to the captain that Peel had been taken 'very queer in the night and won't be able to turn out this morning.' A firm but fair man, Lord Hawke expressed his concern and promised to visit Peel at the close of play.

Middlesex won the toss and elected to bat, but Lord Hawke's compassion for his sick colleague quickly evaporated as a red-faced Peel suddenly joined the team as Hawke led them out. Puzzled by the unexpected recovery and all too aware that Yorkshire now had 12 men on the field, Lord Hawke went over to Peel and immediately realised that he was drunk. 'Leave the field at once,' he ordered, but Peel stood his ground. Accounts differ as to exactly what happened next. Some sources state that Peel had lost the plot so completely that when given the ball, he began bowling at the sightscreen in the erroneous belief that the white shape was a Middlesex batsman; others claim that he proceeded to urinate on the wicket. He may even have done both, but what is certain is that Lord Hawke was compelled to lead him bodily from the field. As Peel himself later recounted in a more sober moment: 'Lord Hawke put his arm round me and helped me off the ground – and out of first-class cricket. What a gentleman!'

Peel might still have been able to extricate himself from his self-inflicted predicament had he apologised but he believed himself to be indispensable to the side. Lord Hawke thought differently, however, and with no indication of remorse from his veteran player, he felt he had no option but to sack him. Thus a glittering career ended in the most unsatisfactory of circumstances.

Bobby Peel was born at Churwell, near Leeds, on 12 February 1857 and first played for Yorkshire in 1882 at a time when the county was rich in slow-bowling talent, notably in the shape of Ted Peate. Consequently, he had to wait patiently for his chance, which came when Peate's weight ballooned to the extent that he fell foul of the disciplinarian Lord Hawke.

Even when relatively inexperienced, Peel was held in such high regard that he was selected for England's tour of Australia in 1884–85, playing in all three Tests and taking 21 wickets. He played in 20 Tests, touring Australia on four occasions, and capturing 101 wickets at 16.98 apiece. He was England's match-winner on more than one occasion. Relishing the sticky wickets that resulted from the wet summer of 1888, he took 24 wickets for less than eight runs each in three Tests against Australia. At Sydney in 1894, he brought about a remarkable turnaround. Set 177 to win, Australia had reached 113 for 2 by the end of the fifth day. Facing almost certain defeat, several of the England players, Peel included, relaxed accordingly but heavy rain fell that night, followed by strong morning sunshine. Having imbibed freely, Peel slept through the storm and when he saw the drying pitch he begged captain Andrew Stoddart to let him bowl. Stoddart instructed Peel to sober up under a cold shower and on that sixth day the refreshed bowler scythed through the Australian batting, taking 6 for 67 to give England a remarkable 10-run triumph. At the Oval in 1896, in what would prove to be his last Test, he took 6 for 23 in Australia's second innings to see England home by 66 runs.

In all first-class matches he took 1,775 wickets at an average of 16.20 and was far too good for most county batsmen. He took 171 wickets in 1888 and 1890 but surpassed that figure with 180 in 1895, when after a slow start to the season in dry weather, his spin and guile made him almost unplayable when the weather broke in July. He took 15 for 50 against Somerset that year, including a career-best 9 for 22 in one innings.

Nor was Peel any slouch with the bat, particularly towards the end of his career when he hit 226 not-out against Leicestershire in 1892 and an unbeaten 210 against Warwickshire in 1896. He scored a total of 12,191 first-class runs, including seven centuries, at an average of a fraction under 20, but also endured his share of failure with the willow at Test level. On the 1894–95 tour of Australia he had the misfortune to record an unprecedented four successive ducks.

Peel's popularity in Yorkshire was such that his benefit match at Bradford in 1894 realised £2,000, although there was a suspicion that he could have raised just as much by taking back his empties. Following his ignominious exit from Yorkshire, he played only one more first-class game, for an England XI in 1899. It comes as no great shock to learn that instead he pursued his other true passion in life and became the landlord of a public house. What is perhaps surprising, however, was that Bobby Peel lived to the ripe old age of 84 before dying in Leeds on 12 August 1941.

Jack Russell
A Creature Of Habit

Some say Robert Charles Russell earned the nickname 'Jack' because he used to scamper between the wickets like a terrier; others reckon it was simply because he is barking mad.

It was his mentor, former Kent and England wicketkeeper Alan Knott, who told Jack Russell to be strong-minded in the way he wanted to keep wicket and never to be afraid to be different. Knott himself was a bundle of restless energy behind the stumps, going through an elaborate routine which sometimes seemed to involve touching every bone in his body before each ball. Russell not only emulated Knott's fastidiousness, he added dozens of new quirks that were all his own invention, especially those relating to dress and diet.

Like Knott, Russell always carried a white handkerchief in the right-hand trouser pocket of his cricketing gear and, for identification, stitched red cotton in one corner. He kept the same handkerchief for eight years until he forgot to remove it before sending his trousers to the hotel laundry while on tour in Australia. The quest to recover it involved endless phone calls and visits to laundries, but all to no avail. The handkerchief was lost. Would Russell's life ever be the same again?

He also insisted on always wearing the same battered white floppy sunhat out in the field – a constant companion from his first-class debut in 1981 right up to his retirement in 2004, by which time it was a decidedly bedraggled specimen. As early as 1997 he wrote: 'There's hardly any of the original left, but I stitch bits on it all the time, using old cricket trousers.' Most people would simply have bought a new hat, but Russell was a superstitious soul and besides, the specially cut rim allowed him to line up the ball when keeping wicket.

The hat was treated with a reverence usually associated with the Crown jewels. Only he and his wife Aileen were allowed to carry out repairs to it. He had it washed religiously twice a season and to dry it he used an apparatus consisting of a glass biscuit jar, a tea cosy and a tea towel. Then, after starching it, he would put the hat in the airing cupboard so that it retained its shape. However, disaster nearly struck on the 1994 tour of the West Indies when he put it in a small oven so that it would dry quicker after starching, but uncharacteristically forgot about it. Luckily room-mate Graeme Hick saw smoke pouring from the kitchen and Russell managed to dive in and retrieve his hat, frantically beating it to extinguish the flames. Resourceful as ever, he repaired the damage by taking pieces from another hat and stitching them on to his. The incident provoked much mirth among his England team-mates, but it was no laughing matter to Russell, whose demand for perfection and routine meant that without his cherished hat, he would not have been able to keep wicket to his customary high standard. 'In many ways,' he admitted, 'my obsession with an ordered, structured world is just a method of getting the best out of myself as an international sportsman.'

That was why he kicked up such a fuss at the 1996 World Cup when informed that he could not wear his usual hat but would instead have to wear coloured headgear to match England's blue strip. Russell refused, and threatened to walk out of the tournament but eventually the authorities relented and allowed him to wear it.

From the age of 16, he wore the same wicketkeeping box (which he had found in the changing rooms at Stroud Cricket Club) and he also wore the same pair of gloves for 10 years until they finally fell apart. 'If I played well in kit I kept using it,' he says. 'The smell in my corner of the dressing room was quite high in the end!'

To keep his cricket gear warm and dry on away trips, Russell, more prepared than any Boy Scout, used to carry a tumble dryer around in the boot of his car. He would drive zipped up in a sleeping bag with the bottom cut out, so as not to get a chill in his back and legs, and he also had a block fitted beneath the accelerator in order to avoid overstretching his Achilles tendon. Along with his daily run, it was all part of Russell's strict fitness regime.

Health was also at the root of his bizarre diet, which consisted largely of chocolate biscuits, baked beans and tea. But they had to be McVitie's jaffa cakes and Heinz baked beans – no other brands would suffice. And if he touched a sandwich, it had to be cheese and pickle. Like Knott, Russell is an ardent tea drinker, usually getting through 30 cups a day. Needless to say, his tea drinking was a regimented affair. He used to dip the tea bag in once, add plenty of milk, then hang the bag on a nail ready for subsequent use. During the 1989 Oval Test, England colleague Derek Pringle counted that Russell used the same bag for all five days, which roughly equated to 150 cups of tea.

He was equally particular about his Weetabix, which had to be soaked in milk for precisely 12 minutes. When playing, he would have Weetabix for breakfast and lunch, adding a mashed banana on the latter occasion. 'I have breakfast cereal at lunch during a day's play, and whoever is twelfth man organises the timing of the milk in the bowl for me. It must be twelve minutes. That's exactly how I like it – it's no different from how someone wants their steak cooked.'

He has been known to eat steak – in fact on tour to India in 1989 he ate cremated steak and chips for dinner on 28 consecutive days. Chicken without the skin was another option, and he spent every night of a Test match at a Chinese restaurant in Perth ordering cashew chicken – without the cashews. He also ate chicken every night on one tour of the West Indies, once going so far as to commandeer Geoffrey Boycott's meal from the hotel kitchen. Boycott, who was almost as fussy about his food as Russell, had reserved the last piece of chicken but Russell got back from the ground before him and managed to convince the kitchen staff that Boycott was eating out. When Boycott discovered that Russell had stolen his meal, he was none too pleased. Russell justifies his unadventurous approach on the grounds that he didn't want to risk getting a stomach upset, which was why when going on tour to India he would take with him copious supplies of beans, biscuits and teabags. 'I just like to feel safe in the food I eat.'

This most individual of cricketers was born in Stroud, Gloucestershire, in 1963. He inherited a fascination with military history from his father and as a boy used to pretend to be a soldier, camping out at night under bushes. This not only inspired his dogged determination as a batsman but also instilled in him a patriotic fervour. Away on tour in Zimbabwe on Christmas Day, 1996, he arranged for his wife to play the Queen's Speech down the phone to his hotel room…

His love of wicketkeeping stemmed from a catch he saw on television two days before his 14th birthday, when Australia's Rick McCosker was caught behind by Knott off the bowling of Tony Greig. 'Low down, one handed, across first slip,' remembers Russell. 'Brilliant. I thought then that I would like to be able to do that.'

His dream came true when he joined Gloucestershire in 1981. At first, on his own admission, he drank too much but the tragic death of his brother David persuaded him to knuckle under and make the very best of his abilities. He was always something of a loner in the Gloucestershire dressing room, his quest for privacy making Greta Garbo seem positively gregarious. None of his team-mates were ever invited to his home, and he claimed that if they ever asked he would only agree on condition that they were blindfolded. Even when builders came to do some work on his house, he thought about blindfolding them and driving them there! Naturally, only his wife, his mother and his agent were entrusted with his home phone number.

Russell quickly developed into an excellent wicketkeeper, adhering to Alan Knott's advice to do things his own way. He adopted a peculiar wide-open stance that left him looking out in the direction of mid-off as the bowler ran in, but it worked, and neither was he afraid to stand up at the wicket to fast bowlers, particularly in one-day games, a move that restricted batsmen enormously. Russell himself was a resolute, rather than spectacular, left-handed batsman with a typically distinctive crab-like stance. 'It does disconcert some bowlers,' he confessed. 'One or two of them find it hard to stop laughing when they first see the crab stance, so I'm already one up on them.'

He made his Test debut against Sri Lanka in 1988 and the following year batted with grit and some style against an Australian team that had pinpointed him as the weakest link. To prepare himself for the anticipated barrage of short deliveries, Russell, accompanied by Knott, turned up early for the Second Test at Lord's and told the MCC groundstaff boys to throw plastic balls at him for 20 minutes. Russell made no attempt to play any strokes, he was just practising ducking out of the way. Frustrated by their attempts to bounce him out, the Australians resorted to sledging, only to find that Russell could return it with interest. After he had scored 64 not-out, they realised he was made of strong stuff and never tried it on with him again. His heroic batting in that series culminated in an unbeaten 128 in the Fourth Test at Old Trafford – his highest-ever first-class score. Russell finished the series third in the England batting averages, prompting *Wisden* to write: 'At the beginning of 1989, Jack Russell had played only one Test for England and was not considered a good enough batsman to merit a place in the one-day squad to face the Australians. By the end of the year he was the only Englishman who could justifiably expect a place in anyone's World XI.'

Russell went on to play in 54 Tests, but all too often, despite his undoubted superiority with the gloves, he was overlooked in favour of the more flamboyant batting of Surrey's Alec Stewart. Russell still had his moments with the bat, however, notably a match-saving 29 not-out in 277 minutes against South Africa at Johannesburg in 1996. He played his last Test in 1998, finishing with a respectable batting average of 27. In total, he scored over 16,000 first-class runs at an average of 30 and claimed more than 1,000 victims. His wicketkeeping ability was never in doubt, and in 2002 he set a world record when conceding no byes in Northamptonshire's mammoth score of 746 for 9.

Having helped his county to great success in the one-day game, Russell retired from cricket in 2004 and immediately concentrated on a highly successful new career as a landscape and portrait artist. He had started painting as a hobby back in 1987 and he uses the cricket pitch as a backdrop to many of his finest works. He now has his own exhibitions and his paintings sell for sizeable sums of money.

So Russell's future looks mapped out with his customary diligent planning. 'I'm such a control freak,' he confesses, 'that I've already organised my own funeral.' In fact he had done so by his 30s. Jack Russell has never been one for leaving anything to chance.

Frank Ryan
Undercover Agent

For those to whom the name is unfamiliar, Frank Ryan was a useful left-arm spinner for Glamorgan in the 1920s and indeed was such an accomplished practitioner of his art that some believe he may have been rewarded with Test recognition had he learned to control his temper and his drinking as well as he controlled the flight of the ball. Instead he ended up in the category of cricket's nearly-men, remembered chiefly for his excesses, which included being found fast asleep under the covers during one away match, having drunk so much that he had completely forgotten where the team were staying. Sadly, this was by no means an isolated incident in the turbulent times of Frank Ryan.

Francis Peter Ryan was born on 14 November 1888 in New Jersey in the United States but came to England early in life and served with the Royal Flying Corps during the First World War. The hostilities delayed his entry into first-class cricket until the age of 30, and it was not until 1919 that he made his debut for Hampshire. A fiery character, he clashed frequently with his county captain, Lionel Tennyson, whose own relaxed approach to life was evidently too strict for Ryan. After two unhappy seasons, he was fired. With no money, he walked to Bristol, sleeping in farm barns on the way, in the hope of landing a contract with Gloucestershire, but none was offered. So he drifted up to Lancashire to play League cricket and enjoyed such success there that Glamorgan were alerted to his potential. Still penniless, he hitch-hiked from Lancashire to Cardiff in 1922 to begin a new chapter of his career in South Wales.

Sensing that this was almost certainly his last chance of playing at county level, Ryan knuckled under initially and displayed a self-discipline that had been conspicuously lacking during his days with Hampshire. He became an integral part of the Glamorgan side, taking 120 wickets in 1924 at an average of 14.58. The following year he fared even better, claiming 133 victims, including a career-best 8 for 41 against Derbyshire at the Arms Park. He again passed the century mark in 1926 and derived considerable satisfaction from showing Gloucestershire what they had missed out on by picking up 12 for 90 at Cheltenham. Then in 1927 at Swansea he and Jack Mercer bowled Nottinghamshire out for 61 on a slow, sandy wicket to stop the visitors winning the County Championship. However, by then his resolve had started to waver and the county hierarchy was expressing displeasure at the way his social diary was affecting his game. He imbibed freely, zealously pursued a succession of Welsh girls, and slept in a variety of improvised beds at the Arms Park. Quite apart from being found under the covers, he disgraced himself on a trip to Lancashire, where he stayed on after the match to drink with friends until the early hours of the morning. He then caught a taxi from Manchester to Cardiff to rejoin his team-mates, swanning into the dressing room with the greeting 'Ryan never lets you down', and handing the bill for the fare to the Glamorgan treasurer. In the light of such incidents it was perhaps not wholly unexpected when Glamorgan decided to release him at the end of the 1931 season as a cost-cutting measure. He had taken 913 wickets for the county (his overall first-class tally was 1,013 at 21.03). As a modest tail-end batsman, he had no trouble in keeping his average in single figures.

Frank Ryan died on 5 January 1954 at Leicester, but half a century later his legendary exploits were revived when he was inducted into the Glamorgan Hall of Fame alongside the likes of Tony Lewis, Wilf Wooller, Peter Walker and Ossie Wheatley. It was not only the barmaids of Cardiff who remembered him.

THE MEN IN
WHITE COATS

Dickie Bird
Star Turn

Matthew Engel once wrote of Dickie Bird: 'He was the first umpire to combine the distinct roles of top-flight umpire and music-hall comedian.' In private, Bird was an unassuming, habitually nervous little man but as soon as he put on that white coat he took centre stage, positively revelling in the spotlight, the extravagant gestures and incessant fidgeting seemingly designed to entertain his global fan club. If there was no hint of high drama or low farce in the offing, Dickie would somehow manufacture it, to the extent that an entire industry has sprung up around Bird-related anecdotes, a handful of them stretched to a point at least an Andrew Flintoff six beyond credibility. Yet there really is no need to embellish the plain facts because chaos and confusion appeared more attracted to Dickie than any other contemporary, with the possible exception of Frank Spencer. As his fellow Barnsley native Michael Parkinson said, Dickie Bird was 'a lightning conductor for misfortune.'

Parkinson should know because he used to open batting with Dickie for Barnsley and experienced the full range of his eccentricities. He remembers how Dickie was always so nervous before an innings that he once inadvertently buckled his pads to each other and fell flat on his face as he went out to bat.

Harold Dennis Bird was born in the Yorkshire town on 19 April 1933, the son of a miner who advised him that, if he wanted to be a sportsman, he should steer clear of cigarettes and women in nightclubs. Dickie has adhered to both dictates with unswerving dedication. He was a promising young footballer until a knee injury sustained at 15 obliged him to pursue his other love, cricket. He was soon opening the batting for Barnsley CC, joined not only by Parkinson but also later by a young Geoffrey Boycott. In 1956 Bird made his first-class debut for Yorkshire but only played when the county's stars were away on Test duty. In 1959 he scored a career-best 181 not-out against Glamorgan at Bradford in a seven-and-a-half-hour knock, at the end of which Yorkshire chairman Brian Sellers told the exhausted batsman: 'Well-played, Dickie lad, but get thee head down – you're in the second team for the next match.' Bird remained the most superstitious of batsmen. If he had a run of low scores with the bat, he would impetuously give away all his cricket gear until on one occasion his team-mates, who had previously always returned it when asked, made him buy it back. The cash outlay cured him of that particular idiosyncrasy.

Bird joined Leicestershire in 1960, only to suffer the ignominy of recording a king pair in the space of a couple of hours against Sussex. Yet even that episode was overshadowed by a Leicestershire match where he was fielding at third man in front of the pavilion. 'The grass there was very lush,' recalled Dickie, 'and I had rubber-soled shoes on. I raced round to field the ball when I suddenly slipped. I flew straight into the pavilion railings and my head became stuck fast. I couldn't move. The game had to be held up until they found a joiner to get my head out.'

After scoring 3,314 first-class runs at an average of 20.71, Bird, still troubled with his right knee, retired from county cricket at the end of the 1964 season and moved into coaching at Plymouth College while continuing to play at the weekends for Paignton Cricket Club. Paignton's opponents included a team captained by former Middlesex and England fast bowler John Warr, and it was he who suggested Bird should consider a career as an umpire. No doubt mindful of the friends who had told him he was far too nervous to be an umpire, Dickie laughed off the idea initially but after giving it serious thought, decided it would be a suitable substitute for playing. Moreover, this most apprehensive of batsmen – acquaintances used to joke that he tried to chew his fingernails through his batting gloves – claims he lost all his nerves when he was umpiring a game. Before the match was a different matter, however.

In the build-up to a game he used to go to the toilet three or four times just to settle himself. For one of his first county matches – Surrey versus Yorkshire at the Oval in 1970 – he arrived at the ground at 5.30am, six hours before play was due to start. Finding the gates still locked, he decided to scale them, but as he reached the top he was spotted by a passing policeman who promptly arrested him. Unsurprisingly, the officer needed some persuading before accepting that Dickie was an eager umpire rather than an incompetent burglar.

He has always had a morbid fear of being late for an appointment, and when planning his journey would take into account all potential pitfalls, from heavy traffic to abduction by aliens. Invited by the Queen for lunch at Buckingham Palace, he arrived at breakfast time and had to spend the intervening five hours in a nearby coffee shop. For a Sunday lunch date with John Major at Chequers that was scheduled for noon, Dickie turned up at 9.30 in the morning. Fortunately the cricket-loving Prime Minister was well aware of Dickie's foibles and had him sent through straight away.

It has to be said that Bird's serenity in the middle was purely relative. Next to Bird the batsman he was calm; next to a caffeine addict he was jumpy. Beneath the trademark flat cap, he was forever fidgeting, relentlessly tugging at the sleeves and tail of his umpire's jacket or at the cap itself in times of stress. In fairness, as Michael Parkinson pointed out, he was beset by bad luck. Not only did the ball seem drawn to him like a magnet, either hitting him painfully or forcing him to take elaborate evasive action, but mother nature appeared to take delight in actively conspiring against him, leading him to complain that 'rain and bad light have followed me around all my life.' He was officiating at Buxton in June 1975 when an unseasonal blizzard prevented play and at Old Trafford 20 years later when he was forced to take the players off the pitch during the Test against the West Indies because the light was too bright! The sun was shining on a greenhouse next to the ground and reflecting on to the stands, as a result of which slip fielders and batsmen were unable to see the ball. Amid much gesturing and agitation, Bird called tea 15 minutes early to allow the groundstaff to block out the reflection with black sheeting. The general consensus of opinion was that it could only have happened to him. The same could be said of the 1988 Headingley Test, also against the West Indies, when a pipe leading into an underground drain ruptured, causing water to spill on to the outfield. Under clear blue skies, Bird had no option but to suspend play, a decision that was greeted with predictable derision from his home crowd. As he and the players walked off to jeers, he shouted by way of apology: 'It's not my fault, it's not my fault.'

If it were not natural causes that put Bird in a flap, there were always man-made problems with which to contend. A bomb scare stopped play during the 1973 Test against the West Indies at Lord's. As the stands evacuated, Dickie wisely stayed out in the middle, sitting on the covers in the belief that it was the safest place to be. For bombs, read pigeons. With England in trouble during the 1976 Test against the West Indies at Trent Bridge, fast bowler John Snow came out after lunch with his pockets stuffed with breadcrumbs, which he proceeded to scatter all over the ground. Pigeons immediately descended on Trent Bridge from right across the Midlands, the avian invasion resulting in play being held up. Bird recalled: 'I just stood there and flapped, I was so flabbergasted.' Given the range of misfortune that beset him, the only surprise is that he was not on duty when the 'George Davis Is Innocent' campaigners sabotaged the Headingley pitch with knives and oil in 1975.

Between 1973 and 1996 Bird umpired 66 Tests and 69 one-day internationals. His natural good humour and unbridled enthusiasm for the game made him a popular figure with even the most temperamental of players, a laugh and a word defusing many a potentially volatile situation. Australia's Merv Hughes, no greater respecter of authority, said simply: 'Dickie Bird, you're a legend.' For players knew that while he took his job extremely seriously and that his impartiality was unquestionable, he always enjoyed a joke and would go out of his way to be helpful, sometimes to his own cost. I have already retold the famous Allan Lamb mobile phone incident, but there were other occasions when players took liberties with him that they would not have tried with other umpires. Often he could be seen swathed in deposited sweaters like an Egyptian mummy, his head barely visible over the top of the pile. On a fiery wicket, Derbyshire batsman Ashley Harvey-Walker once handed his false teeth to Bird while in the middle of the 1974 Old Trafford Test against India, Sunil Gavaskar asked him for a haircut. Resourceful as ever, Bird produced a razor blade from his pocket and halted play to cut off the locks that were blowing into Gavaskar's face and impeding his vision.

Occasionally Bird became so engrossed in the game that he forgot himself. In one of his first umpiring assignments – Surrey against Hampshire at Guildford – he ran from his position behind the stumps and followed a lofted drive right to the boundary's edge, where he tried to catch it. He had momentarily forgotten that he was no longer a player! In that same season he was standing at square leg during a match between Hampshire and Lancashire at Southampton. Seeing Lancashire wicketkeeper Keith Goodwin set off for a suicidal second run, Dickie shouted instinctively: 'No, Goody, no, get back!' When Goodwin failed to make his ground and umpire Bird was obliged to raise his finger, the Hampshire fielders creased up with laughter. He was certainly not above demonstrating his emotions on the field of play. When Pakistan's Mushtaq Mohammed, playing for Northamptonshire against Sussex, produced a magnificent leg-break to bowl Peter Graves, Bird leaped in the air and shouted: 'Mushy, that was a ball of magic. A magic ball, Mushy.' It was akin to a soccer referee kissing a goalscorer.

Bird's popularity never waned, his endearing quirks elevating him to the status of national treasure. At the beginning of the final Test, the two teams – England and India – formed a 'guard of honour' as he came out, and he received a standing ovation from the crowd. Great players – Sobers, Richards, Lillee, to name but three – queued up to pay tribute to the modest Yorkshireman whom they considered to be the world's best umpire. Perhaps the most succinct appraisal came from Ian Botham, who once described him as 'Great bloke, completely bonkers.'

Few sporting figures are held in such affection as Dickie Bird. He gives the impression of having enjoyed every minute of his life in cricket, his one regret being that he never made more of himself as a player. 'I had the ability I can tell you,' he said in a 1998 interview. 'Ray Illingworth said I played as straight as anyone he'd ever seen. If you had compared me to Boycott in the nets, you would have picked me as the Test player.' But the English public does not necessarily warm to greatness; it prefers eccentricity and warmth. And Dickie Bird has both in spades.

Brent 'Billy' Bowden
The Crooked Finger

It has been called the 'crooked finger of death' and it has turned New Zealand umpire Brent 'Billy' Bowden into a cult figure. His highly individual brand of signalling, accompanied by his energy in general around the stumps, has made him the most instantly recognisable of the new wave of umpires. Although the famous finger – he curves his raised finger into the shape of a hook to denote when a batsman is out – was born out of arthritis rather than showmanship, the other signals in his repertoire are pure vaudeville. His method of signalling a four – a sweeping flourish of the arm across the body as the back leg slides out – has been likened variously to wiping breadcrumbs off a table or a turn at La Scala. His signal for leg byes has been compared to a human pogo stick, although Henry Blofeld on *Test Match Special* said of one Bowden leg-bye gesture: 'He taps his leg and shakes it. If it was butter it would be milk by now.' Then there is his hallelujah-like signal for a six, in which he rises from a crouched position, propelling himself into the air, but leaving one leg on the ground while at the same time forcing his two hands, which appear to be using sticks to play a drum, to rise with him. It makes the mating dance of a bird of paradise look positively mundane by comparison.

Bowden suggests that even these exaggerated movements stem partly from the rheumatoid arthritis that brought a premature end to his playing career at the age of 23. If he stands still for too long, he suffers considerable pain, so the gestures are a way of keeping on the move. The crooked finger developed solely because he found it difficult to hold his finger straight. 'When I first started, the fingers were very sore and swollen because of the arthritis, but I've stuck with it and I guess it's fifty-fifty now, part arthritis, part for show.'

Another difficulty caused by his condition is that he is unable to hold items given to him by bowlers – such as sweaters and hats – and so instead he pushes them up the front of his own sweater, with the result that he invariably looks pregnant. However, he cheerfully points out that it is not all doom and gloom as he is usually the first person in the ground to know when bad weather is on the way because his joints creak.

The son of a Baptist minister, Brent Fraser Bowden was born in Henderson, Auckland, on 11 April 1963, earning the nickname 'Billy' at school after Billy Bunter because he was always first to the tuck-shop. He captained his school team to victory in a district competition and graduated to the Auckland squad as a solid batsman and useful off-spin bowler before the arthritis stopped him in his tracks. The condition started when he was 21 and within two years was causing him such pain that he no longer enjoyed playing. Fortunately an advert in the *New Zealand Herald* encouraged him to take up umpiring and by 1992–93 he was on the first-class list. His one-day international debut came in 1995, followed in 2000 by his first Test match, New Zealand versus Australia. Such was his progress that he later became the first New Zealander to be appointed to the International Cricket Council's elite panel.

A religious man who says that God watches over him in the middle – 'he is my third umpire in a way' – Bowden insists that his antics are merely an on-field reflection of his personality. 'There are no preservatives, no additives,' he says. 'I am 100 per cent natural.' While the mannerisms have delighted TV audiences and crowds – after Bowden was felled at square leg by a shot from Geraint Jones in the 2006 Brisbane Test spectators began chanting 'Billy, Billy' – they have not found favour with everyone. His compatriot, former New Zealand Test captain Martin Crowe, has labelled him 'Bozo the clown', while others have suggested that Bowden ought to remember that it is the players, not the umpires, who are supposed to be centre stage. In 2004, on his first Test in India, he was pilloried by the Bangalore press after giving Virender Sehwag out lbw despite a clear inside edge to a ball from Glenn McGrath. Bowden subsequently apologised for the decision, blaming the error on crowd noise that made it difficult to pick up any sounds from the bat. Then in 2007 he was one of four umpires suspended for the inaugural Twenty20 World Championship in South Africa due to his involvement in the showpiece World Cup final earlier in the year that had ended in darkness and farce.

It is to be hoped that the pressures of modern umpiring do not dent the spirit of a genuine character like Billy Bowden. He may play to the gallery but he remains an excellent umpire. Besides, who could not warm to a man who professes his philosophy to be 'Life without sport is like life without underpants'?

Frank Chester
Fearless Frank

During a match between Nottinghamshire and Yorkshire, a ball from Harold Larwood hit Wilfred Rhodes on the toes, causing the Yorkshire batsman to hop around in agony. Rhodes was in such pain that even Larwood stepped forward to apologise and umpire Frank Chester decided to give him a couple of minutes to recover. Eventually, as Rhodes was about to resume was innings, Chester inquired: 'Are you all right, Wilfred?'

'Aye,' replied Rhodes.

'Can you walk?' asked Chester.

'Aye.'

'Well, you can walk to the pavilion. You were lbw!'

The story sums up Chester, a fearless umpire who was no respecter of reputations. In his first county match – Essex versus Somerset at Leyton – he gave both captains out on the first day and was told by the other, more senior, umpire as they walked off that he wouldn't last long if he carried on like that. 'If you give skippers out, you sign your own death warrant,' he was told. Chester ignored the warning and continued giving captains out for the next 33 years. He was so well respected that he stood in 48 Test matches – a world record until it was beaten by Dickie Bird – and was hailed by no less than Don Bradman as 'the greatest umpire under whom I have played.'

Frank Chester was born in Bushey, Hertfordshire, on 20 January 1895. He joined Worcestershire in 1912 as an all-rounder and the following season he scored 703 runs, including three centuries, and took 44 wickets with his slow left-armers. That year *Wisden* wrote of him: 'Nothing stood out more prominently than the remarkable development of Chester, the youngest professional regularly engaged in first-class cricket. Very few players in the history of cricket have shown such form at the age of 17-and-a-half... He bowls with a high, easy action and, commanding an accurate length, can get plenty of spin on the ball. Having begun so well, Chester should continue to improve and it seems only reasonable to expect that when he was filled out and gained more strength, he will be an England cricketer.'

In 1914 he compiled 924 runs – including a career-best 178 not-out against Essex – but then the First World War intervened and, while serving with the British Army in Salonika, Chester lost his right arm just below the elbow. His playing career was over before it had really started – 1,773 runs at an average of 23.95 and 81 wickets (average 31.61) being all he had to show for such a promising talent.

After his terrible injury, his friends encouraged him to take up umpiring and in 1922 he became the youngest name on the first-class list. His youth generally counted in his favour, except on an occasion at Northampton when he was refused entry by the gateman who, unable to believe that he was an umpire, thought he was trying to sneak in without paying. Before his first match – Essex versus Somerset at Leyton – he went into his garden and dug up six stones, which he would use to count the balls of each over. Amazingly, he kept the same six stones throughout his career, storing them in a matchbox during the winter. Chester's stones became a defining image of cricket, particularly as he used to toss them into the air in an exaggerated manner to mark each delivery.

In order to judge lbw decisions, he was the first umpire to crouch down low over the stumps when standing at the bowler's end. However, he was forced to abandon the position temporarily following an unfortunate incident during a match between Surrey and Sussex, when Surrey's Freddie Brown drove a half-volley straight back into Chester's false arm, the force knocking it from its socket. There was an awkward silence as the arm lay on the grass. Unruffled, Chester left the field to have the arm refitted, and on his return, instead of standing right over the stumps, he made a point of standing several yards behind them – an action that immediately broke the ice.

He made his debut as a Test umpire in 1924 – officiating at England versus South Africa at Lord's – and, in the words of *Wisden*, 'raised umpiring to a higher level than had ever been known in the history of cricket.' He took his time over his decisions and earned the title of 'the man who never made a mistake'. Chester evidently deemed himself worthy of such an accolade. Asked once why he had given a batsman the benefit of the doubt, he retorted: 'Doubt? When I'm umpiring, there's never any doubt!'

Chester had always been regarded as scrupulously impartial but although Bradman rated him highly, his fellow Australians began to harbour suspicions, perhaps born out of Chester's assertion that England's intimidating bodyline tactics employed on the 1932–33 series in Australia were perfectly fair. For his part, Chester expected players to conduct themselves properly during a game, and during Australia's 1948 visit to England he felt obliged to rebuke the tourists publicly for their over-aggressive behaviour. Three years later, when South Africa toured England, Chester wanted to no-ball South African fast bowler Cuan McCarthy for throwing but, informed that he would receive no backing from the MCC, he uncharacteristically chose to remain silent.

Chester had long suffered from stomach ulcers, which tended to make him tetchy with bowlers, and when the Australians toured again in 1953 he upset them with his dismissive attitude and habit of rejecting appeals in a mock Australian accent. After the Fourth Test at Headingley, the tourists had become so disillusioned with him that they asked for him to be dropped for the rest of the series. The MCC responded by resting him for the season on grounds of ill health. The stomach problems continued and in 1955 he decided to retire, having officiated in more than 1,000 first-class fixtures. Lord's undoubtedly breathed a huge sigh of relief at the news as Australia were due to visit again in 1956 and the authorities feared the worst if Chester and the Australians locked horns again. Nevertheless the cricket world was stunned when he passed away on 8 April 1957, aged 62.

Frank Chester was essentially a serious man, although when fielding at square leg he did enjoy chatting to nearby fielders about horse racing. He was fond of a flutter and, umpiring at Taunton in 1924, he started to wonder how his hot tip had fared that afternoon. Then George Hunt came out to bat for Somerset, immediately called for an impossible single and was run out. On his way back to the pavilion he called to Chester: 'I was only sent in to tell you your horse has won!'

Cec Pepper
A Sharp Tongue

Even by Australian standards, Cec Pepper was outspoken. Both as a player in his native New South Wales and as an umpire in England, he sent shock waves through the establishment with his blunt speaking, despite the fact that many of his more outrageous remarks were broadly laced with wit. When 5ft 3in Lancashire batsman Harry Pilling asked him for advice on technique, Pepper snapped: 'Go home and ask Snow White!' And when Warwickshire's Dennis Amiss appeared at the wicket carrying a helmet, Pepper asked him where he had parked his moped. Amiss then asked the umpire to hold the helmet while he was at the non-striker's end, to which Pepper replied: 'You hold it, mate, and use it as a pisspot!'

Pepper's uncompromising attitude towards cosseted captains – 'I used to shoot 'em out, no matter who' – also failed to win him friends in high places. When fellow Australian umpire Bill Alley suggested that his ultimate ambition was to stand in an England-Australia Test at Lord's with Pepper, MCC secretary Billy Griffith was horrified by the prospect. 'Oh no,' he wailed. 'We could *never* have that!' So Pepper, whose verbal attack as a leg-spin bowler had once antagonised the Australian Cricket Board, found himself frozen out of the big matches as an umpire. In an unwanted double, the man often regarded as the best Australian player never to win a Test cap went on to become one of the best umpires never to officiate in a Test. No wonder he had a chip on his shoulder the size of a sack of King Edwards.

Cecil George Pepper was born in Forbes, New South Wales, on 15 September 1918. While still a teenager, he hammered 2,834 runs and took 116 wickets for Parkes in one season but still seemed more likely to pursue a career as a tennis player. However, another noted rebel, Sid Barnes, took him under his wing at Petersham Cricket Club in Sydney and by 1938–39 Pepper had graduated to the New South Wales State team. His crafty leg-breaks were complemented by his muscular batting, which once saw him smash a ball out of the Sydney Cricket Ground and into Kippax Lake. During the Second World

War he served his country in the Middle East and New Guinea and became a key member of the 1945 Australian Services team, excelling in the unofficial Tests in England. He clubbed a century in 47 minutes in a one-day match at High Wycombe and, en route to a career-best 168, bludgeoned a ball from Eric Hollies over the houses at Scarborough and into Trafalgar Square, thereby emulating 'Buns' Thornton and winning a bottle of whisky from wicketkeeper Arthur Wood who had goaded him into attempting the big hit. However it all turned sour early in 1946 on the servicemen's farewell tour of their homeland. At Adelaide, Sgt. Pepper became incensed after umpire Jack Scott had rejected three appeals off his bowling against Don Bradman, and he let the official know exactly what he thought of the decisions. He later claimed to have sent an apology to the Australian Cricket Board, but they denied ever receiving it.

He did go to India with the 1949–50 Commonwealth side and returned his best-ever first-class bowling figures of 6 for 33 against Holkar at Indore (including a hat-trick), but he left the tour early, by mutual agreement with his captain, because of frustrations over the standard of umpiring. Instead, he plied his trade in Lancashire League cricket, where he made a name for himself by intimidating umpires and abusing authority. If outright bullying failed to work, he would resort to subtler methods to obtain an lbw decision, saying things like, 'Ooh, that was close, umpire, but you're right – just missing leg-stump. Good decision.' Then the next time he hit the batsman on the pad he would shriek a loud appeal, adding for good measure: 'Must be out this time. Plumb.' And invariably the poor cowed umpire would raise his finger. He still did not take kindly to rejection and while at Rochdale, tweaked the nose of an opposition club member on the pavilion steps over some perceived slight.

Physically and spiritually, Pepper was a huge success in Lancashire. He eventually retired from playing in 1963, and given his track record of run-ins with officialdom, more than a few eyebrows were raised when it emerged that he was joining the umpires' list the following season. Wearing a specially-made cotton coat with loops to hold the bails, and tassled golf shoes, he cut a dashing – if rotund – figure at the wicket. Uncompromising but fair, he took a leaf out of Frank Chester's book by refusing to obey the unwritten law of giving preferential treatment to captains – Lancashire skipper Cyril Washbrook once told him that captaincy was worth up to 400 runs a season – and clamped down hard on batsmen who repeatedly padded up to the ball before the lbw law was changed. 'Three kicks and you're out,' he would tell them.

In spite of his forthright manner, Pepper was popular with the county circuit players, most of whom enjoyed his banter and general abuse. He could be alarmingly irreverent, once announcing a Warwickshire change of bowling from Bill Blenkiron to the Barbadian Bill Bourne as: 'Change of bowler, same action, different colour.' Even when he socialised with a team, it did not affect his impartiality. The day after a heavy drinking session with the Essex boys at Westcliff, he gave seven of them out. Unfortunately, fraternising with players was frowned upon in high places and was another reason why he was denied a Test match appointment. In fact, Pepper became increasingly disillusioned at the way in which Tests were awarded to a small group of establishment figures, and this bitterness led to his eventual retirement from umpiring in 1979.

Upon his death at Littleborough, Lancashire, on 22 March 1993, one friend described Cec Pepper as the only man he knew who could talk, spit, chew, belch and pass wind simultaneously. Above all, he was remembered for his badinage, and in particular for one occasion when he found himself on the receiving end. While bowling in the Lancashire Leagues, having had several appeals rejected by mild-mannered umpire George Long, Pepper questioned Long's eyesight and parentage in his usual inimitable fashion. At the end of the over, realising that perhaps he had gone too far, he apologised, but Long replied: 'Don't worry, Cec. Up here we like a man who speaks his mind.' Believing that he had struck up a rapport with the umpire, Pepper began his next over and when the first ball hit the batsman on the pad, he confidently inquired, 'How's that?' To which Long answered: 'Not out, you fat Australian bastard.'

Bill Reeves
A Way With Words

Overzealous or persistent bowling appeals have long been the bane of an umpire's life, but Bill Reeves was better at most than dealing with them, using his natural wit to put the player firmly in his place. Rejecting yet another appeal from Yorkshire's George Macauley, Reeves remarked dryly: 'There's only one man made more appeals than you, George, and that was Dr Barnardo!' He was equally adept at handling protesting batsmen. If a batsman complained that he was not out, Reeves would smile: 'Weren't you? Wait till you see the papers in the morning.'

It was Reeves who gave a young Denis Compton out on his Middlesex debut in 1936 solely because of an impending call of nature. When Compton's batting partner, Gubby Allen, expressed his surprise at the decision, Reeves replied: 'Don't forget, Mr Allen, that he's a young man capable of scoring a lot more runs. But I'm breaking my neck for a pee!'

Bill Reeves was born in Cambridge on 22 June 1875 and after joining the groundstaff at Leyton, which was then the county's headquarters, he made his debut for Essex in 1897. He soon established himself as a useful all-rounder, bowling at a brisk medium pace and developing into a hard-hitting batsman. He passed 1,000 runs in a season for the only time in 1905, during which he hit two of his three first-class hundreds, the pick of which was 135 against Lancashire in just two hours. The following year he smashed 104 against Sussex, he and Claude Buckenham putting on 163 for the eighth wicket in only 70 minutes. He most productive season with the ball was 1904, when he picked up 106 wickets, although three years earlier he had taken the last five Derbyshire wickets in 11 balls without conceding a run. Yet his best figures – 7 for 33 – were reserved for 1920, when, at the age of 45, he took 62 wickets at 22.59. The next year was his benefit season but he only played in four matches before announcing his retirement in June with a career record of 6,656 runs and 601 wickets.

Having umpired one game the previous summer, he now took up officiating full-time, continuing until 1939. He stood in five England

Tests – two matches against South Africa in 1924, one against Australia in 1926, one against New Zealand in 1937 after an 11-year gap, and one against the West Indies in 1939. He was also due to umpire in the 1938 Test against Australia at Old Trafford, but it was abandoned without a ball being bowled. At whichever level of the game he was umpiring, he invariably demonstrated commendable good humour. When a mix-up resulted in both batsmen running to the same end, Reeves raised his finger as the bails were removed but was unsure which of the two batsmen was actually out. After a lengthy deliberation, he called them over and decided their fate with the toss of a coin. On another occasion he defused a row about an illegal declaration during a match in Glamorgan by stating that he did not think Law 54 applied as they were in a foreign country!

Bill Reeves died in Hammersmith, London, on 22 March 1944, and his tongue-in-cheek wit was much missed. The story was recounted of a young bowler, new to the county game, who, after appealing vociferously for lbw, was told by Reeves: 'You will have more chance in this higher class of cricket if you add "Sir" to your appeal.'

A few overs later, the batsman was again hit on the pads. 'How's that, sir?' asked the eager newcomer.

'That's better, my boy,' grinned Reeves. 'That's out.'

David Shepherd
At The Hop

In 2005, one of the most familiar and best-loved sights disappeared from world cricket – the David Shepherd hop. Spectators from Bristol to Brisbane would be on the lookout whenever the score reached Nelson (111) or one of its multiples to see if umpire Shepherd remembered to do his little hop. He rarely let them down, except on the odd occasions when he was so engrossed in the play to notice the score.

The number of 111 has long been considered unlucky in cricket – one theory being that it resembles a set of stumps without the bails –

and, according to superstition, the only way of preventing something bad happening on a Nelson number is to have no part of the body touching the ground. Shepherd came across the superstition when he was playing village cricket in his native Devon and carried it through his first-class career with Gloucestershire and then his umpiring days. 'You could just lift your feet off the pavilion floor if you weren't in the middle,' he says, 'but if I was on the field of play I would hop or jump. When I took to umpiring, I thought I couldn't keep doing that, but a few friends urged me to carry on. Hardly anyone noticed at first but when I did my second Test, at Edgbaston in 1985, someone had written in to dear old Brian Johnston on *Test Match Special* and said, "Watch this idiot when the score gets on 111." It did, I did my little jump and there was a titter in the crowd. I thought there must be a streaker on the field, but it was Brian telling the world – and the spectators were listening on their radio. From then on, I was lumbered with it.'

Shepherd's superstition about the number 111 has even been his downfall. Batting in a county match against Warwickshire, he had compiled an uncharacteristically patient three-hour century before becoming so anxious to get beyond 111 that he took a liberty with the bowling of Tom Cartwright and was out. After that, he left nothing to chance. When he drove Gloucestershire scorer Bert Avery to Canterbury for a match and pulled up at the hotel, he happened to glance at the mileometer and saw to his horror that he had driven exactly 111 miles. He immediately ordered Avery back in the car and drove him around the block for a mile before returning to the hotel. Time and again county managements tried to put Shepherd into Room 111 or Room 222 at hotels around the country but they never succeeded.

He is equally superstitious about Friday the 13th and fixes a matchstick to his wrist with an elastic band for the day so that he is always touching wood. His fear is not without reason. He last saw his father alive on Friday the 13th, and at the end of a day's umpiring at Lord's on Friday the 13th, he slipped in the shower and fell heavily. To complete his hat-trick of superstitions, whenever he goes up and down the stairs at home, he always ensures that he comes off the last step with his left foot. This is believed to be another Devon myth, but the fact that what is probably no more than an old wives' tale assumes such importance in Shepherd's life helps to explain how this down-to-earth, rustic, ruddy-faced, broad-girthed fellow rose from his West Country roots to become one of the most admired figures in international sport. There was never any front or favouritism with 'Shep', a genial man who became a cricketing colossus but who, no matter where he was officiating in the world, always remained a North Devon boy at heart.

Born at Bideford on 27 December 1940, he worked as a PE and geography teacher for three years while also playing Minor Counties cricket for Devon. He was a comparative latecomer to the first-class game and it was not until 1965 that he joined Gloucestershire, hitting 108 against Oxford University on his debut. His roly-poly build – ample evidence of his fondness for hearty food and a pint – made him a pugnacious middle-order batsman. When Shepherd hit the ball, it winced. Geoffrey Moorhouse wrote of him: 'It is not only his build, though, that calls the deep-rooted countryman to mind. His bottom hand is clamped massively just above the shoulder of the bat, as some ancestor probably held a scythe, or possibly a blacksmith's maul. He stands…head scanning the field of play the way men do by gates when they are contemplating crops.' Some of his most profitable strokes were undeniably agricultural but they proved particularly effective in the one-day game (he appeared in two victorious limited-over finals) where his placing of shots compensated for his lack of speed between the wickets. Any scampered single was followed by much brow-mopping and on one occasion he had to be escorted off suffering from dehydration. By his own admission, he was never the most nimble of fielders, although he did once run out Gary Sobers in a game against Nottinghamshire, not through great agility but because of a mix-up that left both batsmen at the same end. And those huge hands could form a vice-like grip on the ball, making him a safe catcher. After an early session of fielding practice, Gloucestershire skipper Ken Graveney asked vice-captain John Mortimore what Shepherd was like in the field. Mortimore replied that if Shep could get to the ball, he would catch it. On the debit side, he once brought the fencing down at mid-wicket in a vain attempt to stop a four in a Second XI fixture at Worcester. When he retired from playing in 1979, he had hit 10,672 first-class runs (including a dozen centuries) at an average of 24.47. 'Within my limitations I always tried my best,' he said. 'I played with a big tum and a smile on my face.'

He became a first-class umpire in 1980 and went on to stand in 92 Tests and six World Cup tournaments. His decisions, always quietly considered, never rushed, earned him widespread admiration. He was happy to socialise with players, but always on his own terms. He once said: 'There are no barriers – if players want me to share a drink with them at the close of play, I accept, provided the invitation has come from them. Umpires know the players who are inclined to be argumentative or have outsized chips on their shoulders. Discreetly, we keep our distance from them.' His worst umpiring experience was the 2001 Old Trafford Test, which Pakistan won after three England batsmen were out to no-balls missed by Shepherd, who failed to spot bowler Saqlain Mushtaq overstepping the crease. When his errors were pointed out, Shepherd was so mortified that he thought about quitting but reconsidered after receiving the support of the players, the public and the England and Wales Cricket Board.

Between umpiring duties, Shep happily got up before six o'clock in the morning to help out at his brother Bill's newsagent's in Devon and was still delivering papers at the age of 64. After Shepherd had delivered *The Times* to an ex-headmaster, the recipient did a double-take, saying: 'I can't believe this, David. Here I am, reading a report of yesterday's match in Sharjah where you were the umpire, and now you're bringing the paper to my front door!'

In 2005 Shep hopped in public for the last time, choosing to retire on the 200th anniversary of Nelson's death. Fittingly, his final county match was at Bristol, where he had been held in such great affection for 40 years. Tributes poured in for an essentially shy man who tended to shun the limelight. He recalled how a female streaker had run on to the pitch at Lord's during an England versus Australia one-day game in 1989 and made a beeline for the embarrassed umpire, eventually performing a full cartwheel right in front of him. 'I wasn't quite sure what to do,' he said, 'so I shielded my eyes.' The picture made the front page of the *Sun*, but all Shep had been worried about was what his old Mum would think watching on TV back in Devon.

Alec Skelding
The Prince Of Kidders

Alec Skelding was such a maverick umpire that he was never entrusted with a Test match. However, the renowned Leicestershire wit, raconteur and occasional poet stood in over 500 first-class games between 1931 and 1959, officiating until the ripe old age of 72, largely because of his unrivalled entertainment value.

With his thick-lensed glasses perched on a bulbous red nose beneath a shock of white hair, Skelding was an unmistakeable figure, whose wisecracks earned him the nickname of the 'Prince of Kidders'. Inevitably his eyesight was frequently called into question, and he once told Nottinghamshire batsman Joe Hardstaff that there would be no lbw decisions on that particular day because he had brought his reading-glasses by mistake. When Glamorgan were pushing for the county title, their captain Wilf Wooller became frustrated after Skelding turned down a succession of appeals during a key fixture against Middlesex. As the frustration finally boiled over, Wooller angrily turned to Skelding and said: 'For heaven's sake, what was wrong with that one, you blind old bastard?' Refusing to be drawn into a war of words, Skelding just smiled: 'He was not out, Mr Wooller, and it is true that my eyesight is not so good. That is why I wear these strong glasses, but I can assure you that my mother and father were married when I was born, and I'll tell you something else, Mr Wooller – I don't think you and your side are going to win this cricket match!' He was right as Middlesex went on to claim victory and dent Glamorgan's title hopes.

Somerset's combative Australian all-rounder Bill Alley was equally disappointed after Skelding had rejected a confident appeal for lbw off his bowling.

'Sorry, Alec,' he said, apparently accepting the decision. 'I suppose it would not have hit off-stump.'

'You're right, Bill,' replied Skelding.

'And I suppose it would not have hit leg-stump either.'

'You're right again, Bill.'

'But it would definitely have hit bloody middle!'

The other person who famously criticised Skelding's eyesight was the Australian Sid Barnes on his country's 1948 tour of England. Having been given out lbw by Skelding, Barnes remarked loudly: 'That umpire must be blind!' A week later, Skelding, standing in another tour game, sent Barnes a note saying that he had brought with him three pairs of strong spectacles – one for lbw's, one for run-outs, and a third for catches at the wicket. He added that he had also brought a guide dog but that the animal would be left in the pavilion with a steward. As chance would have it, a dog strayed on to the pitch in the course of the game while the Australians were fielding and Barnes gleefully collected the animal before handing it to the umpire. 'Here's your dog, Alec,' said Barnes. 'He must have run away from that steward. Now all you want is a white stick.'

Skelding used to hide a hip flask of brandy beneath his handkerchief and have a secret swig on a chilly day while pretending to blow his nose. He maintained that it kept out the cold and helped him to see straight. However if required to adjudicate on a particularly close run-out, he would sometimes abdicate responsibility altogether, waiting for the appeal to die down before declaring: 'Gentlemen, it's a photo finish. But as I have neither the time nor the equipment, the batsman is not out.' On another occasion Gloucestershire's 'Bomber' Wells – renowned for his chaotic running between wickets – needed a runner, as did his batting partner, with the result that there were four 'batsmen' out in the middle. It was a recipe for disaster, and so it proved. Wells played a ball on to the off side and called for a run but, forgetting that he had a runner, set off himself. His equally inept partner did the same, and then one of them decided that there was the possibility of a second run. Amid shouts of 'Yes', 'No', 'Yes', all four were running and in the ensuing chaos, they all ended up at the same end, whereupon the one fielder who was not convulsed with laughter threw down the stumps at the other end. The matter was referred to umpire Skelding who, after due deliberation, pronounced: 'One of you buggers is out. I don't know which. You decide and inform the bloody scorers!'

He was rarely lost for words. When Derbyshire batsman Dusty Rhodes, who had been celebrating enthusiastically at a function the previous evening, was rapped on the pad by the ball, Hampshire bowler Charlie Knott appealed to the umpire: 'How is he?' Skelding shook his head sadly and replied: 'The bugger's not well at all, and he was even worse last night.'

After Northamptonshire's Dennis Brookes was bowled at Lord's by a ball that cut back viciously to remove the off-stump, Jock Livingston was the next man in. As he took guard, he cheerfully asked umpire Skelding: 'How many balls to go, Alec?' 'Two,' answered Skelding, 'but if the first is as good as the last, one will be enough as far as you are concerned!'

Everyone was fair game to Skelding. Having previously worked on a racecourse, he liked to confuse the scorers by giving signals in tic-tac, but above all he never missed an opportunity to rib the players. One fast bowler had the misfortune to see his false teeth fly out at the moment of delivery, and so his subsequent appeal as the ball hit the batsman's pad was almost unintelligible. Milking the situation for all it was worth, Skelding said: 'I beg your pardon, I cannot understand a word of what you are saying.' The poor bowler tried again, but Skelding still pretended that he could not understand. Finally the bowler bent down, picked up his dentures, replaced them and bellowed his appeal. To which Skelding replied calmly: 'Not out.'

Alexander Skelding was born in Leicester on 5 September 1886 and after playing for local clubs joined the Leicestershire groundstaff in 1905 as a fast bowler. However, the spectacles he habitually wore were considered a handicap on the playing field and he was released at the end of the season. Instead he turned out for Kidderminster in the Birmingham League, where he achieved such success that Leicestershire re-signed him in 1912 and he remained with the county until his retirement from playing in 1929. He was one of those players who improved with age and by the mid-1920s was considered to be just about the fastest bowler in the country, a belief backed up by his haul of 102 wickets in 1927 at the age of 40. He finished with 593 first-class wickets at an average of 24.67, his best performance being 8 for 44 against Nottinghamshire on a perfect pitch in 1924. Asked whether he found playing in spectacles a problem, he admitted: 'I can't see without 'em and on hot days I can't see with 'em, because they get steamed up. So I bowl on hearing only and appeal twice an over!' They certainly did little to improve his vision while batting, for he averaged a meagre 6.76 with the willow and a top score of just 33.

He also operated the Leicestershire scoreboard occasionally but once got into such a mess trying to keep track of proceedings that an angry mob gathered to vent their displeasure at his incompetence.

Hearing the commotion, he poked his head out and called to the nearest protester: 'Do us a favour, cock. Get us an evening paper and let's have the right score.'

But it was as an umpire that Alec Skelding really came into his own. In 1932 he made a little piece of history by becoming the first umpire to give a hat-trick of lbw decisions. The beneficiary was Yorkshire slow left-arm bowler Horace Fisher in the match against Somerset at Sheffield. Having sent two Somerset men back to the pavilion off successive balls, Skelding could hardly believe his eyes when the next ball hit Wally Luckes on the pad. As the appeal went up, Skelding paused, peered down the pitch and almost in disbelief announced: 'As God's my witness, that's out, too!' Afterwards, all three batsmen agreed that they had been plumb.

His sense of fun was evident in a Gentlemen versus Players match. When Eric Hollies, the last man in, came out to face the final over, all the fielders crowded around the bat. As the bowler was about to walk in, Skelding cheekily moved from his position at square leg and crouched down alongside the short leg fielders!

He once wrote a poem called *Duties, Trials and Troubles of County Cricket Umpires*, which contained the lines:

'Most of the time he stands to be shot at;
An immobile creature for mankind to pot at.'

Yet despite being on the receiving end of the occasional show of dissent, there is no doubt that he loved his job and he virtually had to be dragged into retirement. Sadly less than a year later – on 18 April 1960 – he died following a short illness.

The game of cricket had lost one of its most delightful characters, a man who, at the close of play, used to remove the bails with an exaggerated flourish and announce: 'And that, gentlemen, concludes the entertainment for the day.' With Alec Skelding there was never any shortage of entertainment.

BIBLIOGRAPHY

Barry, Paul. *Spun Out: Shane Warne* (Transworld, 2006)

Bird, Dickie. *My Autobiography* (Hodder & Stoughton, 1997)

Blofeld, Henry. *Cricket's Great Entertainers* (Hodder & Stoughton, 2004)

Boon, David. *Under the Southern Cross* (HarperCollins, 1996)

Bowler, Dave. *No Surrender: The Life and Times of Ian Botham* (Orion, 1997)

East, Ray. *Funny Turn: Confessions of a Cricketing Clown* (Unwin, 1983)

Edwards, Alan. *Lionel Tennyson: Regency Buck* (Robson Books, 2001)

Ewbank, Tim. *Andrew Flintoff: The Biography* (John Blake, 2006)

Frith, David. *Silence of the Heart* (Mainstream, 2001)

Gatting, Mike. *Leading From the Front* (Macdonald, 1988)

Green, David. *The History of Gloucestershire County Cricket Club* (Christopher Helm, 1990)

Haynes, Basil and Lucas, John. *The Trent Bridge Battery: The Story of the Sporting Gunns* (Willow Books, 1985)

Heald, Tim. *Denis Compton: The Life of a Sporting Hero* (Aurum, 2006)

Hignell, Andrew. *100 First-Class Umpires* (Tempus, 2003)

Hill, Alan. *Brian Close: Cricket's Lionheart* (Methuen, 2002)

Khan, Imran. *All Round View* (Chatto & Windus, 1988)

Lillee, Dennis. *Menace* (Headline, 2003)

Martin-Jenkins, Christopher. *The Cricketer Book of Cricket Eccentrics and Eccentric Behaviour* (Lennard Books, 1985)

McKinstry, Leo. *Geoff Boycott: A Cricketing Hero* (CollinsWillow, 2000)

McLean, Teresa. *The Men in White Coats* (Stanley Paul, 1987)

Midwinter, Eric. *W.G. Grace: His Life and Times* (George Allen & Unwin, 1981)

Peel, Mark. *Cricketing Falstaff: A Biography of Colin Milburn* (Andrew Deutsch, 1998)

Perry, Roland. *Keith Miller* (Aurum, 2005)

Pietersen, Kevin. *Crossing the Boundary* (Ebury Press, 2006)

Randall, Derek. *The Sun Has Got His Hat On* (Collins, 1984)

Richards, Viv. *Sir Vivian* (Michael Joseph, 2000)

Russell, Jack. *Unleashed* (CollinsWillow, 1997)

Shepherd, David. *Shep: My Autobiography* (Orion, 2001)

Thomson, A.A. *Odd Men In* (Pavilion, 1985)

Tufnell, Phil. *What Now?* (CollinsWillow, 1999)

Wilton, Iain. *C.B. Fry: King of Sport* (Metro, 2002)